Role of Edge Analytics in Sustainable Smart City Development

Scrivener Publishing
100 Cummings Center, Suite 541J
Beverly, MA 01915-6106

Next Generation Computing and Communication Engineering

Series Editor: G. R. Kanagachidambaresan and Kolla Bhanu Prakash

Edge computing has become an active research field supporting low processing power, real-time response time, and more resource capacity than IoT and mobile devices. It has also been considered to effectively mitigate loads on data centers, to assist artificial intelligence (AI) services, and to increase 5G services. Edge computing applications along with the IoT field are essential technical directions in order to open the door to new opportunities enabling smart homes, smart hospitals, smart cities, smart vehicles, smart wearables, smart supply chain, e-health, automation, and a variety of other smart environments.

However, any developments are made more challenging because the involvement of multi-domain technology creates new problems for researchers. Therefore, in order to help meet the challenge, this book series concentrates on next generation computing and communication methodologies involving smart and ambient environment design. It is an effective publishing platform for monographs, handbooks, and edited volumes on Industry 4.0, agriculture, smart city development, new computing and communication paradigms. Although the series mainly focuses on design, it also addresses analytics and investigation of industry-related real-time problems.

Submission to the series:
Dr. G. R. Kanagachidambaresan, ME, PhD
Department of CSE, Vel Tech Rangarajan Dr Sagunthala R&D Institute of Science and Technology, India
E-mail: kanagachidambaresan@gmail.com

Dr. Kolla Bhanu Prakash, ME, PhD, LMISTE, MIAENG, MCSTA, MIEEE
Department of Computer Science Engineering, K L Deemed to be University, India
E-mail: drkbp1981@gmail.com

Publishers at Scrivener
Martin Scrivener (martin@scrivenerpublishing.com)
Phillip Carmical (pcarmical@scrivenerpublishing.com)

Role of Edge Analytics in Sustainable Smart City Development

Challenges and Solutions

Edited by
G. R. Kanagachidambaresan

Scrivener
Publishing

WILEY

Wiley Global Headquarters
111 River Street, Hoboken, NJ 07030, USA

For details of our global editorial offices, customer services, and more information about Wiley products visit us at www.wiley.com.

Limit of Liability/Disclaimer of Warranty
While the publisher and authors have used their best efforts in preparing this work, they make no rep
resentations or warranties with respect to the accuracy or completeness of the contents of this work and
specifically disclaim all warranties, including without limitation any implied warranties of merchant-
ability or fitness for a particular purpose. No warranty may be created or extended by sales representa
tives, written sales materials, or promotional statements for this work. The fact that an organization,
website, or product is referred to in this work as a citation and/or potential source of further information does not mean that the publisher and authors endorse the information or services the organiza
tion, website, or product may provide or recommendations it may make. This work is sold with the
understanding that the publisher is not engaged in rendering professional services. The advice and
strategies contained herein may not be suitable for your situation. You should consult with a specialist
where appropriate. Neither the publisher nor authors shall be liable for any loss of profit or any other
commercial damages, including but not limited to special, incidental, consequential, or other damages.
Further, readers should be aware that websites listed in this work may have changed or disappeared
between when this work was written and when it is read.

Library of Congress Cataloging-in-Publication Data

ISBN 978-1-119-68128-1

Cover image: Pixabay.Com
Cover design by Russell Richardson

Set in size of 11pt and Minion Pro by Manila Typesetting Company, Makati, Philippines

10 9 8 7 6 5 4 3 2 1

Contents

Preface   xv

1   **Smart Health Care Development: Challenges and Solutions**   1
    R. Sujatha, E.P. Ephzibah and S. Sree Dharinya
    1.1   Introduction   2
    1.2   ICT Explosion   3
          1.2.1   RFID   4
          1.2.2   IoT and Big Data   5
          1.2.3   Wearable Sensors—Head to Toe   7
          1.2.4   Cloud Computing   8
    1.3   Intelligent Healthcare   10
    1.4   Home Healthcare   11
    1.5   Data Analytics   11
    1.6   Technologies—Data Cognitive   13
          1.6.1   Machine Learning   13
          1.6.2   Image Processing   14
          1.6.3   Deep Learning   14
    1.7   Adoption Technologies   15
    1.8   Conclusion   15
          References   15

2   **Working of Mobile Intelligent Agents on the Web—A Survey**   21
    P.R. Joe Dhanith and B. Surendiran
    2.1   Introduction   21
    2.2   Mobile Crawler   23
    2.3   Comparative Study of the Mobile Crawlers   47
    2.4   Conclusion   47
          References   47

3 Power Management Scheme for Photovoltaic/Battery Hybrid System in Smart Grid 49
T. Bharani Prakash and S. Nagakumararaj
3.1 Power Management Scheme 50
3.2 Internal Power Flow Management 50
    3.2.1 PI Controller 51
    3.2.2 State of Charge 53
3.3 Voltage Source Control 54
    3.3.1 Phase-Locked Loop 55
    3.3.2 Space Vector Pulse Width Modulation 56
    3.3.3 Park Transformation (abc to dq0) 57
3.4 Simulation Diagram and Results 58
    3.4.1 Simulation Diagram 58
    3.4.2 Simulation Results 63
    Conclusion 65

4 Analysis: A Neural Network Equalizer for Channel Equalization by Particle Swarm Optimization for Various Channel Models 67
M. Muthumari, D.C. Diana and C. Ambika Bhuvaneswari
4.1 Introduction 68
4.2 Channel Equalization 72
    4.2.1 Channel Models 73
        4.2.1.1 Tapped Delay Line Model 74
        4.2.1.2 Stanford University Interim (SUI) Channel Models 75
    4.2.2 Artificial Neural Network 75
4.3 Functional Link Artificial Neural Network 76
4.4 Particle Swarm Optimization 76
4.5 Result and Discussion 77
    4.5.1 Convergence Analysis 77
    4.5.2 Comparison Between Different Parameters 79
    4.5.3 Comparison Between Different Channel Models 80
4.6 Conclusion 81
    References 82

5 Implementing Hadoop Container Migrations in OpenNebula Private Cloud Environment 85
P. Kalyanaraman, K.R. Jothi, P. Balakrishnan, R.G. Navya, A. Shah and V. Pandey
5.1 Introduction 86
    5.1.1 Hadoop Architecture 86
    5.1.2 Hadoop and Big Data 88

5.1.3   Hadoop and Virtualization   88
5.1.4   What is OpenNebula?   89
5.2   Literature Survey   90
    5.2.1   Performance Analysis of Hadoop   90
    5.2.2   Evaluating Map Reduce on Virtual Machines   91
    5.2.3   Virtualizing Hadoop Containers   94
    5.2.4   Optimization of Hadoop Cluster Using Cloud Platform   95
    5.2.5   Heterogeneous Clusters in Cloud Computing   96
    5.2.6   Performance Analysis and Optimization in Hadoop   97
    5.2.7   Virtual Technologies   97
    5.2.8   Scheduling   98
    5.2.9   Scheduling of Hadoop VMs   98
5.3   Discussion   99
5.4   Conclusion   100
    References   101

6   Transmission Line Inspection Using Unmanned Aerial Vehicle   105
A. Mahaboob Subahani, M. Kathiresh and S. Sanjeev
6.1   Introduction   106
    6.1.1   Unmanned Aerial Vehicle   106
    6.1.2   Quadcopter   106
6.2   Literature Survey   107
6.3   System Architecture   108
6.4   ArduPilot   109
6.5   Arduino Mega   111
6.6   Brushless DC Motor   111
6.7   Battery   112
6.8   CMOS Camera   113
6.9   Electronic Speed Control   113
6.10   Power Module   115
6.11   Display Shield   116
6.12   Navigational LEDS   116
6.13   Role of Sensors in the Proposed System   118
    6.13.1   Accelerometer and Gyroscope   118
    6.13.2   Magnetometer   118
    6.13.3   Barometric Pressure Sensor   119
    6.13.4   Global Positioning System   119
6.14   Wireless Communication   120
6.15   Radio Controller   120
6.16   Telemetry Radio   121
6.17   Camera Transmitter   121

6.18 Results and Discussion 121
6.19 Conclusion 124
References 125

7 Smart City Infrastructure Management System Using IoT 127
S. Ramamoorthy, M. Kowsigan, P. Balasubramanie
and P. John Paul
7.1 Introduction 128
7.2 Major Challenges in IoT-Based Technology 129
7.2.1 Peer to Peer Communication Security 129
7.2.2 Objective of Smart Infrastructure 130
7.3 Internet of Things (IoT) 131
7.3.1 Key Components of Components of IoT 131
7.3.1.1 Network Gateway 132
7.3.1.2 HTTP (HyperText Transfer Protocol) 132
7.3.1.3 LoRaWan (Long Range Wide Area Network) 133
7.3.1.4 Bluetooth 133
7.3.1.5 ZigBee 133
7.3.2 IoT Data Protocols 133
7.3.2.1 Message Queue Telemetry Transport (MQTT) 133
7.3.2.2 Constrained Application Protocol (CoAP) 134
7.3.2.3 Advanced Message Queuing Protocol (AMQP) 134
7.3.2.4 Data Analytics 134
7.4 Machine Learning-Based Smart Decision-Making Process 135
7.5 Cloud Computing 136
References 138

8 Lightweight Cryptography Algorithms for IoT Resource-Starving Devices 139
S. Aruna, G. Usha, P. Madhavan and M.V. Ranjith Kumar
8.1 Introduction 139
8.1.1 Need of the Cryptography 140
8.2 Challenges on Lightweight Cryptography 141
8.3 Hashing Techniques on Lightweight Cryptography 142
8.4 Applications on Lighweight Cryptography 152
8.5 Conclusion 167
References 168

9 **Pre-Learning-Based Semantic Segmentation for LiDAR Point Cloud Data Using Self-Organized Map**   **171**
   K. Rajathi and P. Sarasu
   9.1   Introduction   172
   9.2   Related Work   173
         9.2.1   Semantic Segmentation for Images   173
   9.3   Semantic Segmentation for LiDAR Point Cloud   173
   9.4   Proposed Work   175
         9.4.1   Data Acquisition   175
         9.4.2   Our Approach   175
         9.4.3   Pre-Learning Processing   179
   9.5   Region of Interest (RoI)   180
   9.6   Registration of Point Cloud   181
   9.7   Semantic Segmentation   181
   9.8   Self-Organized Map (SOM)   182
   9.9   Experimental Result   183
   9.10 Conclusion   186
         References   187

10 **Smart Load Balancing Algorithms in Cloud Computing—A Review**   **189**
   K.R. Jothi, S. Anto, M. Kohar, M. Chadha and P. Madhavan
   10.1 Introduction   189
   10.2 Research Challenges   192
         10.2.1 Security & Routing   192
         10.2.2 Storage/Replication   192
         10.2.3 Spatial Spread of the Cloud Nodes   192
         10.2.4 Fault Tolerance   193
         10.2.5 Algorithm Complexity   193
   10.3 Literature Survey   193
   10.4 Survey Table   201
   10.5 Discussion & Comparison   202
   10.6 Conclusion   202
         References   216

11 **A Low-Cost Wearable Remote Healthcare Monitoring System**   **219**
   Konguvel Elango and Kannan Muniandi
   11.1 Introduction   219
         11.1.1 Problem Statement   220
         11.1.2 Objective of the Study   221

11.2   Related Works   222
        11.2.1 Remote Healthcare Monitoring Systems   222
        11.2.2 Pulse Rate Detection   224
        11.2.3 Temperate Measurement   225
        11.2.4 Fall Detection   225
11.3   Methodology   226
        11.3.1 NodeMCU   226
        11.3.2 Pulse Rate Detection System   227
        11.3.3 Fall Detection System   230
        11.3.4 Temperature Detection System   231
        11.3.5 LCD Specification   234
        11.3.6 ADC Specification   234
11.4   Results and Discussions   236
        11.4.1 System Implementation   236
        11.4.2 Fall Detection Results   236
        11.4.3 ThingSpeak   236
11.5   Conclusion   239
11.6   Future Scope   240
        References   241

12 **IoT-Based Secure Smart Infrastructure Data Management   243**
   R. Poorvadevi, M. Kowsigan, P. Balasubramanie
   and J. Rajeshkumar
12.1   Introduction   244
        12.1.1 List of Security Threats Related to the Smart IoT
                Network   244
        12.1.2 Major Application Areas of IoT   244
        12.1.3 IoT Threats and Security Issues   245
        12.1.4 Unpatched Vulnerabilities   245
        12.1.5 Weak Authentication   245
        12.1.6 Vulnerable API's   245
12.2   Types of Threats to Users   245
12.3   Internet of Things Security Management   246
        12.3.1 Managing IoT Devices   246
        12.3.2 Role of External Devices in IoT Platform   247
        12.3.3 Threats to Other Computer Networks   248
12.4   Significance of IoT Security   249
        12.4.1 Aspects of Workplace Security   249
        12.4.2 Important IoT Security Breaches and IoT Attacks   250
12.5   IoT Security Tools and Legislation   250

12.6   Protection of IoT Systems and Devices   251
    12.6.1   IoT Issues and Security Challenges   251
    12.6.2   Providing Secured Connections   252
12.7   Five Ways to Secure IoT Devices   253
12.8   Conclusion   255
    References   255

**13 A Study of Addiction Behavior for Smart Psychological
Health Care System**   **257**
V. Sabapathi and K.P. Vijayakumar
13.1   Introduction   258
13.2   Basic Criteria of Addiction   258
13.3   Influencing Factors of Addiction Behavior   259
    13.3.1   Peers Influence   259
    13.3.2   Environment Influence   260
    13.3.3   Media Influence   262
    13.3.4   Family Group and Society   262
13.4   Types of Addiction and Their Effects   262
    13.4.1   Gaming Addiction   263
    13.4.2   Pornography Addiction   264
    13.4.3   Smart Phone Addiction   265
    13.4.4   Gambling Addiction   267
    13.4.5   Food Addiction   267
    13.4.6   Sexual Addiction   268
    13.4.7   Cigarette and Alcohol Addiction   268
    13.4.8   Status Expressive Addiction   269
    13.4.9   Workaholic Addiction   269
13.5   Conclusion   269
    References   270

**14 A Custom Cluster Design With Raspberry Pi for Parallel
Programming and Deployment of Private Cloud**   **273**
Sukesh, B., Venkatesh, K. and Srinivas, L.N.B.
14.1   Introduction   274
14.2   Cluster Design with Raspberry Pi   276
    14.2.1   Assembling Materials for Implementing Cluster   276
        14.2.1.1   Raspberry Pi4   277
        14.2.1.2   RPi 4 Model B Specifications   277
    14.2.2   Setting Up Cluster   278
        14.2.2.1   Installing Raspbian and Configuring
                   Master Node   279

		14.2.2.2	Installing MPICH and MPI4PY	279
		14.2.2.3	Cloning the Slave Nodes	279
14.3	Parallel Computing and MPI on Raspberry Pi Cluster			279
14.4	Deployment of Private Cloud on Raspberry Pi Cluster			281
	14.4.1	NextCloud Software		281
14.5	Implementation			281
	14.5.1	NextCloud on RPi Cluster		281
	14.5.2	Parallel Computing on RPi Cluster		282
14.6	Results and Discussions			286
14.7	Conclusion			287
	References			287

15 Energy Efficient Load Balancing Technique for Distributed Data Transmission Using Edge Computing   **289**
Karthikeyan, K. and Madhavan, P.

15.1	Introduction		290
15.2	Energy Efficiency Offloading Data Transmission		290
	15.2.1	Web-Based Offloading	291
15.3	Energy Harvesting		291
	15.3.1	LODCO Algorithm	292
15.4	User-Level Online Offloading Framework (ULOOF)		293
15.5	Frequency Scaling		294
15.6	Computation Offloading and Resource Allocation		295
15.7	Communication Technology		296
15.8	Ultra-Dense Network		297
15.9	Conclusion		299
	References		299

16 Blockchain-Based SDR Signature Scheme With Time-Stamp   **303**
Swathi Singh, Divya Satish and Sree Rathna Lakshmi

16.1	Introduction			303
16.2	Literature Study			304
	16.2.1	Signatures With Hashes		304
	16.2.2	Signature Scheme With Server Support		305
	16.2.3	Signatures Scheme Based on Interaction		305
16.3	Methodology			306
	16.3.1	Preliminaries		306
		16.3.1.1	Hash Trees	306
		16.3.1.2	Chains of Hashes	306
	16.3.2	Interactive Hash-Based Signature Scheme		307
	16.3.3	Significant Properties of Hash-Based Signature Scheme		309

		16.3.4	Proposed SDR Scheme Structure	310
		16.3.4.1	One-Time Keys	310
		16.3.4.2	Server Behavior Authentication	310
		16.3.4.3	Pre-Authentication by Repository	311
	16.4	SDR Signature Scheme		311
		16.4.1	Pre-Requisites	311
		16.4.2	Key Generation Algorithm	312
		16.4.2.1	Server	313
		16.4.3	Sign Algorithm	313
		16.4.3.1	Signer	313
		16.4.3.2	Server	313
		16.4.3.3	Repository	314
		16.4.4	Verification Algorithm	314
	16.5	Supportive Theory		315
		16.5.1	Signing Algorithm Supported by Server	315
		16.5.2	Repository Deployment	316
		16.5.3	SDR Signature Scheme Setup	316
		16.5.4	Results and Observation	316
	16.6	Conclusion		317
		References		317
Index				**321**

Preface

In the upcoming decades the population is expected to rise exponentially, with population density increasing day by day in cities creating challenges and new infrastructure development. Smart cities are supposed to adopt new technologies on their resources like water management, grid system, transport system and health care industries. The challenge is to provide the experience and facilities in an economic way so as to reach all levels of people in cities. The rapid growth of technology and new smart city development initiatives has made the Internet of Things and Edge analytics an inevitable platform for all engineering domains. Connected devices in a smart environment promises to improve the lifestyle of the people and their living conditions. The sustainable smart city development focuses on five important elements a) citizen, b) infrastructure, technology and data, c) enterprise and innovation, d) leadership and strategy and e) learning and measurement. The needs of sophisticated and ambient environment have resulted in an exponential growth of automation, robustness and artificial intelligence. The involvement of multi-domain technology creates new problems making the development a challenging thing to researchers. Efficient Single Board Computers (SBCs) and advanced VLSI systems have resulted in edge analytics and faster decision making. The QoS parameters like energy, delay, reliability, security, and throughput should be improved on seeking better intelligent expert systems. The resource constraints in the Edge devices, challenges the researchers to meet the required QoS. Since these devices and components work in a remote unattended environment, a best methodology to improve its lifetime has become mandatory. Continuous monitoring of events is mandatory to avoid tragic situations; it can only be enabled by providing high QoS. Monitoring production and creating transparency between production industries enhances trust in productivity and enhances business between the partnering industries. The effective monitoring of resources can give knowledge in productivity and can be used to estimate residual useful lifetime of industry machines. The data generated through sensors in a smart city environment can be widely used for prognostics activities. The applications of IoT in digital twin development, health care, traffic analysis, home surveillance, intelligent agriculture monitoring, defense and all common day to day activities have resulted in pioneering embedded devices, which can offer high computational facilities without much latency and delay. This book addresses such issues along with the solutions. This book also aims to provide a novel literature survey to show a path for new researchers in Edge analytics and Expert systems. Problems in smart grid, data management in cloud system, security concerns and algorithm for edge devices are deeply discussed as well.

G. R. Kanagachidambaresan
May 2020

Smart Health Care Development: Challenges and Solutions

R. Sujatha*, E.P. Ephzibah and S. Sree Dharinya

School of Information Technology & Engineering, Vellore Institute of Technology, Vellore, Tamil Nadu, India

Abstract

Across the globe, every city dreams to become a smart city. Integration of information and communication technologies to optimize the lifestyle of people is the process involved in smart city. Each government thinks and takes various measures to fulfil the necessities of smart city. To achieve this vision statement of smartness in various fields, nations both in developed and developing countries find it a challenging task. The ultimate idea is infrastructure designed by introducing the electronic devices to provide easier access of data and ensuring higher level of communication that will provide a flawless environment. The various tasks include providing required water, electricity, education transportation, safety, good sanitation and health. Taking care of elderly people is a major concern in all the places. Traditional ways of handling files to track the patients' health have slowly entered the phase of digitization. In turn now so many electronic gadgets, sensors etc., are used to make this process so effective and efficient. Smart health care is experiencing the rapid growth with the invention of devices along with technologies like IoT, machine learning, big data, artificial intelligence and so on. Modern era devices for substantiating the smart health are the crux of this chapter.

Keywords: Wearable devices, IoT, machine learning, deep learning, monitoring, patient health care, artificial intelligence

Corresponding author: r.sujatha@vit.ac.in

G. R. Kanagachidambaresan (ed.) Role of Edge Analytics in Sustainable Smart City Development: Challenges and Solutions, (1–20) © 2020 Scrivener Publishing LLC

1.1 Introduction

In developed countries, a smart city is already imbibed and in developing countries establishing a smart city is tough and a time-consuming task. Obviously initiation begins from the federal level. In the fast growing world, the need for smart health is very crucial. Particularly now, the nuclear family setup is growing in a steep phase and the growing population think about their own benefits that in turn increased the gap between the people. Electronic health record is the starting point in the health sector. Health is the great asset for well-being. Evolutionary and exponential change in the lifestyle is the great threat for the health of all living beings. The need for taking care of our living environment is at the alarming factor. Growth of industries and usage of higher level of computing and trending technology have reduced the mobility of the people to a lot. It is the public interest to take this issue as the priority and introduce the integrated health care monitoring aspect in the people's lives. At the outset, awareness to each individual needs to be nurtured.

The rest of the content discusses about the various aspects that substantiates the smart healthcare system and the way it is getting optimized in each phases by intervening the medical health care with Information and Communication Technologies (ICT) [1]. The Internet became the integral part of life years before itself. As the time passed, the utilization of the same became indispensable in manner. Various fields like education, agriculture, marketing, manufacturing, finance, medical and list goes on started relying on the ICT to grow to the next level. Radio frequency identification (RFID) tag is used in the initial stages to track the information in the huge dataset maintenance. The best usage of RFID is found in the library management that helps to find in which location particular book available in huge library infrastructure, ensuring no one is taking the book out of the library without legitimate issue phase. The Herculean task of maintaining the library is made easier. Similarly in the healthcare system, tracking the condition of people is achieved. This marks a milestone in incorporating the Internet of Things (IoT) that is the linking of various devices across the globe. Various architecture evolved due to this process of putting together sensors, RFID tags, computer, expert system, database and so on to converse and provide valuable input based on the situation.

All these produce huge versatile data that need to be handled in perfect manner to gain the benefit of the system. Big data (BD) is the buzz word that made the field of information technology (IT) highly competitive in nature. Stored data needs to be analyzed to provide knowledge based on the requirement. Along with BD many captions like analyst, scientist, and engineering joined to make it very potential area both in job and research perspective [2]. Process of storing at economical manner paved way to cloud computing. Public, private and hybrid clouds evolved based on the capacity of the storage person and purpose [3]. Numerous algorithms, methods passed over the voluminous data that paved way to data mining and in turn branched various concepts like machine learning, soft computing, deep learning, image processing, artificial intelligence. All this depend much on the maths, statistics, business, technology and no doubt domain on which it's applied [4].

By incorporation of the said design the system that consists of input, processing and output that helps in decision making process. In the case of smart healthcare system diagnosis of the diseases by comparing, 'n' number of traits and its value. Based on the insights provided by the system, a suitable treatment provided to control the disease. The ultimate aim of smart healthcare is to ensure sustainable health condition and longevity of the life. By careful requirement gathering followed by analysis of the same, it is the success criteria that define the system.

1.2   ICT Explosion

From the 1990s, the ICT boomed. Later, e-health is the word coined from electronic based health care management which gained popularity by the exponential inventions in the ICT sector. Stakeholders of e-health are patients, physicians, clinicians, researchers and so on. ICT pillars are wireless and wired network, big data analytics, personal devices, sensors, 3d printers. ICT paradigms are mobile cloud, cloud computing, fog computing and IoT. ICT-based healthcare patterns are e-health, pervasive health, ubiquitous health, mobile health and personalized health. Various characteristics like ICT, mobile connectivity, internet, personal smart devices, ubiquitous computing, pervasive computing and context awareness paved the way to different ICT-based healthcare pattern [5–7].

Health data format used different acronyms in research papers like electronic medical record (EMR), electronic health record (EHR), electronic patient record (EPR), clinical data repository (CDR), patient medical record information (PMRI) and so on. Precisely all try to store a patient's personal and history about their visits and follow ups. Since all focus on storing data in a centralized manner, this makes it highly potential to know about status of patient in no time [8, 9]. Various devices utilized in the interactive manner from mobile devices is the boon in gaining efficient output at a low cost in developing countries and great impact is missing of data is minimized [10, 11]. Factors like age, sex, education, residence, living with partner, marital status and other technological factors like network bandwidth, devices capability make the system highly challenging in nature. There is a controversial discussion that adaptability of elderly people for ICT is quiet cumbersome and variation felt across the globe in distribution [12, 13]. Several research works carried on in the US, UK and other countries to know the pulse of elderly people acceptance for ICT. In comparison it seemed that people who were born a lot earlier found the advent of ICT in the health department inconvenient and uncomfortable. Usage of devices in itself is not easy for the elderly age group [14–17]. Easy user interface and extra care and concern to train the elderly people are required in the case of ICT-based healthcare system [18–20].

1.2.1   RFID

The health care industry is facing versatile issues due to the increase in population and types of diseases. The World Health Organization (WHO) has mentioned that medical errors are serious traits that need to be taken into consideration or else it will make the living environment so tough [21]. For this, the Food and Drug Administration (FDA) suggested incorporating IT so the great problem of misidentification could be handled [22]. Often the medical errors include misidentification of patients, wrong medical prescription and follow ups, and inappropriate in the blood transfusion [23, 24].

Patient identification, tracking, monitoring and drug compliance are the phases involved in RFID usage. To ensure perfect treatment given to correct patient is the primary requirement of any healthcare system. Smart RFID makes the system of identifying patient task flawless in nature. Procedures like initial appointment till any surgery in case of casualty will be happening smoothly when tagged properly with RFID. Works are based on the principle of radio frequency [25, 26]. Tracking patient based on emergency is the benefit of the RFID system. Continuity of the treatment is maintained and long waiting time during discharge is waived because of this integration process. A patient is under surveillance such that any crisis is addressed immediately [27, 28]. Implantable RFID helps to monitor and smart bandages used post-surgery aids a lot in monitoring at no time for faster treatment. To provide the correct dose based on severity for correct patient is the milestone in the health information system. RFID integrated with web used for medication along with input of expert for patient is very effective [29, 30]. Barriers are technological challenges, data privacy challenges, structural and financial challenges. Possibility of electromagnetic interference with biomedical devices is the adverse effect. More work carried on data security and handling generated data. Ultimately, adoption of RFID was slowed down. Organization and financial constraints posed an additional problem in the service provider healthcare industry. Return of investment and payback period is not appreciable up to the mark. This paved way to advanced technologies and techniques to make it more viable [31–33].

1.2.2 IoT and Big Data

Data generated in health care industry is growing extensively. With the concept of IoT, various devices are getting interconnected for the purpose of identifying patients and devices to measure blood sugar, pressure, temperature for early diagnose and proving suitable treatment. Tremendous growth is being experienced in health care industry due to the convergence of IoT and big data. Growth in sense that higher accuracy in prediction of diseases, correct combination of drug based on severity, psychological treatment based on various factors from social, economic factor along with huge data that illustrated about patient [35]. IoT is governed by protocol along with software that acts as integration between hardware, middleware and presentation of the same. Hardware comprises of acquiring the data, processing and communicating perfectly. In middleware connection of sensors with application layer and presentation is the main sector that helps to visualize the accumulated data in informative manner [36, 37].

The main feature of IoT is everything communicates, interacts and gets detected. Privacy of the data, availability at any point of time and integration are the dimensions required in case of data security in the world of internet. In perspective of privacy, biometric system is utilized in the health care system to make it more secured and authentication process becomes more stringent. IoT evolution is more interesting in all aspects. In network point of view, in initial stages it sensors and slowly transition to network knowledge [38]. In software algorithms and hardware perspective it transitioned from supervised to unsupervised or intuitive way of processing. Obviously in case of data processing IoT turned out from event-based to invisible. With the optimization over the time the functionalities like intelligence, value creation, connectivity and communication of IoT are appealing in nature. Every feature of the human can be mapped by biometric trait if it is universal, distinct, permanent and collectable in nature. Various biometric techniques are recognition of fingerprint, face, iris, hand geometry, voice, and signature; detection of palms, walk, and behavior and hit the key dynamics [39–41]. Figure 1.1 illustrates the generic way

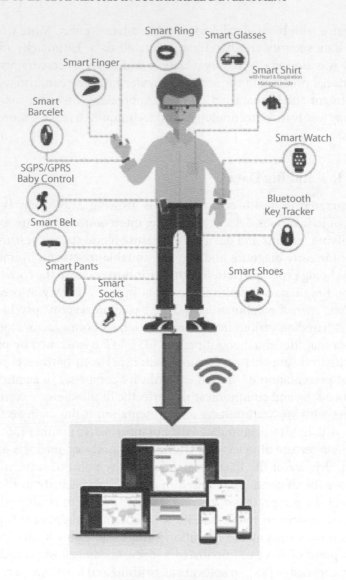

Figure 1.1 Communication flow.

in which various wearable sensor devices prevailing in the market act as a great boon in gathering data and based on threshold value the immediate addressing of the issues. Data visualization through PDA, Laptops, and PC via wireless that is seen by the medical practitioners and members of family ensures everything is perfect. The range of all sorts of devices is in rapid growth due to more research on technology is seen around the world.

1.2.3   Wearable Sensors—Head to Toe

Traditional health care system is the process in which a patient goes to the hospital and meets the practitioner on a regular basis. Huge testing equipment and lengthy waiting time in case of long queue makes the patient still more sick and panic. In the case of chronic disease tracking and monitoring it is a great hurdle in the traditional health care system. Advancement and the need in the medical field with the help of electrical, electronic and other disciplinary profession started putting more effort in creating the wearable sensors to overcome the difficulties and provide medication with great ease [42, 43]. To precisely tell, sensors related to health is evolving in a slow phase because of the complexity involved in a human being. Compatibility is the utmost point followed by durability with conflict that may happen due to abrasion. Bio-signal sensing devices are in phase to cope with the need for tracking of fitness, tracking of health related issues in the highly competitive world. Time spent on the professional stream is being increased and due to that there have been a lot of lifestyle changes. Health is at the jeopardy that initiates diseases in the earlier phase of life. In the olden days, more physical activities, eating habits, level of interaction among the fellow members both in personal and professional life, harmony and several factors had great impact on health of people. But the vast development in science, engineering and technology has changed the setup of life to a completely different perspective. Living a fast life made the need for this entire smart health sector to be optimized. Several researchers work in this field of nano-materials, advanced materials along with bio background professionals to make it reliable [44].

Interoperability and dynamic concept were introduced in the communication framework for the smart health care system. Health sensors are implanted inside to make the system highly perceivable in nature. Wearable sensors are small computing devices that interact with various devices and transmit the sensed information from the surface of its placement in body. The structure is miniature in nature to serve the purpose of compatibility and ease in service. In recent years many sensors started footing the medical industry. Extensive research and testing is required since it is used in highly critical application to save guard human life [45, 46]. Table 1.1 provides insight of the various wearable sensors to construct the smart healthcare in the latest years. Certain specification standard for the parameter range (temperature) and frequency is provided by the manufacturing sectors. Various setup like time interval to capture data and varied postures make it more informative to take decision and act accordingly.

Salient features that make wearable devices in healthcare more novel are: stretchability—the way device gets intact perfectly requires it to be elastic and tensile, ultrathin—structure and size should be in miniature form, bio-compatibility and degradability obviously tells about the location of the device placement on skin or organ so it should be sensitive to human and healing in nature [47–50].

1.2.4   Cloud Computing

The advent of big data in the health care sector has paved way to a heterogeneous and voluminous dataset that need to be analyzed to reach the goal. The storing of gathered data is the phenomenal task followed by pre-processing to make the dataset clean. Velocity of data is also a challenging task. Analyzing the repository of dataset based on the scenario and domain

Table 1.1 Wearable sensors.

Sensors	Application
Smart lens	Tear monitoring
Temperature sensors	Temperature monitoring
Tooth guard	Saliva monitoring
Face mask	Breath monitoring
Biosensors	Sweat monitoring
Strain sensors	Motion monitoring
Triboelectronic generators	Self-powered monitoring
Pressure sensors	Blood pressure monitoring
Photodetectors	PPG monitoring
EEG sensors	Wound monitoring

is the pervasive task with lots of queries. To smoothen this process, relying on hardware and software is inevitable and the usage of cloud computing provides a helping hand in managing it in an economical manner. On demand service are provided by cloud computing that is part of IT service paradigm. Based on the technology, organization, resources, environment data/information, stakeholders, physicians, and vendor categories detailed analysis have been made. Ultimately to provide quality care, financial improvement, support all stakeholders like patients, physicians and other medical related corners [51–53].

Cloud computing as an IT based approach delivers the following services:

- Agility in implementation
- Broad network access
- Distribution and resource pooling for a range of applications
- Dynamicity
- Elasticity
- Fast services conformation
- Heterogeneity
- Higher reliability
- Location independence
- Lower capital expenditure
- Scalability
- Transparency
- Uncertainty
- Voluntariness.

The application of smart healthcare by inputting the use of advanced technologies helps in assisting diagnosis and treatment, managing the complete zone of health, preventing disease and monitoring of risk, drug research optimized with the huge data for analyzing and aids virtual assistants [54–57]. Big healthcare is a great step and with the concepts of mapping reduced from cloud computing it is being managed. For each and every disease, the dedicated system is at the verge of development. For a few diseases like heart disease, Parkinson disease, and thyroid disease, the intelligent health care system is live. Continuous optimization is required and factors influencing needs to be catered. A hybrid system for the health care system as a whole is also a need of the hour in the health industry [58, 59]. Many cloud-computing providers are actively working in the field to provide the customization and cater to the environment based on the requirements of the end user and in the case of health industry privacy, secrecy are the additional pillars that needs to be in frame to make it hassle-free.

1.3   Intelligent Healthcare

Due to the advancement and integration of information technology in traditional healthcare, routine doctor visits in the case of chronic diseases is getting changed. Remote help of the smart healthcare management can now be done with both regular and acute conditions. Avenue started with big data by storing all sorts of data from the initial patient getting inside the clinic, making registration, follow-ups, treatments, drug delivery, and surgery and so on. Analyzing the data is possible with basic data mining concepts like machine learning, image processing and in place of decision making expert system with the help of artificial intelligence that pitches various knowledge in the healthcare arena.

Keyword co-occurrence in the past 20 years by checking the articles of science direct provides great support about the smart healthcare in the open source journal. The search is limited to open source journal only. Co-occurrence analysis is depicted in the Figure 1.2 compiled with VOSviewer [60].

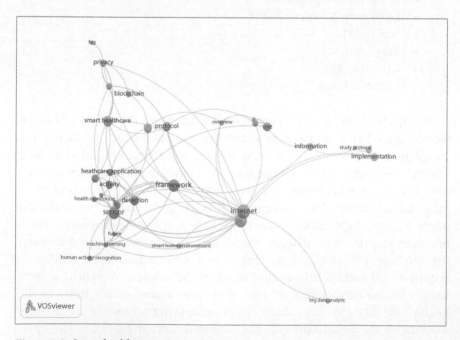

Figure 1.2 Smart healthcare—Co-occurrence.

1.4 Home Healthcare

Part of smart healthcare is usage of diagnostic devices in the home to help in chronic conditions. Long waiting time, distance and amount incurred in the medical bills are too high led to possess the equipment and use it as per the requirement. The number of people affected by diabetics, blood pressure and cholesterol is an increasing trend due to food habits and working style. The office work entered inside the house in the name of work from home and that eventually made the physical movements less that paved to way several issues. Particularly in the IT industry, the working style has made the great impact in the lifestyle of the people. It not only reduced the physical activities but also the interaction with the outer world that creates the internal pressure and depression in due course of time. Slowly the health condition of the people gets down and their body shows several dis-abnormalities. To save time in tracking and monitoring their health condition both in case of old age or young age, the equipment usage has grown exponentially. Diabetic care unit for diabetic patient, BP monitor for blood pressure patient and similarly for each ailment, concerned equipment are being used. The U.S. Bureau of Labor Statistics has published the statistics stating that anticipated usage of aids for personal care in home will reach 13.0 million by 2020 that is approximately 70.0% up from 2010. Figure 1.3 illustrates the market of US home healthcare diagnostic component [61].

1.5 Data Analytics

It's very evident from the discussion that with the smart healthcare system devices huge data is collected and its next stage is analyses followed by

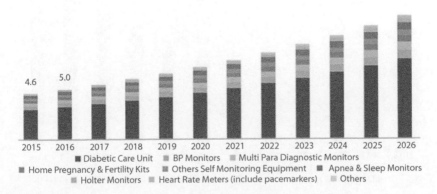

Figure 1.3 US home healthcare diagnostic component, 2015–2026 (USD Billion).

decision-making process. Big data occupied important place in all avenue and no doubt in case of healthcare too. Data gathering, storing, preprocessing gets its completion only on retrieving potential results from them. Analytics is the buzz word that narrates about decision making process [62–64].

Data analytics broadly falls in to

Descriptive analytics—answers "what happened?"
Purpose—Visualization, reporting and data mining.
Predictive analytics—answers "what will happen?"
Purpose—Simulation, regression analysis and causal forecasting.
Prescriptive analytics—answers "what should I do?"
Purpose—Optimization, heuristics, & rule-based system.

Big data processing and analytics goes hand in hand. Analytics provided is the way of representing in so abstract manner but to accomplish it the number of machine learning algorithms, population based algorithms, evolutionary algorithms, bio-inspired algorithms, meta-heuristic algorithms are applied over the dataset to mine the knowledgeable ideas. The medical field is facing the high level of challenge due to the growth of indefinite size of data pertaining to practitioner, patient, diseases and other related traits. Life expectancy is on increased fashion in spite of controversy prevailing on comparison to traditional olden day's life. Physical and psychological factors contribute to the wellness of person in a nutshell. Various modules of each phase are integrated to develop novel frameworks in optimized manner. The research in the Germany healthcare industry, illustrating the trend over the year with the analytics is given in Figure 1.4 [65–67].

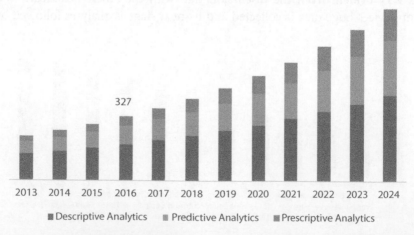

Figure 1.4 Germany healthcare analytics.

1.6   Technologies—Data Cognitive

Data mining is the key process that acts as the backbone for the many industries that handles huge data for analytic purpose. Knowledge discovery occurs in the stored data base after preliminary stages of cleaning and transforming the raw data. Statistics, machine learning and artificial intelligence are the main subsets of the data mining. Cognitive intelligence and ambient intelligence help in carving the healthcare industry to next level by adapting perfect techniques for attending the patient at golden hours without delay. Figure 1.5 provides a clear curve indicating the technologies' growth pertaining to managing and handling huge data.

1.6.1   Machine Learning

Algorithms applied over dataset are largely categorized into supervised learning, unsupervised learning, semi-supervised and reinforcement learning for the purpose of regression, classification, prediction, association, forecasting and clustering. In the supervised algorithm type outcome is expected and common examples are Nearest Neighbor, Naive Bayes, Decision Trees, Linear Regression, Support Vector Machines (SVM), and Neural Networks and so on. Unsupervised algorithm output is not the goal but to make the grouping based on occurrences and are commonly referred to as k-means algorithm, association rule, etc. Between these two qualities are semi-supervised learning functions. A branch of artificial intelligence is the reinforcement learning based on performance optimization, within

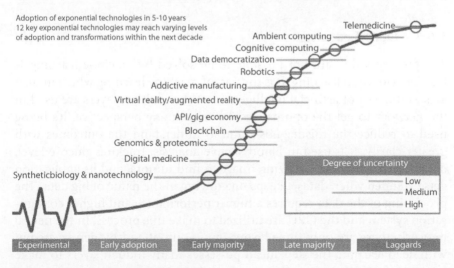

Figure 1.5 Key exponential technologies.

the specific context, where machines and software agents take the decision [68, 69]. The benchmark datasets for various diseases are provided to motivate and create awareness among the researchers. Features they consider for their analysis provide great insight to get moved to the next stage. Popular data repository is UCI that comprises of heart disease dataset, cancer dataset, diabetics dataset, thyroid dataset, kidney disease dataset, diabetic retinopathy dataset and the recent addition to this is Parkinson dataset. Big data is provided in a few links based on the request and purpose of request. In general the combination of bio experts and IT experts that drives the smart healthcare management system [70, 71].

1.6.2   Image Processing

In the healthcare field a lot of data exist in the image format that requires careful analysis by the experts to derive the conclusion about the seriousness of the disease. Each disease will be on different critical levels based on the intensity. Interpreting a pure number-based dataset is entirely different from the processing of the images. Similarly to the numerical based dataset, data preprocessing should be done to remove the noise signals in the image. In any set of the datasets, handling missing values is another potential area of research work. Acquiring such image with preprocessing enhances the image quality. Image restoration, segmentation, morphological processing and in the case of smart healthcare location-based processing and identification is core work. Modeling and training the dataset will help to provide more accuracy on the determination part. Cancer-related work relies more on the image processing [72].

1.6.3   Deep Learning

The problems that are not possible to be solved by machine learning is feasible with deep learning. It is the part of machine learning which in turn acts as the part of artificial intelligence but the multiple layers are used in the network to get the optimal results in accuracy perspective. It's being used to reduce the misdiagnosis and to understand the outcomes with greater clarity. It is used in blood sample analysis, tracking glucose level, detect heart ailments, analyzing image to find tumors, and its application gets extended when dataset keeps on growing in the name of big data. The processing of the data requires a higher performance and higher configuration system and the GPU are utilized to make this process. In the neural network, there are only three layers: input, output and hidden layers but with deep learning the step ahead possesses many hidden layers to make deep analysis. Fast computation and number of iterations provide higher accuracy and better outline to the smart health care system [73, 74].

1.7   Adoption Technologies

Each and every decade the technology is growing stupendously. The various stakeholders in the smart healthcare are patients, doctors, lab technicians, nurses, management people, care takers and emergency helpers. Location and space of the healthcare units are becoming tougher due to an increase of the patients and diseases. Deloitte makes the great contribution in the healthcare sector and their recent research mapped the possible key exponential technologies that will be adopted in the forthcoming years to provide help in good timely treatment [75, 76].

1.8   Conclusion

By integrating all the discussed sectors in the perfect streamline the smart healthcare system will become a highly supportive pillar in the nation's growth. Ultimately, output will provide an expert-based decision support system that makes the correct disease diagnosis and optimizes the drug management phase. Healthcare sustainability is the dream of all the people and by proper collaboration and hard core research with maximum research, it is possible.

References

1. Aceto, G., Persico, V., Pescapé, A., The role of Information and Communication Technologies in healthcare: taxonomies, perspectives, and challenges. *J. Netw. Comput. Appl.*, 107, 125–154, 2018.
2. Archenaa, J. and Mary Anita, E.A., A survey of big data analytics in healthcare and government. *Procedia Comput. Sci.*, 50, 408–413, 2015.
3. Botta, A., De Donato, W., Persico, V., Pescapé, A., Integration of cloud computing and internet of things: a survey. *Future Gener. Comput. Sy.*, 56, 684–700, 2016.
4. Smolij, K. and Dun, K., Patient health information management: searching for the right model. *Perspect. Health Inf. Manag./AHIMA*, American Health Information Management Association, 3, 3, 2006.

5. Germanakos, P., Mourlas, C., Samaras, G., A mobile agent approach for ubiquitous and personalized eHealth information systems. *Proceedings of the Workshop on 'Personalization for e-Health' of the 10th International Conference on User Modeling (UM'05)*, Edinburgh, 2005.

6. Lee Ventola, C., Mobile devices and apps for health care professionals: uses and benefits. *Pharm. Ther.*, 39, 5, 356, 2014.

7. Thuemmler, C. and Bai, C. (Eds.), *Health 4.0: How virtualization and big data are revolutionizing healthcare*, Springer, New York, NY, 2017.

8. Mitchell, J., *From telehealth to e-health: the unstoppable rise of e-health*, Department of Communications, Information Technology and the Arts, Canberra, Australia, 1999.

9. Awad, A., Mohamed, A., Chiasserini, C.F., Elfouly, T., Distributed in-network processing and resource optimization over mobile-health systems. *J. Netw. Comput. Appl.*, 82, 65–76, 2017.

10. Kaplan, W.A., Can the ubiquitous power of mobile phones be used to improve health outcomes in developing countries? *Glob. Health*, 2, 1, 9, 2006.

11. Fedha, T., Impact of mobile telephone on maternal health service care: a case of Njoro division. *Open J. Prev. Med.*, 4, 05, 365, 2014.

12. Haddon, L., *Information and communication technologies in everyday life: A concise introduction and research guide*, Berg, Oxford, 2004.

13. Wilson, E.V. and Lankton, N.K., Modeling patients' acceptance of provider-delivered e-health. *J. Am. Med. Inform. Assoc.*, 11, 4, 241–248, 2004.

14. Jones, S. and Fox, S., *Generations online in 2009*, Pew Internet & American Life Project, Washington, DC, 2009.

15. Adams, N., Stubbs, D., Woods, V., Psychological barriers to Internet usage among older adults in the UK. *Med. Inform. Internet*, 30, 1, 3–17, 2005.

16. Heart, T. and Kalderon, E., Older adults: Are they ready to adopt health-related ICT? *Int. J. Med. Inform.*, 82, 11, e209–e231, 2013.

17. Mann, W.C., Ottenbacher, K.J., Fraas, L., Tomita, M., Granger, C.V., Effectiveness of assistive technology and environmental interventions in maintaining independence and reducing home care costs for the frail elderly: A randomized controlled trial. *Arch. Fam. Med.*, 8, 210–217, 1999.

18. Hill, R., Beynon-Davies, P., Williams, M.D., Older people and internet engagement: Acknowledging social moderators of internet adoption, access and use. *Inform. Tech. People*, 21, 3, 244–266, 2008.

19. Vimarlund, V. and Olve, N.-G., Economic analyses for ICT in elderly health-care: questions and challenges. *Health Inform. J.*, 11, 4, 309–321, 2005.

20. Selwyn, N., The information aged: A qualitative study of older adults' use of information and communications technology. *J. Aging Stud.*, 18, 4, 369–384, 2004.

21. WHO, Patient Safety. World Health Organization, Geneva, Switzerland, 2018.

22. Aguilar, A., Van Der Putten, W., Kirrane, F. (Eds.), Positive patient identification using RFID and wireless networks. *HISI 11th Annual Conference*

and *Scientific Symposium, Dublin, Ireland*, Semantic Scholar, Seattle, Washington, U.S., 2006.

23. Mehrjerdi, Y.Z., RFID Role in Efficient Management of Healthcare Systems: A System Thinking Perspective. *IJIEPR*, 26, 1, 45–61, 2015.

24. Yao, W., Chu, C.-H., Li, Z., The Adoption and Implementation of RFID Technologies in Healthcare: A Literature Review. *J. Med. Syst.*, 36, 3507–25, 2012.

25. Khalid, M., Afzaal, H., Hassan, S., Zafar, N.A., Analysis and Formal Model of RFID-Based Patient Registration System. *Analysis*, 8, 11, 2017.

26. Liao, Y.-T., Chen, T.-L., Chen, T.-S., Zhong, Z.-H., Hwang, J.-H., The Application of RFID to Healthcare Management of Nursing House. *Wireless Pers. Commun.*, 1, 3, 1237–57, 2016.

27. Pérez, M.M., Cabrero-Canosa, M., Hermida, J.V., García, L.C., Gómez, D.L., González, G.V., Application of RFID technology in patient tracking and medication traceability in emergency care. *J. Med. Syst.*, 36, 6, 3983–93, 2012.

28. Azevedo, S.G. and Ferreira, J.J., Radio frequency identification: a case study of healthcare organisations. *IJSN*, 5, 2–3, 147–55, 2010.

29. Manzoor, A., *RFID in Health Care-Building Smart Hospitals for Quality Healthcare, Health Care Delivery and Clinical Science: Concepts, Methodologies, Tools, and Applications*, Pennsylvania, USA, pp. 839–67, IGI Global, 2018.

30. Dey, A., Vijayaraman, B., Choi, J.H., RFID in US hospitals: an exploratory investigation of technology adoption. *Manag. Res. Rev.*, 39, 4, 399–424, 2016.

31. Rosenbaum, B.P., Radio frequency identification (RFID) in health care: privacy and security concerns limiting adoption. *J. Med. Syst.*, 38, 3, 19, 2014.

32. Rahman, F., Bhuiyan, M.Z.A., Ahamed, S.I., A privacy preserving framework for RFID based healthcare systems. *Future Gener. Comput. Sy.*, 72, 339–52, 2017.

33. Ma, H. and Wang, K., Research on application of RFID technology in health care. *WIT Trans. Eng. Sci.*, 113, 209–16, 2016.

34. Bhatt, Y. and Bhatt, C., Internet of things in healthcare, in: *Internet of things and big data technologies for next generation healthcare*, pp. 13–33, Springer, Cham, 2017.

35. Khajeheian, D., Friedrichsen, M., Mödinger, W. (Eds.), *Competitiveness in Emerging Markets*, Springer International Publishing, Berlin, Germany, 2018.

36. Moreno-Camacho, J.L., Calva-Espinosa, D.Y., Leal-Leyva, Y.Y., Elizalde-Olivas, D.C., Campos-Romero, A., Alcántar-Fernández, J., Transformation from a conventional clinical microbiology laboratory to full automation. *Lab. Med.*, 49, 1, e1–e8, 2017.

37. Buyya, R. and Dastjerdi, A.V. (Eds.), *Internet of Things: Principles and paradigms*, Elsevier, Amsterdam, Netherland, 2016.

38. Hossain, M.S. and Muhammad, G., Cloud-assisted industrial internet of things (IIoT)—enabled framework for health monitoring. *Comput. Netw.*, 101, 192–202, 2016.

39. Jain, A., Nandakumar, K., Ross, A., Score normalization in multimodal biometric systems. *Pattern Recognit.*, 38, 12, 2270–2285, 2005.

40. Di Nardo, J.V., Biometric technologies: functionality, emerging trends, and vulnerabilities. *J. Appl. Secur. Res.*, 4, 1–2, 194–216, 2008.

41. Hamidi, H., An approach to develop the smart health using Internet of Things and authentication based on biometric technology. *Future Gener. Comput. Sy.*, 91, 434–449, 2019.

42. Yan, J., Yang, X., Sun, X., Chen, Z., Liu, H., A lightweight ultrasound probe for wearable human-machine interfaces. *IEEE Sens. J.*, 19, 14, 5895–5903, 2019.

43. Pang, Y., Jian, J., Tu, T., Yang, Z., Ling, J., Li, Y., Wang, X., Qiao, Y., Tian, H., Yang, Y., Ren, T.-L., Wearable humidity sensor based on porous graphene network for respiration monitoring. *Biosens. Bioelectron.*, 116, 123–129, 2018.

44. Zang, Y., Zhang, F., Di, C.-A., Zhu, D., Advances of flexible pressure sensors toward artificial intelligence and health care applications. *Mater. Horiz.*, 2, 2, 140–156, 2015.

45. Yao, S., Swetha, P., Zhu, Y., Nanomaterial-Enabled wearable sensors for healthcare. *Adv. Healthc. Mater.*, 7, 1, 2018.

46. Baskar, S., Shakeel, P.M., Kumar, R., Burhanuddin, M.A., Sampath, R., A dynamic and interoperable communication framework for controlling the operations of wearable sensors in smart healthcare applications. *Comput. Commun.*, 149, 17–26, 2020.

47. Amjadi, M., Pichitpajongkit, A., Lee, S., Ryu, S., Park, I., Highly stretchable and sensitive strain sensor based on silver nanowire-elastomer nanocomposite. *ACS Nano*, 8, 5, 27, 5154–5163, 2014.

48. Triplett, M., Nishimura, H., Ombaba, M., Logeeswarren, V.J., Yee, M., Polat, K.G., Oh, J.Y., Fuyuki, T., Léonard, F., Islam, M.S., High-precision transfer-printing and integration of vertically oriented semiconductor arrays for flexible device fabrication. *Nano Res.*, 7, 998–1006, 2014.

49. Sun, Q., Qian, B., Uto, K., Chen, J., Liu, X., Minari, T., Functional biomaterials towards flexible electronics and sensors. *Biosens. Bioelectron.*, 119, 237–251, 2018.

50. Son, D., Kang, J., Vardoulis, O., Kim, Y., Matsuhisa, N., Oh, J.Y., McGuire, A.F., An integrated self-healable electronic skin system fabricated via dynamic reconstruction of a nanostructured conducting network. *Nat. Nanotechnol.*, 13, 11, 1057, 2018.

51. Gao, F. and Sunyaev, A., Context matters: a review of the determinant factors in the decision to adopt cloud computing in healthcare. *Int. J. Inf. Manage.*, 48, 120–138, 2019.

52. Marston, S., Li, Z., Bandyopadhyay, S., Zhang, J., Ghalsasi, A., Cloud computing—The business perspective. *Decis. Support Syst.*, 51, 1, 176–189, 2011.

53. Gao, F., Thiebes, S., Sunyaev, A., Rethinking the meaning of cloud computing for health care: A taxonomic perspective and future research directions. *J. Med. Internet Res.*, 20, 7, e10041, 2018.

54. Almogren, A., An automated and intelligent Parkinson disease monitoring system using wearable computing and cloud technology. *Cluster Comput.*, 22, 1, 2309–2316, 2019.
55. Furda, R. and Gregus, M., Conceptual View on Healthcare Digitalization: An Extended Thematic Analysis. *IJBDAH*, 2, 1, 35–54, 2017.
56. Gupta, A.K. and Mann, K.S., Sharing of medical information on cloud platform—a review. *IOSR-JCE*, 16, 2, 08–11, 2014.
57. Hossain, M.S. and Muhammad, G., Cloud-assisted speech and face recognition framework for health monitoring. *Mobile Netw. Appl.*, 20, 3, 391–399, 2015.
58. Tian, S., Yang, W., Le Grange, J.M., Wang, P., Huang, W., Ye, Z., Smart healthcare: making medical care more intelligent. *Glob. Health J.*, 17, 11, 9, 2019.
59. Rajabion, L., Shaltooki, A.A., Taghikhah, M., Ghasemi, A., Badfar, A., Healthcare big data processing mechanisms: the role of cloud computing. *Int. J. Inf. Manage.*, 49, 271–289, 2019.
60. https://www.vosviewer.com/accessed December 29, 2019.
61. https://www.grandviewresearch.com/industry-analysis/home-healthcare-industry accessed December 29, 2019.
62. Mehta, N., Pandit, A., Shukla, S., Transforming healthcare with big data analytics and artificial intelligence: A systematic mapping study. *J. Biomed. Inform.*, 100, 103311, 2019.
63. Raghupathi, W. and Raghupathi, V., Big data analytics in healthcare: promise and potential. *Health Inf. Sci. Syst.*, 2, 1, 3, 2014.
64. Costa, F.F., Big data in biomedicine. *Drug Discov. Today*, 19, 4, 433–440, 2014.
65. https://www.asianhhm.com/healthcare-reports/healthcare-analytics-market-to-witness-phenomenal-growth accessed December 29, 2019
66. Dey, N., Hassanien, A.E., Bhatt, C., Ashour, A.S., Satapathy, S.C. (Eds.), *Internet of things and big data analytics toward next-generation intelligence*, Springer, Berlin, 2018.
67. Saheb, T. and Izadi, L., Paradigm of IoT big data analytics in healthcare industry: a review of scientific literature and mapping of research trends. *Telemat. Inform.*, 41, 12, 2019.
68. Sakr, S. and Elgammal, A., Towards a comprehensive data analytics framework for smart healthcare services. *Big Data Res.*, 4, 44–58, 2016.
69. Wu, X., Zhu, X., Wu, G.Q., Ding, W., Data mining with big data. *IEEE Trans. Knowl. Data Eng.*, 26, 1, 97–107, 2013.
70. Chen, M., Hao, Y., Hwang, K., Wang, L., Wang, L., Disease prediction by machine learning over big data from healthcare communities. *IEEE Access*, 5, 8869–8879, 2017.
71. Mehta, N. and Pandit, A., Concurrence of big data analytics and healthcare: A systematic review. *Int. J. Med. Inform.*, 11, 457–65, 2018.
72. Marshall, K.W., Mikulis, D.J., Guthrie, B.M., Quantitation of articular cartilage using magnetic resonance imaging and three dimensional reconstruction. *J. Orthop. Res.*, 13, 6, 814–823, 1995.

73. Chen, M., Zhang, Y., Qiu, M., Guizani, N., Hao, Y., SPHA: Smart personal health advisor based on deep analytics. *IEEE Commun. Mag.*, 56, 3, 164–169, 2018.

74. Downing, N.S., Cloninger, A., Venkatesh, A.K., Hsieh, A., Drye, E.E., Coifman, R.R., Krumholz, H.M., Describing the performance of US hospitals by applying big data analytics. *PLoS One*, 12, 6, e0179603, 2017.

75. Ghani, K.R., Zheng, K., Wei, J.T., Friedman, C.P., Harnessing big data for health care and research: are urologists ready. *Eur. Urol.*, 66, 6, 975–977, 2014.

76. https://www2.deloitte.com/content/dam/Deloitte/global/Documents/Life-Sciences-Health-Care/gx-lshc-hc-outlook-2018.pdf, 2018.

2

Working of Mobile Intelligent Agents on the Web—A Survey

P.R. Joe Dhanith* and B. Surendiran

National Institute of Technology Puducherry, Karaikal, India

Abstract

Due to the exponential growth of dynamic internet contents, demand for efficient and economical crawling methods has also increased. Consequently, many new techniques have been proposed; among them the most important one is mobile crawling. The mobile crawlers are capable of downloading only relevant web pages at the source of the data to reduce the HTTP request overhead. Mobile crawler attracted many search engines because of its efficient filtering and reduced memory and time consumption. This chapter provides a survey on mobile crawling. A bunch of twenty mobile crawlers from the available literature are presented in this chapter. The necessity and influence of each metric with respect to network load are discussed. Future directions, limitations and strategies are also presented for the viewers.

Keywords: Web, web crawler, mobility, agents, mobile crawler, mobile intelligent agents

2.1 Introduction

Due to the rapid growth of the internet, a search engine needs a good crawling mechanism for indexing the web pages. There are seven different types of crawlers. They are universal crawler, preferential crawler, hidden crawler, mobile crawler, incremental crawler, distributed crawler and parallel crawler. Except for mobile crawler, all the other crawlers execute from

---

Corresponding author: joe.dhanith@gmail.com

G. R. Kanagachidambaresan (ed.) Role of Edge Analytics in Sustainable Smart City Development: Challenges and Solutions, (21–48) © 2020 Scrivener Publishing LLC

the client side. It causes network overload and high latency. These drawbacks can be reduced in mobile crawlers. The mobile crawler sends mobile agents to remote locations for local access of web pages. Mobile agent is the prime part of the mobile crawler.

According to D. Chess [1], Mobile agents are programs written in a script language that can be sent to a remote server computer for execution from a client computer.

Figure 2.1 shows the basic architecture of mobile agents. The communication between client and server by migrating around the entire network is the basic idea behind mobile agents. The client application communicates the server application through agent subsystem. The agent subsystem sends the message from client application through communication medium with the help of messaging system. The agents at the server side receive the message with the help of messaging subsystem. The agent at the server side processes the message and sends it to the server application. The major advantages of mobile agents are given as follows:

(i)   reduces the network overload and latency
(ii) encapsulate protocols and execute autonomously through the network
(iii) robust and fault tolerant.

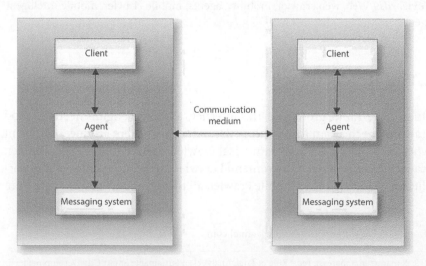

Figure 2.1 Mobile agent infrastructure.

The various real-time applications such as e-commerce, personal assistance, secure brokering, mobile crawler, etc., make the mobile agents popular among researchers.

In this work, a survey focuses on challenges and future scope of mobile based crawlers. Twenty mobile crawlers have been exposed. A comprehensive assessment is done focusing on four dimensions (Network Load, Precision, crawling time and CPU cycles). The survey is concluded with a relation table elucidating the combination of inputs and expected outputs.

2.2 Mobile Crawler

The aim of mobile crawler is to download web pages locally at the remote server side.

Otman *et al.* [2] proposed a decision-making environment based on Naive Bayes classification using mobile agents. Figure 2.2 shows the proposed mobile crawler architecture of Otman *et al.* These mobile agents identify the available offers in the online for business and it will filter out the most suitable offers for the company. The main purpose of these mobile agents is to participate in online bidding is to grab the most related offers to the company. These agents identify and access the tenders through the HTTP client protocol. After retrieving all the offers from the website it stores them in a MySQL database. Then transform the MySQL data to HDFS. Then the multi agent system starts its process by

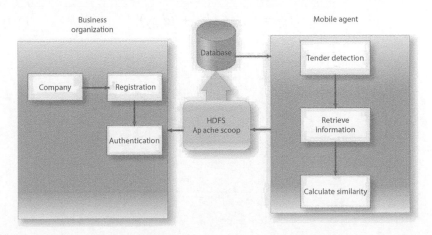

Figure 2.2 Mobile agent for online bidding.

sharing the information for coordination of their activities. These agents then compute the semantic similarity between the offer and the area of specialization of the company. If the similarity is above 0.7 then it starts participating in bidding. The similarity between the offer and the area of specialization of the company can be calculated by using the following formula:

$$f_s = (w_1 * f_{tf}) * (w_2 * f_{idf}) \tag{2.1}$$

where f_s is the similarity score function, w_1 is the weight of term-frequency, f_{tf} is the term-frequency function, w_2 is the weight value of Inverse-Document-Frequency, and f_{idf} is the Inverse-Document-Frequency function. The semantic similarity module in this crawler improves the performance of the bidding process.

The weight factors w_1, w_2 in Equation (1) aids in removing the irrelevant offers at the early stage. This factor in mobile crawler helps to achieve good precision and recall in crawling.

Niraj *et al.* [3] proposed a mobile crawler to optimize the frequency of mobile agents for visiting web sites based on user interest. Figure 2.3 shows the proposed mobile crawler architecture of Niraj *et al.* In this work, the web page on which the user is more interested is downloaded at a faster rate than those on which the user is less interested. But in practical, the user's interest in the web pages is not at the same rate. Consider four documents d1, d2, d3, and d4. d2 is visited by 3 users and d1, d3 and d4 visited only by 1 user. So, d2 should be revisited first. The revisit frequency can be calculated by using the following formula:

$$f_{art} = f_{crt} + (fd_{crt1} + fd_{crt2}) \tag{2.2}$$

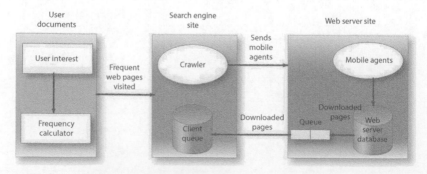

Figure 2.3 Mobile crawler based on user interest.

Where f_{art} is the adjusted refresh time function, f_{crt} is the current refresh time function, fd_{crt1} is the change in refresh time in contents, and fd_{crt2} is the change in refresh time shown in websites.

If the user's interest increases in a specific website then the revisit frequency can be calculated by using the following formula:

$$fd_{crt2} = (f_{ubc} + f_{lbc}) * f_{crt} \qquad (2.3)$$

where f_{crt} is the current refresh time function, fd_{crt2} is the change in refresh time shown in websites, f_{ubc} is the upper threshold value function and the f_{lbc} is the lower threshold value function.

The frequency revisit module in this crawler identifies the best suited web pages at the early stage helps to avoid the network traffic and improves the quality of downloading.

Rajendar Nath *et al.* [4] proposed a mobile crawler to reduce the bandwidth consumption and increases the efficiency of indexing. Figure 2.4 shows the proposed mobile crawler architecture of Rajendar Nath *et al.* This crawler starts downloading from the seed URLs and stores these URLs in a queue. If the queue is empty, it stops the crawling and sends the web pages to the search engine. If the queue is not empty, it gets the next URL from the queue and retrieves its statistics from the ODBFM. If statistics not available, it retrieves the web page and stores it for sending to the search engine. Otherwise it checks whether Last Modified Date (LMD) did not retrieve the web page, scans and analyzes it to count the number of URLs

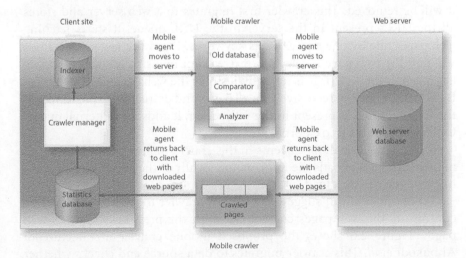

Figure 2.4 Mobile crawler to filter out non-modified web pages.

and number of keywords. It checks whether the number of URLs mismatch. If some URLs mismatch then it stores the web page and sends it to the search engine. Otherwise, it rejects the web page. If LMD is available, it fetches the CMD and then checks whether the CMD is different from the one previously crawled. If yes then it retrieves the web page. Otherwise it rejects the web page. The number of web pages indexed can be calculated by using the formula:

$$f_n = f_l + (f_m * f_{m1}) + f_h \qquad (2.4)$$

where f_n is the total number of web pages indexed, f_l is the probabilistic function of a web page whose rate of change is less than 0.10, f_m is the probabilistic function of a web page whose rate of change is between 0.10 and 0.80, f_{m1} is the average of probabilistic function of a web page whose rate of change is between 0.10 and 0.80 and f_h is the probabilistic function of a web page whose rate of change is greater than 0.80.

The LMD module in this crawler rejects the un-modified web pages at the early stage helps to improve the network load and bandwidth.

Joachim Hammer *et al.* [5] proposed a mobile crawler which migrates to various data sources for downloading web pages. Figure 2.5 shows the proposed mobile crawler architecture of Joachim Hammer *et al.* This crawler reduces the HTTP request overhead by moving the mobile crawler to the data source directly to enable the localized data access. In this work, query shipping approach is used to find the relevance of a web page at the source of the data. If the web page is relevant it will be downloaded. Otherwise it will be removed. This crawler first migrates to a web server and stores all the URLs present in the server in the URL queue. It starts fetching web pages one by one and extracts keywords. From the keyword, it finds whether the web page is relevant or irrelevant by using a query-shipping approach. If the web page is relevant, it stores the web page in the page list. It performs crawling recursively on all pages and extracts web page links. If the web page link is present in the web server, it adds it to internal queue. Otherwise, it adds it to external queue.

The ability of the mobile agents in this crawler moves around the entire network and downloads the information locally at the server side helps to improve the network load.

Anbukodi *et al.* [6] suggested a mobile crawler to reduce overhead by contrasting the web page's current size with the previously crawled web pages. Figure 2.6 shows the proposed mobile crawler architecture of Anbukodi *et al.* This crawler migrates to data source and checks whether there is any URL present in the ODBFM. If not URLs present stop crawling,

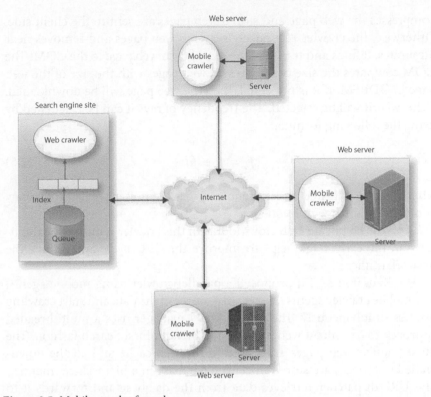

Figure 2.5 Mobile crawler for web.

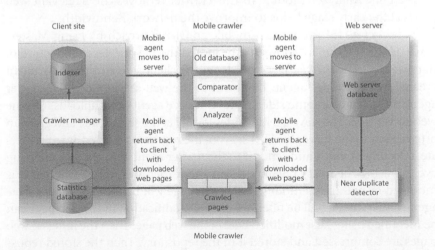

Figure 2.6 Mobile crawler using NDD.

compresses the web page and stored web pages are sent to the client side. Otherwise, the crawler recursively searches web pages and removes near duplicates. It finds and transfers the size of each web page to the COM. The COM compares the size of the present web pages with the size of the web page in ODBFM. If it is not equal, then the web page will be downloaded. Otherwise it will be rejected. The frequency of revisit can be calculated by using the following formula:

$$f_a = f_c + fd \qquad (2.5)$$

where f_a is the adjusted revisit frequency, f_c is the present revisit frequency and $f d$ is the change in frequency.

The Near Duplicate Detector Module in this crawler removes the duplicates in the early stage helps to improve the CPU cycle and reduce the network traffic.

Abu Kausar *et al.* [7] proposed a parallel crawler using mobile agents. The mobile crawler agents migrate to a source of the data and start crawling process simultaneously. The central crawl manager uses a multithreaded approach to download web pages in the Breadth First Search fashion. The most popular web pages are stored in the web cache and all the downloaded web pages are stored in central database in a hierarchical manner. The URL dispatcher retrieves data from the database and forwards it to crawling. Then the crawling starts downloading from the seed URLs. These URLs are assigned with page rank and store it in the repository. The link analyzer analyzes the web page and removes if it is irrelevant.

The Link Analyzer Module in this crawler removes the irrelevant web pages at the early stage helps to improve the network Bandwidth.

Badawi *et al.* [8] proposed a mobile crawler approach by using Master-Slave design. Figure 2.7 shows the proposed mobile crawler architecture of Badawi *et al.* The master agent resides at the client side and the slave agent created by the master agent, then sent to the web server side. The master agent at the search engine side creates the slave agents and uploads it to the web server side. The slave agent resides locally at the server side and gives an http request to the server for URLs. From the response received, it will generate a document index and sends it to the master agent after the first crawling cycle. During the next crawling, it will check each web pages whether it is modified or not. If it is modified, the web page will be indexed by the slave agent. Otherwise, it will be filtered out. The modification in the web page can be identified using Last modified date of the web page. Then the indexed web pages are compressed and stored it in the repository. Then the stored repository will be sent to the master agent. The crawling will continue recursively.

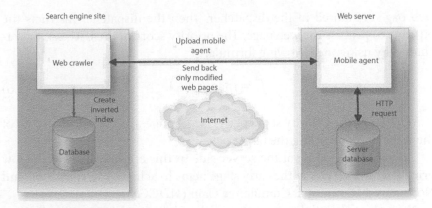

Figure 2.7 Mobile agent to maintain search engine freshness.

The Indexing module at the slave side in this crawler removes the un-modified web pages at the early stage helps to improve the network load.

JY Chen *et al.* [9] proposed a mobile crawler for the Tianji tracking engine. Figure 2.8 shows the proposed mobile crawler architecture of JY Chen *et al.* This crawler scheduler maintains the queue of downloaded and un-downloaded links. Once a web page is downloaded, the scheduler finds the priority score of the web page and stores it in the priority queue in the sorted order. The controller controls the entire system. The controller retrieves URL from the scheduler and given it to the dispatcher. The dispatcher requests the processor to download the web page. The downloaded

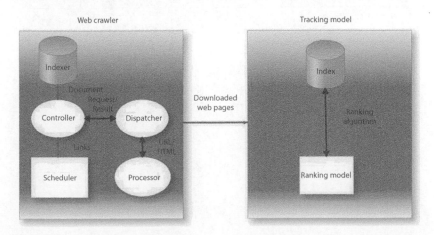

Figure 2.8 Tianji tracking model.

web page are stored in the dispatcher. Then the dispatcher instructs the pipeline to process the web page. The priority score of the URL can be calculated by using the following formula:

$$f_p = \max(f_l) - 1 \qquad (2.6)$$

Where f_p is the priority score of the target page, f_l is the priority score of the web page containing the target page.

The ranking module at the server side in this crawler removes the low prioritized web pages at the early stage helps to achieve high precision and Normalized Discounted Cumulative Gain (NDCG).

A. Singh *et al.* [10] designed a parallel mobile crawler to reduce the time and bandwidth of crawling. Figure 2.9 shows the proposed mobile crawler architecture of A. Singh *et al.* The central crawler maintains a list of URLs for crawl. The URLs are sent in batches to the Crawl frontier. The crawl frontier starts fetching web pages in a Breadth First Fashion. The downloaded URLs are stored in a Local Document Database. Once all the parallel processes are over, the downloaded documents from all the processes are stored in a central database.

The Local Document Database at the server side in this crawler supports parallel process helps to improve the crawling time.

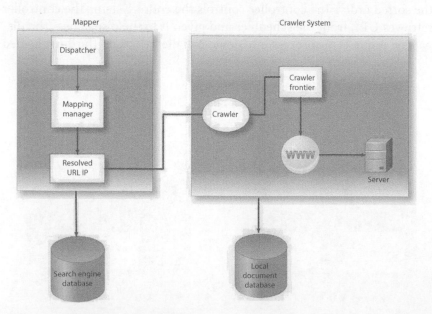

Figure 2.9 Parallel migrating crawler.

Abu Kausar *et al.* [11] proposed a mobile crawler using Java Aglet. Figure 2.10 shows the proposed mobile crawler architecture of Abu Kausar *et al.* This crawler initially moves to the data source and then starts crawling. Once it reaches the web server, it checks the local URL queue. If the queue is empty, it stops crawling the web page and compresses the data stored then forwards it to the search engine. Otherwise, it continues retrieving web pages recursively until the completion and also removes the duplicates. While downloading it finds the size of the web page and compares the size with the previously downloaded web page. If it is equal, then the crawler rejects the web page. Otherwise, it downloads it.

The Last Modified Size Module of this crawler helps to remove the un-modified web pages at the early stage helps to improve the CPU cycles.

Manish Kumar *et al.* [12] proposed a mobile crawler for hidden web environment. Figure 2.11 shows the proposed mobile crawler architecture of Manish Kumar *et al.* In this crawler, the central coordinator generated a job list. Once a job list is generated, the mobile agent moves to the source data. Then the queries are fired database for retrieving data. In this query generation phase, the queries are generated from a set of keywords. Then Map-Reduce is applied to get the index. If the data is sufficient to index, then it will stop its crawling. Otherwise, the queries are recursively fired to the database to the generation of index.

The Communication Layer in this crawler reduces the volume of downloaded web pages helps to improve the coverage percentage.

H.M. Chuang *et al.* [13] proposed a mechanism to construct POI database to store POI search maps using deep crawler. Figure 2.12 shows the proposed mobile crawler architecture of H.M. Chuang *et al.* A Named

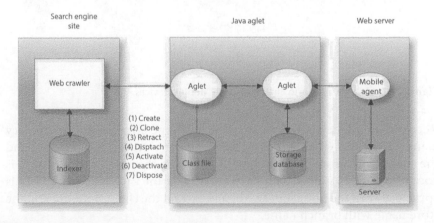

Figure 2.10 Mobile crawler using Java Aglets.

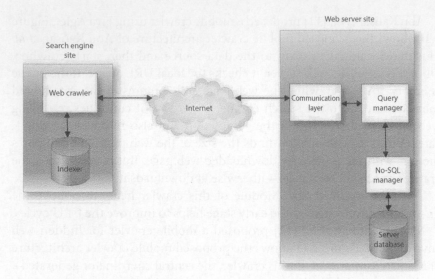

Figure 2.11 Mobile crawler for hidden web.

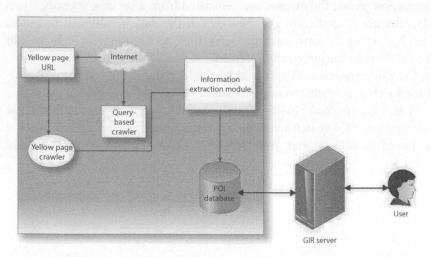

Figure 2.12 Mobile Crawler to enable Maps in Mobile Devices.

Recognition Model is trained to search snippets to form a vocabulary using GIR server. Then a query-based crawler extracts the addresses and the store names from the server. In this crawler, the initial query pattern is composed of city names with keywords. Then the category of the store is appended with the initial query. Then to extract the chain store, append the store name with branch name.

The Named Recognition Model module in this crawler extracts the information using snippets helps to improve the Address Bearing Ratio.

T. Kawamura *et al.* [14] proposed a mobile based recommendation mechanism called Word-of-Mouth Scouter. This mechanism, supports the user to analyze the product. Once the user takes a photo of a product's barcode, the mechanism immediately extracts the useful information such as name, manufacturer, etc., of a company, traverses the web, finds the relevant blogs and review of the product. This review can be identified by applying NLP techniques by integrating with ontologies. The Positive/Negative determination module can be used to determine the correlation between different blogs. Then the associate topic module extracts the similarity between the different products using TF-IDF. The similarity can be calculated by using the following formula:

$$f_s(p_1, p_2) = f_{tf} * f_{idf} \qquad (2.7)$$

where $f_s(p_1, p_2)$ is the relevance score between p_1 and p_2, f_{tf} is the term-frequency function and f_{idf} is the Inverse-Document-Frequency function.

Then the Boolean filter and the stochastic filter are used to remove the ads and the spam documents.

The Positive/Negative determination module in this crawler helps to identify the positive subset correlation of products and the negative subset correlation among the products at the early stage helps to improve the precision rate.

M. Butkiewicz *et al.* [15] suggested Klotski to boost mobile user experience. Figure 2.13 shows the proposed mobile crawler architecture of M. Butkiewicz *et al.* KLOTSKI's front-end is an optimized internet proxy that prioritizes user-relevant URLs. It uses legacy HTTP to connect with web servers and uses SPDY to communicate with users. When a client u query for a page w arrives, the front end uses the preferences of the user and a load time estimator to determine the collection of prioritized resources. The back-end of KLOTSKI is responsible for capturing page dependencies and dynamics using measuring agents via offline measurements through fingerprint generator. The agents document and report key properties such as the dependencies between fetched resources, the size of each resource, the waterfall load list, and the location of each resource on the rendered display for each page fetched.

The dependency properties generated by the finger print generator removes the irrelevant web pages at the early stage helps to improve the computation time.

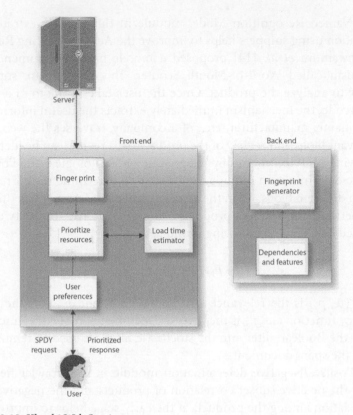

Figure 2.13 Klotski Web Service.

M. Butkiewicz [16] suggested a websieve to create friendly mobile websites, enabling even small web providers to support mobile devices without spending substantial resources to do so. Figure 2.14 shows the proposed mobile crawler architecture of M. Butkiewicz *et al.* Websieve's main goal is to select all possible web pages subsets whose load time should be lower than the maximum load time allowed. The websieve architecture contains three important components. The first one is dependency extraction, second is utility inference and third is object selection. For each web page the backend of the websieve generates fingerprint. The fingerprint includes dependency structures, load time information of objects and object utilities by the service provider. For dependency extraction a nearest neighbor algorithm is used to match the reloaded object with the original web page, to find the missing objects.

$$d = match(o_i, o) \& match(o, o_i) \qquad (2.8)$$

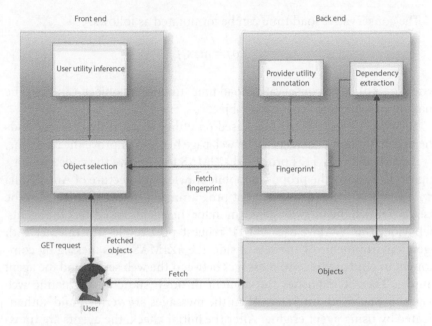

Figure 2.14 Websieve.

where d is the dependency extraction, o_i is the subset of object in the blocked web page, o is the subset of object in the original image and match represents the one-to-one mapping of objects.

Then to find the utility score, features such as location of the object, type of the object and clickable information of the object are taken as features. These features are then learned by predictive classifier to produce the utility score.

$$f_{utilscore} = L(f_i) \ where \ i = 1, 2, \ldots, n \qquad (2.9)$$

where $f_{utilscore}$ is the utility score, L represents the learning classifier and f_i is the features selected from the objects.

Then the object selection can be done by using integer linear programming by combining two approaches conservative load time and heuristic estimate of load time.

$$\forall_i : f_o \leq f_p \qquad (2.10)$$

where f_o is the selected object and f_p is the logical parent of the selected object.

The conservative load time can be formulated as follows:

$$f_{load}(o) = \max_{i \in o} f_{ti} \qquad (2.11)$$

where $f_{load}(o)$ is the conservative load time function of object o and f_{ti} is the maximum load time function of object o_i.

The object selection module based on utility score in this crawler finds the optimal subset of objects in the web page helps to improve the load time.

Amar Nalla *et al.* [17] proposed aZIMAS to improve the code mobility. Figure 2.15 shows the proposed mobile crawler architecture of Amar Nalla *et al.* At the client side, web agent programming model (WAPM) can be used to launch the mobile agents, monitor the agents and direct the agents' behavior. This WAPM uses HTTP request post request to interact with agent environment. At the server side, the aZIMAS uses messaging component to send and receive messages between the web server and the agent engine. Then it publishes the content through static and dynamic web pages through web interface. Then the messages are verified and authenticated by using agent engine. After the initial check, the agents are transferred to agent space. Then the aZIMAS agent API provides security. The agent space provides security. The agent space provides all the functionality needed by the agents for migration. The agent space registers the agents in name registry. Then the memory allocation for agents is handled by resource controller. The communication manager handles communication

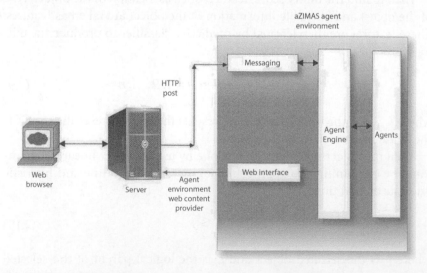

Figure 2.15 aZIMAS Agent.

between the agents. The agent in aZIMAS contains the attributes such as ID, home base, credentials, data and code.

The agent space in this crawler maintains the web pages downloaded by the mobile agents helps to improve the response time.

Prasannaa Thati *et al.* [18] proposed an efficient crawling mechanism called as crawlets. Figure 2.16 shows the proposed mobile crawler architecture of Prasannaa Thati *et al.* The basic idea of crawlets is to crawl web pages at the website locally and send back the preprocessed web pages to the search engine. The web crawler maintains two queues, one for storing the already crawled web pages and the other one to store the un-crawled web pages. Before it starts downloading the web page, the crawler will check whether the URL supports crawling or not. If it supports, then the crawler uploads the crawlets into the website. The crawlets carries two queues, the first one is list of seed URLs queue and the second is the list of already crawled queues to the web site. The crawler can dispatch a crawlet with a larger set of seed URLs to avoid multiple visits to a website. The crawlet is not able to crawl all the web pages in the site at the first visit. During its second visit, it tries to crawl almost all the web pages in the site. Once a crawlet is uploaded, the crawler will not crawl until it hears from the crawlet. For security reasons, to prevent malicious attacks, there is a need for mutual authentication between search engine and website. Once a mutual authentication is successful, then only the websites allows the crawlet to upload. For authentication, it uses public key cryptography and mutual key encryption to protect data transmission.

The increase in seed URL helps to avoid duplication which helps the crawler to improve crawling time.

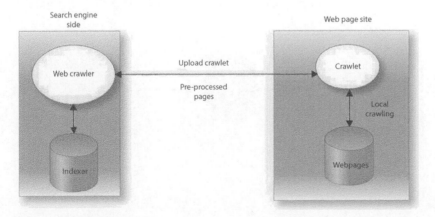

Figure 2.16 Crawlet.

S. Funfrocken *et al.* [19] proposed a mobile agent based methodology called as web agent based service providing (WASP). Figure 2.17 shows the proposed mobile crawler architecture of S. Funfrocken *et al.* When the user gives a normal HTTP request to the web server, it immediately retrieves the information from the file and response back to the user. When the user tries to request the web server through agents it immediately forwards the request to server agent environment (SAE). The SAE request does not affect the implementation of web server. This WASP environment consists of two agent requests, one for agent startup and the other for agent transfer. In the startup and configuration phase, the agent gets started by SAE to configure the user requested data. In the service phase, the agent is executed to provide the user requested service. In this phase, to locally access the data, the agent moves from web server to other web server.

P. Marques *et al.* [20] proposed the M & M approach which is based on no agent platform where the applications itself becomes agent-enabled. Figure 2.18 shows the proposed mobile crawler architecture of

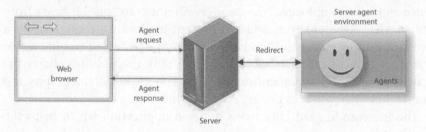

Figure 2.17 WASP Infrastructure.

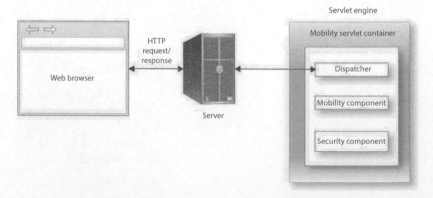

Figure 2.18 Mobility servlet container.

P. Marques *et al*. Once the web server receives the HTTP request, it forwards the request to mobility servlet container (MSC). This MSC publishes the information on the web. The dispatcher in the MSC, receives the HTTP request from the web server and passes it to the mobility component. The mobility component receives the request and retrieves the information from the local server and sends back to the dispatcher. The dispatcher sends HTTP response to the web server. To publish the information agent requires full HTTP request. This request includes IP of the client, MIME type and session information. This can be used to distinguish the clients. The security component in MSC allows the agent to migrate between hosts using SSL.

T. Goddard *et al*. [21] proposed a mobile agent based mechanism called as webvector. Figure 2.19 shows the proposed mobile crawler architecture of T. Goddard *et al*. It combines URL based agent identification with flexible communication model. While retrieving files from web server locally, agents retrieve documents along with the URLs associated with them. The webvector makes use of these URLs to identify a specific port to make the URL available for connection. The x-tcp and x-udp are the two protocols proposed in webvector. These protocols provide security and assistance for other agents. The webvector is composed of three major components. The first component webvector.cgi is used to execute the agents on the server side. The second components security manager is used to provide security for the agents and

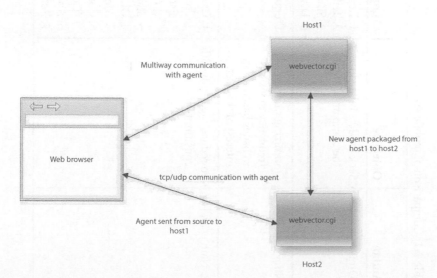

Figure 2.19 WebVector.

Table 2.1 Comparison of mobile crawlers.

Author	Objective	Components	Target variables	Evaluation metrics used
Otman *et al.* [2]	Seek tenders related to the company	1. Registration 2. Tenders Detection 3. Similarity Calculation 4. Distributed storage	Company information stored in mysql database	Precision
Niraj *et al.* [3]	Optimizing migrant frequency to visit websites based on the interest of the user.	Frequency Calculator	Current refresh time, adjusted refresh time, change in refresh time	Quantity, quality and network traffic
R. Nath *et al.* [4]	To reduce the bandwidth consumption	1. Crawler Manager (CM) 2. Frequency Change Estimator Module (FCEM) 3. Statistics Database (SD) 4. Old Database File Module (ODBFM) 5. Comparator Module (CoM) 6. Analyzer Module (AM). 7. Remote Site/Server (RS)	1. Name of URL 2. Last Modified Date 3. Number of URLs in the page 4. Number of keywords in the page	1. Page change behavior. 2. Load on the network. 3. Bandwidth preserved

(Continued)

Table 2.1 Comparison of mobile crawlers. (*Continued*)

Author	Objective	Components	Target variables	Evaluation metrics used
Joachim Hammer *et al.* [5]	To download web pages at the server side	1. Crawler Manager 2. Archive Manager 3. Query Engine 4. Database Command Manager 5. Connection Manager	1. Status Code 2. Location 3. Last modified size 4. Content 5. Content type 6. Content length	1. Total Load 2. Network Load
Anbukodi S. *et al.* [6]	To identify the pages updated for download on the remote site.	1. Crawler Manager 2. Statistics Database Module 3. Old Database File Module (ODBFM) 4. Comparator Module (CoM) 5. Near Duplicate detector Module	1. Current revisit frequency 2. Change in frequency 3. Adjusted revisit frequency	1. CPU cycles 2. Average network traffic 3. Actual network traffic

(*Continued*)

Table 2.1 Comparison of mobile crawlers. (*Continued*)

Author	Objective	Components	Target variables	Evaluation metrics used
Md. Abu Kausar *et al.* [7]	To analyze the downloading locally at the server side	1. Scheduler 2. New ordered Queues 3. Site ordering module 4. URL Queues/ Known URLs 5. Multithreaded downloader 6. URL Collector 7. Link Extractor 8. Link analyzer	1. URLs 2. Customized page rank of web pages 3. doc_id 4. length of document	1. Network Bandwidth
Marwa Badawi *et al.* [8]	Detecting major web page adjustments that effectively represent the index of the search engine and reducing network load.	1. Master Agent (MA) 2. Slave Agent (SA)	1. No. of pages added 2. No. of pages deleted 3. No. of pages modified 4. Last modified date 5. Page size in bytes 6. Hash value 7. Keyword count 8. No. of bytes downloaded	1. Network load

(*Continued*)

Table 2.1 Comparison of mobile crawlers. (*Continued*)

Author	Objective	Components	Target variables	Evaluation metrics used
Jin-Yuan Chen et al. [9]	To crawl web pages on the basis of time preferences	1. Scheduler 2. Controller 3. Dispatcher 4. Processor 5. Pipeline	1. Time slot 2. Page Rank 3. Priority value for each link 4. Decay Ratio over time	1. Precision 2. Normalized Discounted Cumulative Gain
Akansha Singh et al. [10]	The crawler's job is divided into several separate and parallel crawlers that move to different machines to increase network capacity and accelerate upload.	1. Central Crawler 2. Crawl Frontiers 3. Local Document Database 4. Central Database: 5. Web Server	1. URL-IP pairs 2. URL	1. Crawl limit 2. Content downloaded in MB 3. Content After compression in KB 4. Time in seconds
Md. Abu Kausar et al. [11]	It has the unusual ability to transfer itself to another system from one system in a network.	1. Crawl Manager 2. Indexer 3. HTTP Server 4. Persistence Manager 5. Cache Manager 6. Security Manager	1. URL 2. Title 3. Modification date 4. Keywords	1. CPU cycles

(*Continued*)

Table 2.1 Comparison of mobile crawlers. (*Continued*)

Author	Objective	Components	Target variables	Evaluation metrics used
Manish Kumar *et al.* [12]	Send the mobile crawler to the remote server to gather information of large size in the hidden network.	1. Outbox 2. Query building database 3. Query manager 4. Archive manager 5. NoSQL manager	1. Labelled value set 2. Field 3. Value 4. Probability	1. Coverage Percentage
Hsiu-Min Chuang *et al.* [13]	To locate pages that could be used to retrieve addresses and shop names.	1. POI Database 2. GIR Server 3. Store Name Model 4. Yellow and query based crawler	1. Store name 2. Store address	1. Address bearing ratio 2. Region of Interest
Kawamura *et al.* [14]	To extract only the information necessary depending on the situation of the client.	1. P/N Determination 2. Associate Topic Extraction 3. Sorting and Filtering	1. Opinions of authors and trackbacks 2. Trackbacks and comments 3. Timestamps 4. Frequency of opinions	Precision

(*Continued*)

Table 2.1 Comparison of mobile crawlers. (*Continued*)

Author	Objective	Components	Target variables	Evaluation metrics used
M. Butkiewicz et al. [15]	A framework that prioritizes information that is most important to the needs of the user.	1. Fingerprint Generator 2. Prioritize 3. Load Estimator	1. Identical Parent 2. Lone child 3. Surrounding text 4. Position of URLs	1. Absolute Error 2. Relative Error
M. Butkiewicz et al. [16]	To detect the dynamic interdependencies on today's web pages automatically.	1. User Utility Inference 2. Object Selection 3. Dependency Extraction 4. Fingerprint	1. Web page content 2. Set of objects before and after blocking 3. Type of object	Load Time
Amar Nalla et al. [17]	To allow lightweight mobile agents to be executed on the Internet and to remove some of the restrictions imposed by existing systems	1. Web Interface 2. Messaging 3. Agent Engine 4. Agent Space	1. ID 2. Home Base 3. Credentials 4. Data 5. Code Fragment 6. Appletcontext	1. Response Time 2. Available Memory
P. Thati et al. [18]	Crawl pages locally at a location and return a concise description to the search engine	1. Extract URLs 2. Dispatch Crawlet 3. Download URLs	1. Web Page Text 2. URLs 3. Authentication Key	1. Crawling Time 2. Data Transfer Rate 3. CPU Time

(*Continued*)

Table 2.1 Comparison of mobile crawlers. (*Continued*)

Author	Objective	Components	Target variables	Evaluation metrics used
S. Funckfrocken *et al.* [19]	By switching from server to server, mobile agents can access local web server information.	1. WASP HTTP Client 2. Server Agent Environment 3. Agent Startup 4. Migration 5. Web Data Interface	1. Agent Request 2. Agent Response 3. Configuration Information 4. GUI Request 5. GUI Response	CPU Cycles
P. Marques *et al.* [20]	to enable web servers to send and receive agents	1. Web Server 2. Mobility Servlet Container 3. Mobility Component	1. IP of the client 2. MIME Types 3. Session Information	Resource Control
T. Goddard *et al.* [21]	Combines a dynamic interaction framework with the detection of URL-based agents.	1. webvector.cgi 2. webvector 3. securitymanager	1. URL 2. tcp/udp port	Computational Power

the third component webvector which will interact directly with the agents. The agents' activities are monitored in tracker.lookup function.

2.3   Comparative Study of the Mobile Crawlers

A comparative study focusing objective, components used, target variables, and Evaluation metrics as four different features for comparison are discussed. The comparison gives a overview and weight of individual inputs as given in Table 2.1.

2.4   Conclusion

This chapter provides a survey over the existing mobile web crawlers. There are many suggestions in the literature for crawling mobile web sites, but unfortunately there is no survey that makes thorough comparison. In this chapter, we surveyed and compared mobile Web crawling proposals on various aspects, namely: objectives, components target variables, and the measures used to assess their performance. The crawler that has the common points of change are Network Load, Precision, crawling time and CPU cycles. A relation of each input and output was also presented to readers for possible future directions.

References

1. Chess, D., Harrison, C., Kershenbaum, A., Mobile agents: Are they a good idea? *Lect. Notes Comput. Sci. (including Subser. Lect. Notes Artif. Intell. Lect. Notes Bioinform.)*, 1222, 25–45, 1997.
2. Maarouf, O., Madani, Y., Errtali, M., Elayachi, R., Detecting tenders based on Mobile agents. *Procedia Comput. Sci.*, 151, 2018, 1114–1119, 2019.
3. Singhal, R., Dixit, A., Agarwal, R.P., Sharma, A.K., Regulating frequency of a migrating web crawler based on users interest. *Int. J. Eng. Technol.*, 4, 4, 246–253, 2012.
4. Nath, R. and Bal, S., A novel mobile crawler system based on filtering off non-modified pages for reducing load on the network. *Int. Arab J. Inf. Technol.*, 8, 3, 272–279, 2011.
5. Hammer, J. and Fiedler, J., Using Mobile Crawlers to Search the Web Efficiently. *Int. J. Comput. Inf. Sci.*, 1, 1, 36–58, 2000.
6. Anbukodi, S. and Muthu Manickam, K., Reducing web crawler overhead using mobile crawler, in: *2011 Int. Conf. Emerg. Trends Electr. Comput. Technol. ICETECT 2011*, pp. 926–932, 2011.

7. Kausar, M.A., Dhaka, V.S., Singh, S.K., An Effective Parallel Web Crawler based on Mobile Agent and Incremental Crawling. *J. Ind. Intell. Inf.*, January 2013, 1, 86–90, 2013.

8. Badawi, M., Mohamed, A., Hussein, A., Gheith, M., Maintaining the search engine freshness using mobile agent. *Egypt. Informatics J.*, 14, 1, 27–36, 2013.

9. Chen, J.Y., Zheng, H.T., Xiao, X., Sangaiah, A.K., Jiang, Y., Zhao, C.Z., Tianji: Implementation of an Efficient Tracking Engine in the Mobile Internet Era. *IEEE Access*, 5, c, 16592–16600, 2017.

10. Singh, A. and Singh, K.K., Faster and Efficient Web Crawling with Parallel Migrating Web Crawler. *Int. J. Comput. Sci. Issues*, 7, 3, 28–32, 2010.

11. Kausar, M.A., Dhaka, V.S., Singh, S.K., Web Crawler Based on Mobile Agent and Java Aglets. *Int. J. Inf. Technol. Comput. Sci.*, 5, 10, 85–91, 2013.

12. Kumar, M. and Bhatia, R., Design of a mobile Web crawler for hidden Web, in: *2016 3rd Int. Conf. Recent Adv. Inf. Technol. RAIT 2016*, pp. 186–190, 2016.

13. Chuang, H.M., Chang, C.H., Kao, T.Y., Cheng, C.T., Huang, Y.Y., Cheong, K.P., "Enabling maps/location searches on mobile devices: constructing a POI database via focused crawling and information extraction," *Int. J. Geogr. Inf. Sci.*, 30, 7, 1405–1425, 2016.

14. Kawamura, T., Nagano, S., Inaba, M., Mizoguchi, Y., WOM Scouter: Mobile service for reputation extraction from weblogs. *Int. J. Metadata, Semant. Ontol.*, 3, 2, 132–141, 2008.

15. Butkiewicz, M., Wang, D., Wu, Z., Madhyastha, H.V., Sekar, V., K LOTSKI: Reprioritizing Web Content to Improve User Experience on Mobile Devices. NSDI'15: Proceedings of the 12th USENIX Conference on Networked Systems Design and Implementation, 439–453, 2015.

16. Butkiewicz, M. *et al.*, Enabling the transition to the mobile web with WebSieve. *ACM HotMobile 2013 14th Work. Mob. Comput. Syst. Appl.*, 14, 2–7, 2013.

17. Nalla, A., Helal, A., Renganarayanan, V., AZIMAs—Almost Zero Infrastructure Mobile Agent System. *IEEE Wirel. Commun. Netw. Conf. WCNC*, 1, 36–43, 2002.

18. Thati, P., Chang, P.H., Agha, G., Crawlets: Agents for high performance web search engines. *Lect. Notes Comput. Sci. (including Subser. Lect. Notes Artif. Intell. Lect. Notes Bioinform.)*, 2240, 119–134, 2001.

19. Funfrocken, S., "How to integrate mobile agents into Web servers,". WET-ICE '97: Proceedings of the 6th Workshop on Enabling Technologies on Infrastructure for Collaborative Enterprises. *J. Eng. Appl. Sci.*, 94–99, 1997.

20. Marques, P., Fonseca, R., Simões, P., Silva, L., Silva, J., Integrating mobile agents into off-the-shelf web servers: The M&M approach. *Proc.—Int. Work. Database Exp. Syst. Appl. DEXA*, 677–681, 2001.

21. Goddard, T. and Sunderam, V.S., WebVector: agents with URLs. WET-ICE '97: Proceedings of the 6th Workshop on Enabling Technologies on Infrastructure for Collaborative Enterprises. *J. Eng. Appl. Sci.*, 100–105, 1997.

3

Power Management Scheme for Photovoltaic/Battery Hybrid System in Smart Grid

T. Bharani Prakash* and S. Nagakumararaj

Department of EEE, Sri Krishna College of Technology, Coimbatore, India

Abstract

This chapter illustrates the power management scheme for hybrid systems in microgrids. The adaptive droop control and the power flow management is done to maintain the grid voltage and frequency that are considered to be the main feature of power management that is employed in the proposed scheme.

This proposed control strategy is applied for sharing of load with other sources while charging the battery system. The PV/battery unit which can not only track the maximum power like MPPT (Maximum Power Point Tracking) but also supply the maximum PV power to the microgrids as long as there is sufficient load to be supplied with the power generated by the hybrid system. The control strategy employed is designed to modify the operating point of PV autonomously whenever the available PV power is higher than the load and the battery is completely charged. Moreover, the battery can operates as separate storage unit that can regulate voltage and frequency and supply deficit power to the microgrid.

The various strategies employed are PI and MPPT along with Phase-Locked Loop (PLL) is employed in the management of power in a hybrid system. The system performance is studied by using MATLAB software and the output is analyzed.

Keywords: MPPT, PI controller, phase locked loop, microgrid, internal power flow management, voltage source control, space vector pulse width modulation, state of charge

*Corresponding author: bharani.ffb@gmail.com

G. R. Kanagachidambaresan (ed.) *Role of Edge Analytics in Sustainable Smart City Development: Challenges and Solutions*, (49–66) © 2020 Scrivener Publishing LLC

3.1 Power Management Scheme

In a grid connected system the battery storage is crucial in the operation of microgrids, which is used for the regulation of frequency and voltage when there is no alternate generation. It is also necessary to ensure that the load is supplied with sufficient power even in the absence of intermediate power. In such a case an energy storage unit is employed that is connected to microgrids through voltage source controller.

To avoid this problem power management strategy has been employed between PV and battery units. Normally the battery and the other sources connected to the grid is controlled by certain droop control strategies when there is an occurrence of insufficient from the PV to the microgrid. This droop control strategy is used to prevent the battery from depletion. The depletion of battery may cause damage in the loads connected to microgrids. The main purpose of battery is not only for the storage purpose but also used to supply or absorb power during fault conditions. This control scheme is used to coordinate the features of the grid connected system with the microgrid system. This paper principally involves two basic power management strategies as shown below:

- Internal Power Flow Management
- Voltage Control Scheme.

3.2 Internal Power Flow Management

The voltage at the DC-link is regulated by the battery bidirectional boost converter while the PV boost converter is controlled to regulate the voltage at the PV array terminal. The PV array voltage reference vpv-ref is generated by the PV power controller based on the battery SOC, the PV maximum power, and the load power.

Based on these variables, the power flow within the system can be categorized into two operating scenarios: the MPPT scenario, and the internal SOC upper limit control scenario. During the MPPT scenario, the voltage vpv-ref is generated by the MPPT algorithm, which assumes that the SOC of the battery is less than the maximum limit SOCmax. When the SOC increases beyond the specified SOCmax, the SOC upper

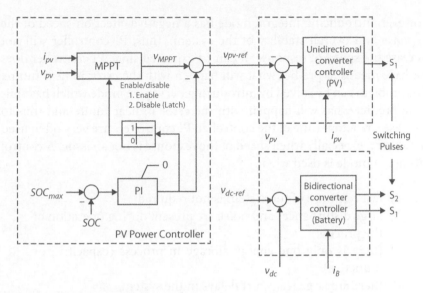

Figure 3.1 Internal power flow management.

limit control starts to control the PV power by moving the PV operating point away from the maximum power point (MPP) towards the voltage source operating region of the PV characteristic curve. Therefore, this loop will keep reducing the power extracted from the PV array until the battery current iB drops to zero and the SOC settles at SOCmax as shown in Figure 3.1.

Under this condition, the PI output will be used to disable the MPPT algorithm and force it to stay at the current vM P P T; otherwise it will keep searching for the maximum power causing vM P P T to drift away from the MPP region. This control loop is called the internal SOC control loop, as opposed to the external loop discussed in Section 3.5. In this operating scenario, the PI controller continuously adjusts the PV operating point to follow the load as long as the power available from the PV array can match the load demand. If the load becomes larger than the PV power, the battery will supply the deficit power and the internal SOC upper limit control loop becomes idle again.

3.2.1 PI Controller

PI controller will eliminate forced oscillations and steady state error resulting in operation of on-off controller and P controller respectively.

However, introducing integral mode has a negative effect on speed of the response and overall stability of the system. Thus, PI controller will not increase the speed of response. It can be expected since PI controller does not have means to predict what will happen with the error in near future. This problem can be solved by introducing derivative mode which has ability to predict what will happen with the error in near future and thus to decrease a reaction time of the controller. PI controllers are very often used in industry, especially when speed of the response is not an issue. A control without D mode is used when:

a) fast response of the system is not required
b) large disturbances and noise are present during operation of the process
c) there is only one energy storage in process (capacitive or inductive)
d) there are large transport delays in the system.

The integral or reset action allows the controller to eliminate steady-state offset. There is no need for a bias term, as the controller output will change as needed to drive to zero. The controller transfer function is given by τI is called the *integral time constant* and determines the weight given to the integral action relative to the proportional part. As K_c is increased or t_I is decreased (i.e., more aggressive control), the closed loop dynamics goes through the same sequence of changes as the P-only controller: overdamped,

General approach to tuning PI:

1. Initially have no integral gain (TI large)
2. Increase KP until get satisfactory response
3. Start to add in integral (decreasing TI) until the steady state error.

With PI controller, we are able to eliminate the steady state error. In summary with small value of Ki (Ki = 0.01), we have smaller percentage of overshoot (about 13.5%) and larger steady state error (about 0.1). As we increase the gain of Ki, we have larger percentage of overshoot (about 38%) and manage to obtain zero steady error and faster response. With the response depicted in Figures 3.2 and 3.3, P-I-D controller can be introduced in order to reduce the overshoot and to ensure the response converge to the specified design objectives.

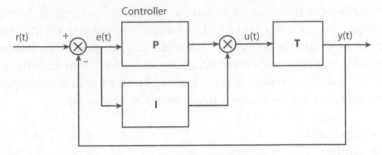

Figure 3.2 PI controller.

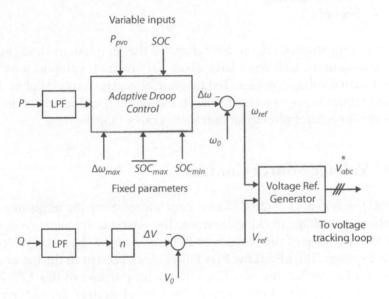

Figure 3.3 Voltage source control.

3.2.2   State of Charge

State of charge (SOC) is the equivalent of a fuel gauge for the battery pack in a battery electric vehicle (BEV), hybrid vehicle (HEV), or plug-in hybrid electric vehicle (PHEV). The units of SOC are percentage points (0% = empty; 100% = full). An alternate form of the same measure is the depth of discharge (DoD), the inverse of SOC (100% = empty; 0% = full). SOC is normally used when discussing the current state of a battery in use, while DoD is most often seen when discussing the lifetime of the battery after repeated use. Usually, SoC cannot be measured directly but it can be estimated from direct measurement variables in two ways: offline and online. In offline techniques, the battery desires to be charged and discharged in constant rate such as Coulomb-counting. This method gives precise estimation of battery SoC, but they are protracted, costly, and interrupt main battery performance. Therefore, researchers are looking for some online techniques. In general there are five methods to determine SOC indirectly:

- chemical
- voltage
- current integration
- Kalman filtering
- Pressure.

Measuring state-of-charge by voltage is the simplest method, but it can be inaccurate. Cell types have dissimilar chemical compositions that deliver varied voltage profiles. Temperature also plays a role. Higher temperature raises the open-circuit voltage, a lower temperature lowers it, and this phenomenon applies to all chemistries in varying degrees.

3.3   Voltage Source Control

In VSC the system is controlled as voltage source. Here the frequency and the reference voltage tracking are done. The reference frequency is generated with the help of the real power in the system by the adaptive droop control system. The LPF (Low Pass Filter) block present in the below diagram is a first order low pass filter. The main purpose of this LPF is to remove the harmonics in the output. The control strategy depends on the SOC of the battery. When the SOC of the battery is below the minimum limit then the control strategy the first priority is given to the charge of the battery and next to the power sharing. On the other hand, when the SOC of the battery is between the minimum and maximum of the charge of the battery. Else the microgrid is shared with the hybrid unit and the excess PV power is stored in the battery. If the SOC exceeds the maximum value the hybrid system will supply the power to the microgrid as long as there is sufficient load otherwise it will store the excess in the battery. There are certain cases where conditions from different criteria as mentioned above takes place. In such a case the internal power management loop control is performed which reduces the ability of PV to extract Maximum Power Point Tracking (MPPT). By reducing the power output of the PV the system can effectively follow the load change that occurs in the system.

Various operating scenario based on the SOC (State Of Charge) of the battery is described in Figure 3.3. Space vector pulse width modulation technique is employed in the closed loop control scheme as one of the effective PWM (Pulse Width Modulation) technique. Space Vector Pulse Width Modulation (SV-PWM) is actually just a modulation algorithm which translates phase voltage (phase to neutral) references, coming from the controller, into modulation times/duty-cycles to be applied to the PWM peripheral. It is a general technique for any three-phase load, although it has been developed for motor control. SV-PWM maximizes DC bus voltage exploitation and uses the "nearest" vectors, which translates into a minimization of the harmonic content. The classical application of SV-PWM is vector motor control, which is based on the control of currents' projection on two orthogonal coordinates (direct and quadrature, dq), called Field Oriented Control (FOC). The basic concept is that with a known motor and known voltage output pulses you can accurately determine rotor slip by monitoring current and phase shift. The controller can then modify the PWM "sine" wave shape, frequency or amplitude to achieve the desired result.

3.3.1 Phase-Locked Loop

A phase-locked loop or phase lock loop (PLL) is a control system that generates an output signal whose phase is related to the phase of an input signal. While there are several differing types, it is easy to initially visualize as an electronic circuit consisting of a variable frequency oscillator and a phase detector. The oscillator generates a periodic signal. The phase detector compares the phase of that signal with the phase of the input periodic signal and adjusts the oscillator to keep the phases matched. Bringing the output signal back toward the input signal for comparison is called a feedback loop since the output is 'fed back' toward the input forming a loop as shown in Figure 3.4. Keeping the input and output phase in lock step also implies keeping the input and output frequencies the same. Consequently, in addition to synchronizing signals, a phase-locked loop can track an input frequency, or it can generate a frequency that is a multiple of the input frequency. These properties are used for computer clock synchronization, demodulation, and frequency synthesis. Phase-locked loops are widely employed in radio, telecommunications, computers and other electronic applications. They can be used to demodulate a signal, recover a signal from a noisy communication channel, generate a stable frequency at multiples of an input frequency (frequency synthesis), or distribute precisely timed clock pulses in digital logic circuits such

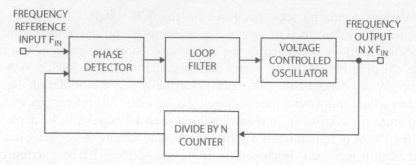

Figure 3.4 Phase-locked loop.

as microprocessors. Since a single integrated circuit can provide a complete phase-locked-loop building block, the technique is widely used in modern electronic devices, with output frequencies from a fraction of a hertz up to many gigahertz.

There are several variations of PLLs. Some terms that are used are analog phase-locked loop (APLL) also referred to as a linear phase-locked loop (LPLL), digital phase-locked loop (DPLL), all digital phase-locked loop (ADPLL), and software phase-locked loop (SPLL).

3.3.2 Space Vector Pulse Width Modulation

Space vector modulation (SVM) is an algorithm for the control of pulse width modulation (PWM). It is used for the creation of alternating current (AC) waveforms; most commonly to drive 3 phase AC powered motors at varying speeds from DC using multiple class-D amplifiers. There are various variations of SVM that result in different quality and computational requirements. One active area of development is in the reduction of total harmonic distortion (THD) created by the rapid switching inherent to these algorithms. A three phase inverter as shown to the right converts a DC supply, via a series of switches, to three output legs which could be connected to a three-phase motor. The switches must be controlled so that at no time are both switches in the same leg turned on or else the DC supply would be shorted. The reference signal may be generated from three separate phase references using the αβγ transform. The reference vector is then synthesized using a combination of the two adjacent active switching vectors and one or both of the zero vectors.

Various strategies of selecting the order of the vectors and which zero vector(s) to use exist. Strategy selection will affect the harmonic content and the switching losses.

3.3.3   Park Transformation (abc to dq0)

In electrical engineering, direct–quadrature–zero (or $dq0$ or dqo) transformation or zero–direct–quadrature (or $0dqo$ or odq) transformation is a mathematical transformation that rotates the reference frame of three-phase systems in an effort to simplify the analysis of three-phase circuits. In the case of balanced three-phase circuits, application of the dqo transform reduces the three AC quantities to two DC quantities. Simplified calculations can then be carried out on these DC quantities before performing the inverse transform to recover the actual three-phase AC results. It is often used in order to simplify the analysis of three-phase synchronous machines or to simplify calculations for the control of three-phase inverters. In analysis of three-phase synchronous machines park transformation transfers three phase stator and rotor quantities in to a single rotating reference frame to eliminate the effect of time varying inductances. The dqo transform presented here is exceedingly similar to the transform first proposed in 1929 by Robert H. Park. In fact, the dqo transform is often referred to as Park's transformation. The power-invariant, right-handed dqo transform applied to any three-phase quantities (e.g. voltages, currents, flux linkages, etc.) is shown below in matrix form:

$$
x_{dqo} = Kx_{abc} = \sqrt{\frac{2}{3}}
\begin{bmatrix}
\cos(\theta) & \cos\left(\theta - \dfrac{2\pi}{3}\right) & \cos\left(\theta + \dfrac{2\pi}{3}\right) \\
-\sin(\theta) & -\sin\left(\theta - \dfrac{2\pi}{3}\right) & -\sin\left(\theta + \dfrac{2\pi}{3}\right) \\
\dfrac{\sqrt{2}}{2} & \dfrac{\sqrt{2}}{2} & \dfrac{\sqrt{2}}{2}
\end{bmatrix}
\begin{bmatrix}
x_a \\
x_b \\
x_c
\end{bmatrix}
$$

The inverse transform is:

$$
x_{abc} = K^{-1}x_{dqo} = \sqrt{\frac{2}{3}}
\begin{bmatrix}
\cos(\theta) & -\sin(\theta) & \dfrac{\sqrt{2}}{2} \\
\cos\left(\theta - \dfrac{2\pi}{3}\right) & -\sin\left(\theta - \dfrac{2\pi}{3}\right) & \dfrac{\sqrt{2}}{2} \\
\cos\left(\theta + \dfrac{2\pi}{3}\right) & -\sin\left(\theta + \dfrac{2\pi}{3}\right) & \dfrac{\sqrt{2}}{2}
\end{bmatrix}
\begin{bmatrix}
x_d \\
x_q \\
x_o
\end{bmatrix}
$$

3.4   Simulation Diagram and Results

3.4.1   Simulation Diagram

The wind energy renewable source is employed along with the PV/Battery hybrid system in the proposed paper. The management of power is effectively carried out in the middle of the solar power, wind and the battery as shown in Figure 3.5 and Figure 3.6. The output Measurement block gives the signal to the flow control block that consists of ideal switches that operates as per as the

Vector	A+	B+	C+	A−	B−	C−	V_{AB}	V_{BC}	V_{CA}	
$V_0 = \{000\}$	OFF	OFF	OFF	ON	ON	ON	0	0	0	zero vector
$V_1 = \{100\}$	ON	OFF	OFF	OFF	ON	ON	$+V_{dc}$	0	$-V_{dc}$	active vector
$V_2 = \{110\}$	ON	ON	OFF	OFF	OFF	ON	0	$+V_{dc}$	$-V_{dc}$	active vector
$V_3 = \{010\}$	OFF	ON	OFF	ON	OFF	ON	$-V_{dc}$	$+V_{dc}$	0	active vector
$V_4 = \{011\}$	OFF	ON	ON	ON	OFF	OFF	$-V_{dc}$	0	$+V_{dc}$	active vector
$V_5 = \{001\}$	OFF	OFF	ON	ON	ON	OFF	0	$-V_{dc}$	$+V_{dc}$	active vector
$V_6 = \{101\}$	ON	OFF	ON	OFF	ON	OFF	$+V_{dc}$	$-V_{dc}$	0	active vector
$V_7 = \{111\}$	ON	ON	ON	OFF	OFF	OFF	0	0	0	zero vector

Figure 3.5 SVPWM switching sequences.

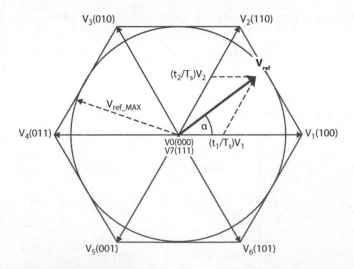

Figure 3.6 SVPWM switching vectors.

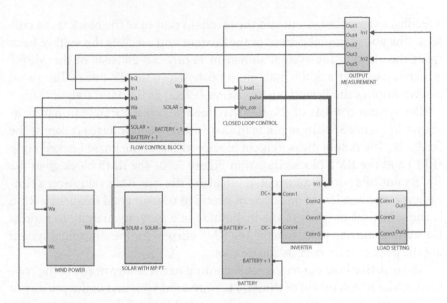

Figure 3.7 Simulation diagram.

signal from the output measurement. Based on the switching performance the sources act to follow the change in load conditions.

Based on the load value the sources are given priorities according to the switching signals from the flow control block. During the off load period the battery that has been charged continues to deliver the power to the load. During the peak hours the renewable sources continues to deliver the power to the load. The simulation diagram of proposed model is shown in Figure 3.7.

The PV system is a constant DC source. The system consists of three inputs such as irradiance, temperature and voltage input that is coming as

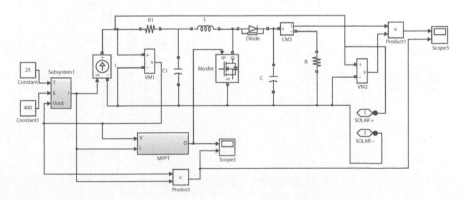

Figure 3.8 PV with MPPT.

a feedback from the system and the resultant output of the block is the current. The above model generates the current and receives the voltage back from the circuit. The system shown in Figure 3.8 consists of the MPPT which is used to track the maximum power from the PV panel. The above system implies the Perturb and Observe (P&O) as the MPPT algorithm.

The system consists of the Resistive load which is variable in nature as shown in Figure 3.9. The ouput of the load current and voltage is taken as the feedback. The output measurement block consists of the Phase Locked Loop (PLL) and the RMS blocks shown in Figure 3.10. The RMS block gives the RMS value of a periodic current. It calculates the true RMS value over a running average window of one cycle of specified fundamental frequency. RMS is the statistical measure of the magnitude of a varying quantity to express the average current in ac system. The RMS current for the sinusoidal system are the peak current over its square root.

The resistive load current is set according to the utility needs of the consumer. The RMS current of the load is compared with that of the priority of the sources given by the customer. The switching signals are generated by the relational operator that is given to the flow control block.

The closed loop control consists of the PI controller and the SVPWM (Space Vector Pulse Width Modulation) which is employed for the generation of pulses which are fed to the inverter shown in Figure 3.11. In the closed loop control the abc to dq0 transformation is done on a set of three phase signals as given below,

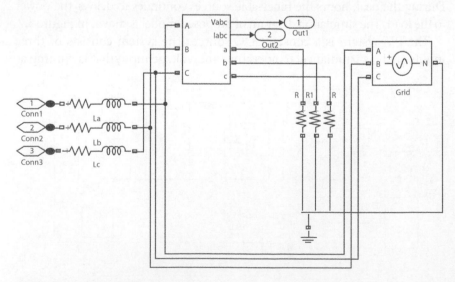

Figure 3.9 Resistive load.

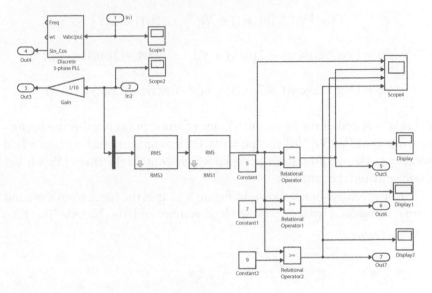

Figure 3.10 Output measurement block.

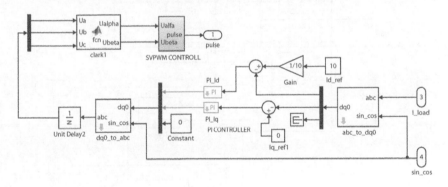

Figure 3.11 Closed loop control.

$$Vd = 2/3 * [Va * \sin(wt) + Vb * \sin(wt - 2pi/3) + Vc * \sin(wt + 2pi/3)]$$

$$Vq = 2/3 * [Va * \cos(wt) + Vb * \cos(wt - 2pi/3) + Vc * \cos(wt + 2pi/3)]$$

$$V0 = 1/3 * [Va + Vb + Vc]$$

For the dq0 to abc transformation the block transforms three quantities (direct axis, quadrature axis and zero-sequence components) expressed in a two axis reference frame back to phase quantities. The following transformation is used,

$$Va = [Vd * \sin(wt) + Vq * \cos(wt) + Vo]$$

$$Vb = [Vq * \cos(wt - 2pi/3) + Vd * \sin(wt - 2pi/3) + Vo)$$

$$Vc = [Vq * \cos(wt + 2pi/3) + Vd * \sin(wt + 2pi/3) + Vo)$$

where w = speed of rotation (rad/s).One of the inputs contains the vectorized signal of [Vd Vq V0] components. Other input should contain a [sin (wt) cos (wt)] two dimensional signal which contain the three [Va Vb Vc] phase sinusoidal quantities.

The flow control block shown in Figure 3.12 gets the input from the wind energy conversion system, Photovoltaic system and the battery. The flow

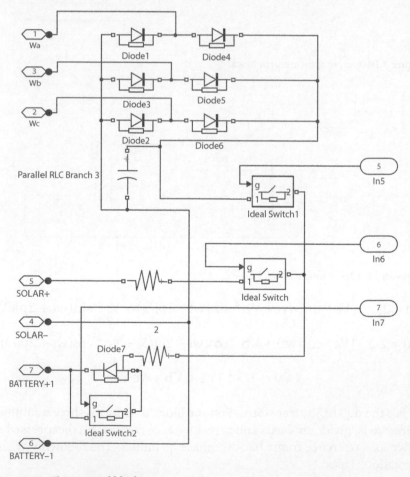

Figure 3.12 Flow control block.

control block consists of three ideal switches which operates according to the switching signals that are been generated in the output measurement block that depends on the load current. According to the load current the switching signals are generated and the ideal switches are turned on such that the power reaches the inverter through the battery that in turn maintains the SOC of the battery. The sources are in turn connected parallel with the load.

The Priority of the sources available can be defined by the user and according to the priority conditions the relational operator acts and the switching signals are given to the ideal switches. In this system the priority of the sources are given in the order given below:

- Wind Power
- PV Power
- Battery.

3.4.2   Simulation Results

The PV output power with and without Maximum Power Point Tracking algorithm is shown below in Figure 3.13:

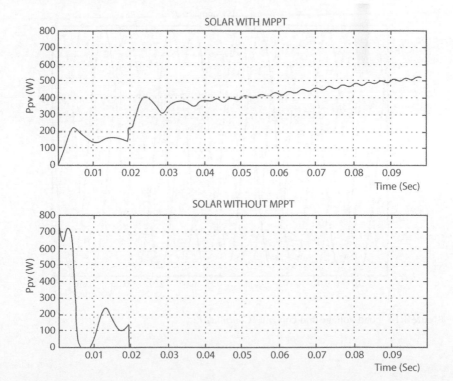

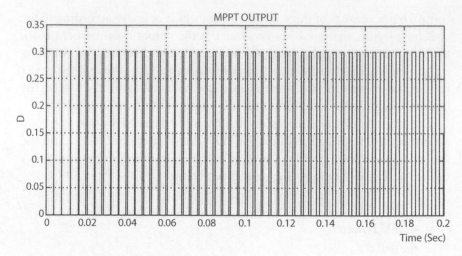

Figure 3.13 PV power with and without MPPT.

The load current and the load voltage are given below in Figure 3.14:

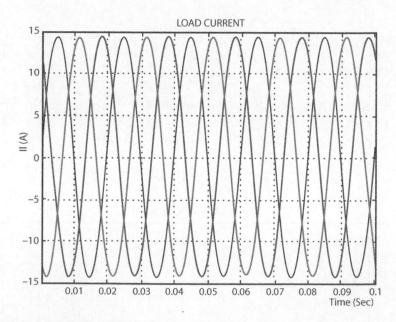

Figure 3.14 Load voltage and current. *(Continued)*

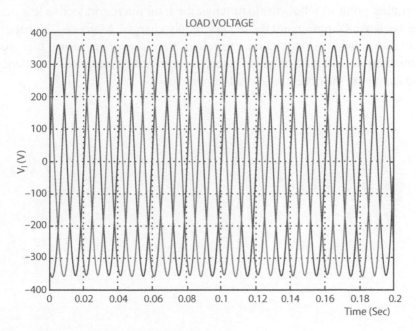

Figure 3.14 (Continued) Load voltage and current.

Conclusion

In this paper a power management strategy for PV/battery hybrid units in an islanded microgrid has been proposed. The PV/battery unit is controlled to operate as a voltage source that employs an adaptive droop control strategy, in contrast to the PV control strategies in the literature where the PV units are controlled to operate as current controlled sources (PQ control). It has been shown that controlling the PV/battery unit as a voltage source with the proposed adaptive droop provides the PV/battery hybrid unit with several unique features. First, the hybrid unit has the ability to share the load power with other sources while storing any excess energy in the battery. Second, it can track and supply the maximum PV power to the microgrid provided that there is sufficient load demand in the microgrid. Otherwise, the hybrid unit will autonomously match the available load while charging the battery with the excess energy as in standalone strategies. Third, the control strategy modifies the PV operating point to follow the load when the total microgrid load is less than the available PV power and the battery is fully charged. Moreover, the battery may also provide the operational functions that a separate storage unit may provide in an islanded microgrid, such as regulating voltage and frequency, and supplying the deficit power in the microgrid.

4

Analysis: A Neural Network Equalizer for Channel Equalization by Particle Swarm Optimization for Various Channel Models

M. Muthumari[1]*, D.C. Diana[2] and C. Ambika Bhuvaneswari[3]

[1,3]Assistant Professor, School of Electrical and Communication, Veltech Rangarajan Dr. Sagunthala R and D Institute of Science and Technology, Avadi, Chennai, India
[2]Associate Professor, Electronics and Communication Engineering, Easwari Engineering College, Ramapuram, Chennai, India

Abstract

The data transmission rate over the communication system is affected because of the distortion that occurs in the channel. Normally distortion occurs due to the dispersive nature of the channel in terms of Inter-Symbol Interference (ISI) and additive white Gaussian noise. For high-speed and reliable communication in channel the equalization technique is applied at the end of the receiver. Comparing to other equalizers, an adaptive channel equalizer plays an important role in a communication process. Functional Link Artificial Neural Network (FLANN) performs better in all noise condition than other conventional method and neural network. Due to absence of hidden neurons in functional link artificial neural network it can be able to reduce computational complexity that arises in networks. An adaptive equalizer is trained with Particle Swam Optimization (PSO) algorithm to finding the performance of equalization for better optimization and to achieve minimum mean square error.

Keywords: Inter-Symbol Interference, equalization, Functional Link Artificial Neural Network, Particle Swarm Optimization, mean square error, AWGN, adaptive equalizer

*Corresponding author: muthu2s94@gmail.com

G. R. Kanagachidambaresan (ed.) Role of Edge Analytics in Sustainable Smart City Development: Challenges and Solutions, (67–84) © 2020 Scrivener Publishing LLC

4.1 Introduction

The data transfer rates and spectrum efficiency of wireless communication have been significantly improved over the past decades. In the past five decades there has a phenomenal growth in communication services. High-speed communication services are provided by satellite and fiber optic networks. In the communication channel, the data transmission should be efficient with high speed. The process of providing this kind of reliable communication is a big challenging task for the engineers and scientists. In digital communication, the transmission of symbols should have good intention i.e. with minimum errors. If the speed of digital communication is high then we need to transfer a signal with large bandwidth, but this is impossible because of the limited resources availability.

The main aim is to design a good equalizer for developing the artificial neural network type of equalizer. This then is trained by the better optimization algorithms with different modulation techniques. By using this, the error caused in the desired signal is going to be eliminated.

Patra *et al.* [1], proposed a computational efficient artificial neural network for adaptive channel equalization with a 4-QAM signal constellation in a digital communication system. Here a single layer Chebyshev neural network (ChNN) is used to expand the input by using Chebyshev polynomials. The performance evolution and comparison is done by the extensive simulations with a linear LMS-based equalizer. Using Chebyshev polynomials makes it a complicated analysis while equalization is done. Zeng *et al.* [2] analyzed a feedback recurrent neural network for a complex-valued non-linear equalizer—which is based on the pipelined decision network (CPDFRNN). It is also a kind of non-linear channel equalization. This pipelined decision network has a complex network for equalizing the data and has a long mathematical operation.

Potter *et al.* [3] proposed a particle swarm optimization (PSO) algorithm with novel hybrid PSO-EA-DEPSO algorithm for channel equalization. The evolutionary algorithm (EA) and differential evolution (DE) is presented for multiple-input–multiple-output (MIMO) channel prediction and is used to train a recurrent neural network (RNN). Zhao *et al.* [4] discussed a pipelined recurrent neural network (JPRNN) with modified RTRL algorithm that is used to train a novel joint-processing adaptive nonlinear equalizer that will be able to eliminate nonlinear channel distortion that occurs in a communication system. The RTRL algorithm is only adapted for RNN.

Every power system is required to solve the optimization problems in one or more nonlinear function. In most of the cases analytical systems might suffer due to slow convergence; for that a heuristics-based swarm intelligence method is used as an efficient alternative. Del Valle *et al.* [7] present a detailed operation of PSO and its variants, and it also provides an effective survey on the power system applications that have a powerful nature of PSO as an optimization technique. Hong *et al.* [8] analyzed a nonlinear data pattern that occurs due to rainfall forecasting. To get accurate forecasting of rainfall there are lots of novel forecasting approaches, among that Recurrent artificial neural networks (RNNS) which have played an important role. To solve nonlinear regression, support vector machines (SVMs) have also been applied with such. To forecast the different rainfall depth values, different hybrid model of RNNs and SVMs, namely RSVR, were used.

Patra *et al.* [9] looked to solve the problem of channel equalization in a digital communication system, thus the artificial neural network (ANN) structures have been established. The problem associated with channel non-linearities has been overcome by applying equalizers which has the capability of producing arbitrarily complex decision regions. To solve that the functional link ANN (FLANN) has been established. The comparison between the performance analyses of the proposed network with two other ANN structures has been done with the LMS-based channel equalizer in terms of bit-error rate (BER) and attainable MSB, signal to noise ratio and channel nonlinearities. Lee *et al.* [11] proposed a hybrid electromagnetism-based particle swarm optimization HEMPSO, to design a functional-link-based Petri recurrent fuzzy neural system (FLPRFNS) for each input calculation. To receive the best current information about each particle updates, HEMPSO combines have the advantage over multiple-agent-based searching, global optimization and they also indicate that the FLPRFNS exhibits with the high accuracy.

Liang *et al.* [12] proposed a weighted slice algorithm for the problem of linear channel estimation with unknown channel input signals, which has cumulated slices of different orders that are linearly combined and estimated single-input–single-output channels. A weight computation criterion approach incorporates a certain matrix structure to improve the reliability of estimation. To control the channel order overestimation, this generalized algorithm has advantage over Fonollosa and Vidal's algorithm.

Lin *et al.* [13] proposed the SENFIN (self-evolving neural fuzzy inference networks) model, which combines the orthogonal polynomials and linearly independent functions in a functional expansion of the FLNN. For structure learning and parameter learning there is an efficient algorithm named as reinforcement evolutionary learning algorithm (REL). Structure learning is used to determine the number of fuzzy rules that can adopt a subgroup symbiotic evolution to generate several variable fuzzy systems and parameter learning is used to adjust parameters of the SENFIN: which is a one of the hybrid evolutionary algorithms, which means combining the cooperative particle swarm optimization and the cultural algorithm, produces the cultural cooperative particle swarm optimization (CCPSO). From the result, it has been concluded that the CCPSO method can improve the global search capacity. Lin *et al.* [14] proposed an innovative technique to compensate the backlight images. There are two processing stages to compensate: the first one is the backlight level detection, in that feature weighting first transferred the color space into gray space and the second one is backlight image compensation. By using the proposed functional-link-based neuro-fuzzy network (FNFN) with immune particle swarm optimization (IPSO), these two backlight factors can detect the compensation degree. In the backlight image compensation stage, according to the compensation degree of each image, the adaptive cubic curve method has been proposed to compensate. At backlight level detection stage, the backlight degree has been indicated by histograms of the luminance distribution.

Mingo López *et al.* [15] analyzed the differential evolution algorithm with the particle swarm optimization, instead of training the classic back propagation algorithm. This proposed method trains a neural network based algorithm to get optimal solutions. Based on the choice of the processing elements, the performance of a neural network for particular problems is varying, and the performance is based on the net architecture and the learning algorithm. To optimize topology and structure of connectivity the proposed method were analyzed. Ribeiro *et al.* [16] discussed a methodology, to select optimal inputs, topologies, and transfer functions for ANN with the help of Particle Swarm Optimization (PSO) rather than the standard technique like a back-propagation [of errors].

Sandhya Yogi *et al.* [17] proposed a new approach to equalization done in a communication channel with the help of Functional Link Artificial Neural Networks (FLANNs), where the training of FLANNs using PSO Algorithm has been done and the performance of the FLANNs compared with the conventional LMS based channel equalizer. From the experimental results, it can be clearly identified that the proposed equalizer improves the classification capability with differentiating the received data.

Dehuria *et al.* [18] analyzed an improved particle swarm optimization (IPSO) which has been used to train the functional link artificial neural network (FLANN). It is named as ISO-FLANN. Here the complexity of the network increases with the number of layers increases, as well as it is increased by the number of nodes in layers increases. From that it is noticed, the required number of nodes in a layer and the required number of layers in the network to solve a given problem is very difficult to decide. Further, the global classification capabilities of IPSO can be relied on to explore the entire weight in that space, which is plagued by a host of local optima with the help of the functionally expanded features like FLANN overcomes the non-linear nature of problems. In this approach the comparison study is made with the following methods like MLP, support vector machine (SVM) with algorithm to train is radial basis function (RBF) kernel, FLANN trained with gradient descent learning.

Touri *et al.* [19] discussed a methodology for perfect reconstruction of discrete data transmission which has a deterministic worst-case framework done through a dispersive communication channel. It is an extended version of capture time-varying transmission dynamics, which also has the case of linear time-varying preprocessing the data, without increasing the power of the transmitted signal. The necessary and sufficient conditions were presented for perfect reconstruct ability and formulated a framework. This provides a design procedure which is based on optimization for periodic preprocessing with DFE at the receiving end.

Zhao *et al.* [20] proposed a novel computational efficient adaptive nonlinear channel equalizer, to compensate linear and nonlinear distortion that occurs in nonlinear communication channel which is based on a combination of FIR filter and FLANN (CFFLANN). In this CFFLANN network, there is no need of hidden layers, and has a simpler structure rather than other traditional neural networks (NNs) and during the training mode it requires less computational burden. Results were obtained from the simulations and comparisons of the MSE, BER, and the effect of eigen value ratio (EVR).

Zhao *et al.* [21] analyzed a novel methodology with low computational complexity, pipelined decision feedback RNN equalizer (PDFRNE). Because of having DFRNN with the decision feedback structure in each module, it can eliminate the past error remaining in the network. With that by improving the performance, it can be able to overcome the unstableness due to its nature of the IIR structure.

Zeng *et al.* [22] presented a novel method for the design of a nonlinear channel equalizer with computationally efficient nonlinear adaptive filter by a pipelined FLA decision feedback RNN. This method has been done to reduce computational burden and to improve the nonlinear processing capabilities of the functional link artificial recurrent neural network (FLANN). Since it has a module nesting architecture that interconnected like a chained form, it can reduce the computational complexity and improve the performance. Moreover, the nature of infinite impulse response structure in that equalizer with a decision feedback recurrent it overcomes the unstableness. Finally, the performance of the PFLADFRNN modules has been evaluated with the help of a modified real-time recurrent learning algorithm through the extensive simulations for a different channel models in digital communication systems. The performance comparisons of multilayer perceptron, FLANN and reduced decision feedback FLANN equalizers as clearly indicated by the multiple parameters like the convergence rate, bit error rate, steady-state error.

Zhao *et al.* [23] proposed a novel adaptive decision feedback equalizer (DFE) with the combination of finite impulse response (FIR) filter and FLNN to compensate the linear and nonlinear distortions that occur in digital communication systems. The result due to the convex nonlinear combination improves the convergence speed. A novel simplified modified normalized least mean square (SMNLMS) algorithm has been derived to further improve the performance of the nonlinear equalizer and the analysis of the convergence properties of the proposed algorithm has been done. Finally, computer simulation results support the analysis of the proposed equalizers to evaluate the performance of that equalizer over the multiple structures for example functional link neural network (FLNN), RBF neural network and LMS decision feedback for both the time-invariant and the time-variant nonlinear channel models.

Das *et al.* [5] analyzed a Particle Swarm Optimization (PSO) [6] algorithm in order to eliminate the problem of channel equalization while training the Artificial Neural Network (ANN). From that it can be able to optimize all the parameters. From the analysis, it shows that an ANN equalizer works better in all noise conditions and providing better performance as compared with the other kinds of ANN-based equalizers. With that ANN is going to analyze in different modulation conditions and by different channel models.

4.2   Channel Equalization

In a communication channel, the receiver side can't eliminate the multiple reflections of the transmitted signal at different times. This resulted in the creation of the inter symbol interference that happens at the receiver end. Due to this, the performance of a communication system is degraded in terms of time dispersion and is known as multipath delay spread. To compensate these distortions that occur in communication systems, equalizers are designed. It is composed of two phases. The first one is the

Supervised Learning method, where the input signals that we are given is represented as s (t). Then those input signals go into the channel which may be linear or nonlinear channel. Most probably the tapped delay line model is using to model a multi-path channel. The output of that multipath channel y (t) is corrupted with AWGN as shown in Figure 4.2. Then the error between this corrupted output signals and the delay versions of input signal is noticed by comparing those two signals. After that comparison that error signal by using some adaptive algorithm (PSO) it is going to update the adaptable parameters of the equalizer (FLANN). Next these steps are continuing for different modulation techniques to the train the equalizer. By comparing equalizer output with some threshold value the decision is made at the receiver side.

4.2.1 Channel Models

The transmitter and the receiver are going to connect through a medium known as a channel as shown in Figure 4.1. When the wireless signal is traveling from the transmitter antenna to the receiver antenna characteristics chances occur in a signal. This kind of change occurs due to following factors

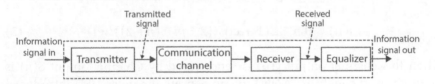

Figure 4.1 Block diagram of the communication system.

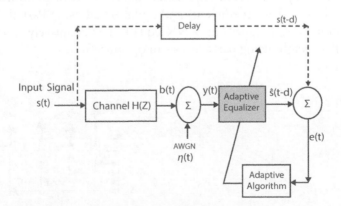

Figure 4.2 Block diagram of the channel equalization.

like two antennas separating range i.e. distance, the signal path, and the environment used for communication. A channel between the transmitter and receiver can only be able to obtain the characteristics of received signal from the transmitted signal. This is known as a channel model.

- Tapped Delay line (TDL) Model
- Stanford University Interim (SUI) Channel Models

4.2.1.1   Tapped Delay Line Model

A delay line has been represented in this model with N taps. The channel shown in Figure 4.3(a) is represented by an N taps and the channel shown in Figure 4.3(b) is represented by a 4-tap. This is mathematically expressed as with AWGN noise,

$$y(n) = \{x(n) * h(0) + x(n-1) * h(1) + \ldots + x(0) * h(n)\} + \eta(n) \quad (1)$$

Where,

- $x(n)$—input signal to the channel
- $h(n)$—channel impulse response it is represented by,

$$h(n) = 0.5 * \Sigma(1 + \cos((2 * pi * (n-2))/w)) \quad (2)$$

Then this channel output $y(n)$ is represented by Channel output $S(n)$ is then given to equalizer (ANN) to compensate the noise (ISI) introduced in the channel i.e. to get the original input sequence at the receiver. From the equalizer output calculates the mean square error for optimization. It initializes the equalizer coefficients and updates that using Particle Swarm Optimization (PSO) algorithm. ANN equalizer is adaptively trained for best possible weight using particle swarm optimization.

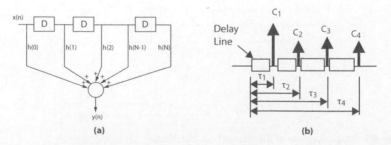

Figure 4.3 (a) Tapped-Delay-Line model, (b) 4-Tap model.

4.2.1.2   Stanford University Interim (SUI) Channel Models

In this model, the total channel gain is not normalized. Before using a SUI model, the specified normalization factors have to be added with each tap to arrive at 0 dB total mean power. This model has maximum frequency parameter for a specified Doppler. The comparison of an Omni antenna with the total mean power reduction for a 30° antenna is known as Gain Reduction Factor (GRF). There is a need to add the specified GRF to the path loss if it has a 30° antenna.

4.2.2   Artificial Neural Network

A neural network is a representation of transfer network for simulating learning process. This is just like an artificial representation of a human. "Neural network" is normally used to process and transmit the information. Because of the changing of the structure of network based on external and internal information, this artificial neural network is called as an adaptive system.

ANN is a feed forward network. ANNs are organized into three types of layers as shown in Figure 4.4. They are input layer, output layer and hidden layers. Based on the computation process of the hidden layers ANN is performing, the output of the network $v(n)$ an be calculated from following:

$$v(n) = f((h(n) * w_{ho}) + B) \qquad (3)$$

Where the $h(n)$—hidden node, it is defined as

$$h(n) = f((y(n) * w_{ih}) + B) \qquad (4)$$

- $y(n)$ input of the network.
- w_{ho} weight between hidden node to output.

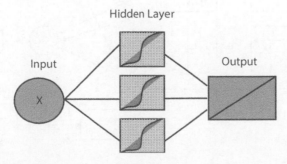

Figure 4.4 Structure of ANN.

- w_{hi} weight between input to hidden node.
- B—Biases weight.
- (f)—Transfer function.

4.3 Functional Link Artificial Neural Network

An alternative structure of ANN is known as functional link ANN (FLANN). As shown in Figure 4.5 the FLANN has no hidden layer like ANN. This is known as a single layer network. Due to this single layer structure, it can obtain less computational complexity and higher convergence speed compared to MLP. All neurons are operating on the layer with a transfer function. A sigmoid function is a one kind of good transfer function for neural networks. It has a mapping range of the input to the [0, 1].

$$\text{Sigmoid}(x) = \frac{1}{1+e^{-\infty.x}} \quad (5)$$

4.4 Particle Swarm Optimization

The random particles (solutions) which are formed as a group that can be initialized using PSO algorithm it is mainly used to search for optima solution. By using the two different types of "best" values it is able to update every iteration of each particle. One of the best solutions is used to achieve the fitness as well as store. This first value is called as pbest. Second best

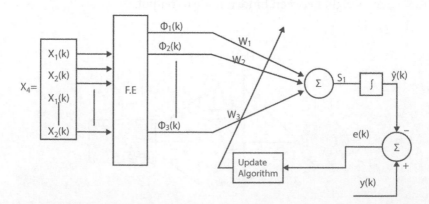

Figure 4.5 Structure of FLANN.

value is tracked by the particle swarm optimizer that can be obtained by any particle in the population. When each and every particle are flown through the multidimensional search space it will change their position depends on its neighbors [10]. In a multidimensional search space, the position vector of particle is represented by x_i^t then each particle position is updated by using following representation,

$$x_i^{t+1} = x_i^t + v_i^{t+1} \qquad (6)$$

Where v_i^t —velocity vector of particle

$$v_{ij}^{t+1} = v_{ij}^t + c_1 r_{1j}^t \left[P_{best,i}^t - x_{ij}^t \right] + c_2 r_{2j}^t \left[G_{best} - x_{ij}^t \right] \qquad (7)$$

Where

- v_{ij}^t —velocity vector of particle
- x_{ij}^t —position vector of particle i in dimension j at time t
- $P_{best,i}^t$ —personal best position
- G_{best} —global best position of particle i in dimension j
- c_1 and c_2—cognitive and social components respectively i.e. positive acceleration constants
- r_{1j}^t and r_{2j}^t —random numbers from uniform distribution U(0,1) at time t.

4.5   Result and Discussion

The performance analysis of equalizers is observed through a convergence plot. In this section the simulation analysis is taken for PSO algorithm with different neural networks and different combination of the coefficient of PSO algorithm for FLANN with both BPSK and QAM modulation. For each criterion other parameters are kept constant. Also, the comparison between different channel model (Tapped delay line and SUI models) for FLANN with both BPSK and QAM modulation is done in this section.

4.5.1   Convergence Analysis

Performance analysis of FLANN, ANN and RNN equalizers have been done in different channel conditions. The comparison of convergence rate of these three equalizers is shown in Figure 4.6. From this convergence curve analysis, it is clear that the mean square value for functional link artificial neural network

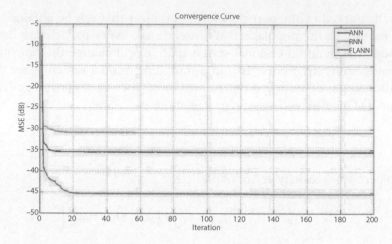

Figure 4.6 Comparison between FLANN, ANN and RNN equalizers.

is −45 dB artificial neural networks is −36 dB and recurrent neural network has a −31dB. By comparing different types of neural network, FLANN gives a better convergence. For further comparison of different parameters in PSO algorithm is done by using FLANN as shown in Figures 4.7–4.12.

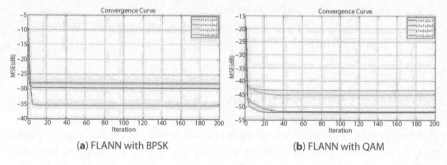

(a) FLANN with BPSK   (b) FLANN with QAM

Figure 4.7 Convergence curve of FLANN with different cognitive and social constants.

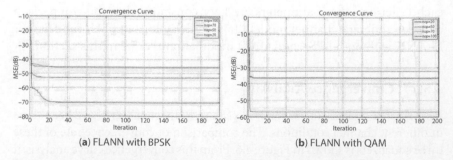

(a) FLANN with BPSK   (b) FLANN with QAM

Figure 4.8 Convergence curve of FLANN with varying number of particles.

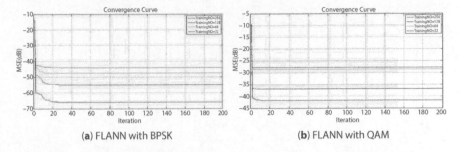

(**a**) FLANN with BPSK   (**b**) FLANN with QAM

Figure 4.9 Convergence curve of FLANN with varying number of training samples.

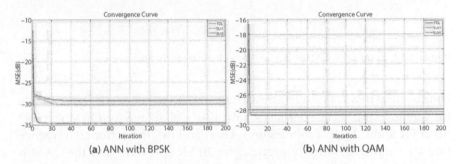

(**a**) ANN with BPSK   (**b**) ANN with QAM

Figure 4.10 Convergence curve of ANN with different channel models.

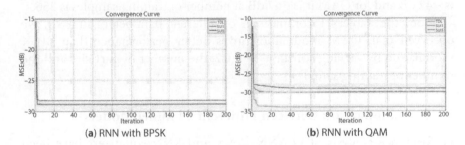

(**a**) RNN with BPSK   (**b**) RNN with QAM

Figure 4.11 Convergence curve of RNN with different channel models.

4.5.2   Comparison Between Different Parameters

By using c1 and c2, we are able to determine the respective strength. From the comparison we observed that, QAM modulation gives better performance than BPSK modulation by varying these two constants convergence characteristics of equalizer as shown in Figures 4.7(a) and (b) respectively. The number of particles n in the swarm is known as Swarm size or population size. From this we are able to generate large search space with the help of a big swarm.

From the above convergence characteristics it is clear that the different parameter in PSO algorithm with better optimization is achieved QAM

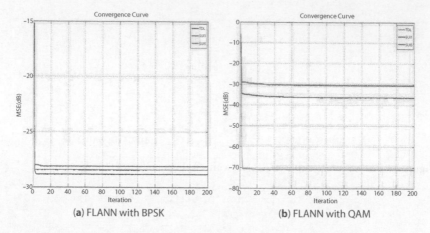

Figure 4.12 Convergence curve of FLANN with different channel models.

compared to BPSK. From Figure 4.7(a) and (b), the better convergence rate for cognitive and social constant for BPSK is −36 dB and for QAM it is −57 dB at C1 and C2 is 1. From Figures 4.8(a) and (b), the better convergence rate for varying number of particles for BPSK is −58 dB and for QAM it is −70 dB at number of particles is 100. From Figures 4.9(a) and (b), the better convergence rate for varying number of training samples for BPSK is −42 dB and for QAM it is −67 dB at number of training samples is 256.

From the Table 4.1 comparison of different parameters in PSO, we observed that, QAM modulation gives better performance than BPSK modulation by varying constants C1, C2, the number of particles and the number of training samples.

4.5.3   Comparison Between Different Channel Models

Performance analysis of FLANN, ANN and RNN equalizers have been done in different channel conditions. In FLANN there is no hidden layer like ANN and this is known as a single layer network. Due to this single layer structure, it can obtain less computational complexity and higher convergence speed compared to MLP. The comparisons of different channel models are made for all three networks with both BPSK and QAM.

Tapped delay model represents the channel by a delay line with N taps, here a 4-tap delay line model is used. The performance evaluation of various channel models for all kind of equalizers belongs to both BPSK and QAM as shown in Figures 4.10, 4.11 and 4.12, respectively. From these three figures, Tapped delay line model has a fast convergence than these two SUI channel models for all equalizers.

Table 4.1 Comparison of convergence characteristics for FLANN with different parameters in both BPSK and QAM.

Modulation techniques using FLANN	Cognitive and social constant (C1, C2)	Varying number of particles	Varying number of training samples
BPSK	−36 dB	−58 dB	−42 dB
QAM	−57 dB	−70 dB	−67 dB

Table 4.2 Comparison of convergence characteristics by using channel model TDL with different NN in both BPSK and QAM.

Modulation techniques using FLANN	RNN (TDL)	ANN (TDL)	FLANN (TDL)
BPSK	−28 dB	−28.5 dB	−29 dB
QAM	−34 dB	−35 dB	−70 dB

From the performance analysis made for all above parameters and terms which used for channel equalization, Functional link artificial neural network gives a better results in all noise condition compared with other neural networks in both BPSK and QAM system, especially QAM with FLANN which gives a better convergence, that is clearly shown in Table 4.2.

4.6   Conclusion

The major challenge which affects communication system is Inter-symbol Interference. In order to eliminate the effect of ISI and improve signal quality, an adaptive equalization technique is used at the receiver side. In this proposed method Functional Link Artificial Neural Network (FLANN) equalizer based on Particle Swarm Optimization (PSO) algorithm is analyzed for various values of particles, training sequence and acceleration coefficients. From the analysis Functional link artificial neural network performs well in all kind of parameter comparison. FLANN equalization with QAM modulation achieves a minimum MSE when compared with ANN and RNN equalizers for both BPSK and QAM. In existing methodology, the PSO algorithm is used to train a neural network with only finding the optimal weights of the network i.e. we can able to optimize all the variables, network weights and network parameters by using PSO. Detailed output presented here is a FLANN based equalizer trained with PSO as compared with other neural network equalizers like ANN and RNN influence of different channel models for each neural network with BPSK and QAM modulation. In future current optimization (Particle Swarm Optimization) technique will be compared with different optimization technique.

References

1. Patra, J.C., Poh, W.B., Chaudhari, N.S., Das, A., Nonlinear channel equalization with QAM signal using Chebyshev artificial neural network, in: *Proceedings. 2005 IEEE International Joint Conference on Neural Networks*, 5, pp. 3214–3219, 2005.
2. Zhao, H., Zeng, X.P., He, Z.Y., Jin, W.D., Li, T.R., Complex-valued pipelined decision feedback recurrent neural 6 International Journal of Engineering & Technology network for nonlinear channel equalization. *IET Commun.*, 6, 9, 1082–1096, 2012.
3. Potter, C., Venayagamoorthy, G.K., Kosbar, K., RNN based MIMO channel prediction. *Signal Process.*, 90, 2, 440–450, 2010.
4. Zhao, H., Zeng, X., Zhang, J., Li, Y., Wang, X., Li, T., A novel joint-processing adaptive nonlinear equalizer using a modular recurrent neural network for chaotic communication systems. *Neural Netw.*, 24, 12–18, 2011a.
5. Das, G., Pattnaik, P.K., Kumari Padhy, S., Artificial Neural Network trained by Particle Swarm Optimization for non-linear channel equalization. *Expert Syst. Appl.*, 41, 3491–3496, 2014.
6. Chau, K.W., Particle swarm optimization training algorithm for ANNs in stage prediction of Shing Mun River. *J. Hydrol.*, 329, 363–367, 2006.
7. Del Valle, Y., Venayagamoorthy, G.K., Mohagheghi, S., Hernandez, J.-C., Harley, R.G., Particle swarm optimization: Basic concepts, variants and applications in power systems. *IEEE Trans. Evol. Comput.*, 12, 171–195, 2008.
8. Hong, W.-C., Rainfall forecasting by technological machine learning models. *Appl. Math. Comput.*, 200, 1, 41–57, 2008.
9. Patra, J.C. and Pal, R.N., A functional link artificial neural network for adaptive channel equalization. *Signal Process.*, 43, 181–195, 1995.
10. Kennedy, J. and Eberhart, R., Particle swarm optimization, in: *Proceedings of ICNN'95-International Conference on Neural Networks*, 4, pp. 1942–1948, 1995.
11. Lee, C.-H. and Lee, Y.-C., Nonlinear systems design by a novel fuzzy neural system via hybridization of electromagnetism-like mechanism and particle swarm optimization algorithms. *Inf. Sci.*, 186, 1, 59–72, 2012.

12. Liang, J. and Zhi, D., FIR channel estimation through generalized cumulant slice weighting. *IEEE Trans. Signal Process.*, 52, 3, 657–667, 2004.

13. Lin, C.-J. and Chen, C.-H., Nonlinear system control using self-evolving neural fuzzy inference networks with reinforcement evolutionary learning. *Appl. Soft Comput.*, 11, 8, 5463–5476, 2011.

14. Lin, C.-J. and Liu, Y.-C., Image backlight compensation using neuro-fuzzy networks with immune particle swarm optimization. *Expert Syst. Appl.*, 36, 3, Part 1, 5212–5220, 2009.

15. Mingo López, L.F., Blas, N.G., Arteta, A., The optimal combination: Grammatical swarm, particle swarm optimization and neural networks. *J. Comput. Sci.*, 3, 1–2, 46–55, 2012.

16. Ribeiro, P.F. and Schlansker, W.K., *A hybrid particle swarm and neural network approach for reactive power control.* p. 6, IEEE, 2004.

17. Yogi, S., Subhashini, K.R., Satapathy, J.K., A PSO based functional link artificial neural network training algorithm for equalization of digital communication channels, in: *2010 5th International Conference on Industrial and Information Systems*, pp. 107–112, 2010.

18. Dehuri, S., Royb, R., Choc, S.-B., Ghosh, A., An improved swarm optimized functional link artificial neural network (ISO-FLANN) for classification. *J. Syst. Softw.*, 85, 6, 1333–1345, 2012.

19. Touri, R., Voulgaris, P.G., Hadjicostis, C.N., Time varying power limited preprocessing for perfect reconstruction of binary signals, in: *Proc. of the 2006 American Control Conference*, pp. 5722–5727, IEEE, Minneapolis, USA, 2006.

20. Zhao, H. and Zhang, J., Adaptively combined FIR and functional link neural network equalizer for nonlinear communication channel. *IEEE Trans. Neural Netw.*, 20, 4, 665–674, 2009.

21. Zhao, H., Zhang, X., Zhang, J., Li, T., Nonlinear adaptive equalizer using a pipelined decision feedback recurrent neural network in communication systems. *IEEE Trans. Commun.*, 58, 8, 2193–2198, 2010b.

22. Zhao, H., Zeng, X., Zhang, J., Li, T., Liu, Y., Ruan, D., Pipelined functional link artificial recurrent neural network with the decision feedback structure for nonlinear channel equalization. *Inf. Sci.*, 181, 3677–3692, 2011c.

23. Zhao, H., Zeng, X., Zhang, X., Zhang, J., Liu, Y., Wei, T., An adaptive decision feedback equalizer based on the combination of the FIR and FLANN. *Digit. Signal Process.*, 21, 6, 679–689, 2011b.

5

Implementing Hadoop Container Migrations in OpenNebula Private Cloud Environment

P. Kalyanaraman, K.R. Jothi*, P. Balakrishnan,
R.G. Navya, A. Shah and V. Pandey

*School of Computer Science and Engineering (SCOPE), Vellore Institute of
Technology, Vellore, India*

Abstract

The cloud platform provides access to virtual machines, networks, and storage as a service. Virtualization enabled datacenters to pave the way for better resource utilization, server consolidation and scalability. Further, the scalable data-intensive applications such as Elastic Map Reduce (EMR) are deployed on the cloud. MapReduce uses two operations in programming languages namely, functional map, and reduce. These functions allow us to implement distributed and parallel computing. The methodology used while deploying Hadoop on a virtual cluster is obtained from CloudStack from where virtual machines are obtained, which stresses creating a template based on which all nodes are created. When heterogeneous computing resources are required by the target workloads to satisfy real-time requirements, virtual Hadoop can be used. The efficiency of Virtual Hadoop is examined and determined. This makes it easier to conduct systematic big data processing by adopting heterogeneous computing. By making use of cloud computing, an efficient and convenient parallel programming environment can be set up to improve resource utilization. Data-intensive processing can be done in the cloud (virtual machines) using Hadoop, which is an implementation of MapReduce. In a virtual cluster, resource utilization is more efficient when compared to a physical cluster, management is more accessible, power can be saved, and the reliability is improved.

Keywords: Hadoop, Containers, OpenNebula, Docker, Linux

Corresponding author: prof.krj@gmail.com

G. R. Kanagachidambaresan (ed.) Role of Edge Analytics in Sustainable Smart City Development:
Challenges and Solutions, (85–104) © 2020 Scrivener Publishing LLC

5.1 Introduction

Hadoop is a distributed handling structure which is open source. It directs data planning and limits with regards to gigantic data applications in versatile gatherings of PC servers. It is the epitome of an environment of enormous information processing that is used to assist applications that require significant data computation in areas that include data mining, prescient examination, and AI. Hadoop frameworks can handle vast amounts of shaped and unshaped data, which gives users increased freedom for handling, gathering, and breaking down information as opposed to traditional relational databases and information distribution center. Hadoop's potential for processing and storing various kinds of data packets makes it a perfect match for vast information scenarios. They usually include a lot of information and in addition to it, a blend of segregated exchange data, unstructured and semi-structured data, for instance, web server, web clickstream records, and versatile app logs, online networking posts sensor information from the Internet of things (IoT) and client messages. It is an innovation created inside the Apache Software Foundation as a component of an open-source venture, officially known as Apache Hadoop. Various merchants offer business Hadoop appropriations, in spite of the fact that the quantity of Hadoop sellers has declined in light of a packed market and after that, focused weights driven by the expanded sending of huge information frameworks in the cloud. The move to the cloud likewise empowers clients to store information in lower-cost cloud object stockpiling administrations rather than Hadoop's namesake document framework; accordingly, Hadoop's job is being decreased in some immense information structures [1].

5.1.1 Hadoop Architecture

Hadoop is a Java-based framework (Figure 5.1) that can be installed on top of an Operating System. Hadoop has to be installed in all the nodes to use the distributed processing features. An easier way to do this would be to clone VM's or use templates. These nodes can be classified into three categories:

- Client machines:
  When Hadoop is installed, the required cluster configuration settings are inbuilt. It is accountable for loading all the structured/unstructured data onto the Hadoop cluster on command. Client node requests to process data and the MapReduce engine completes the work, and then this output is fetched by the client node.

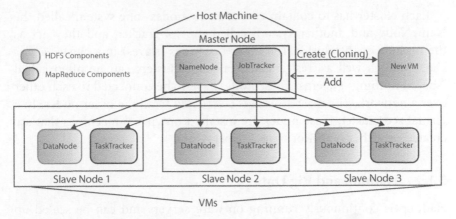

Figure 5.1 Architecture of virtualized hadoop cluster. Source: [22].

- Master nodes:
  The master node in a Hadoop cluster is accountable for storing data in a Hadoop distributed file system (HDFS). It is also responsible for parallel computation on the stored information using MapReduce functionality. A master Node has three daemons within it–
- JobTracker:
  The JobTracker keeps track of the execution of parallel processing of data utilizing MapReduce.
- NameNode:
  NameNode takes care of the storing of data in HDFS. It monitors all the data about files (i.e., the metadata for files) like which the user is accessing a particular file at a point of time, which file is saved in which Hadoop cluster and the access time of the file.
- Secondary NameNode:
  Secondary NameNode is used for storing a backup of the NameNode data.
  - Slave nodes (worker nodes):
    The slave nodes in a Hadoop cluster are accountable for performing computations and data storage. Every slave node runs two services—a TaskTracker and a DataNode service for communicating with the Master node in the Hadoop cluster. The TaskTracker service is handled by the JobTracker, and the DataNode service is handled by the NameNode.

Each cluster has to contain two primary nodes- one system called the NameNode and another system called the JobTracker, and they act as the masters of the cluster. The other machines (slaves) in a cluster act as DataNode as well as TaskTracker. Hadoop clusters can be often called "shared nothing" systems. These nodes have to be connected to each other over a network. The master node is connected to all the other nodes. In a virtualized cluster, these nodes are installed on virtual machines that are created on either type-1 or type-2 hypervisors.

5.1.2 Hadoop and Big Data

Hadoop is continuously running on ware servers and can be scaled up to support a large number of equipment hubs. The Hadoop Distributed File System (HDFS) is calculated to provide high-speed data access over all the hubs in a group. It is also intended for high blame tolerant capacities so applications can keep executing if one of the hubs fail. These key points pushed Hadoop to become information so fundamental, and the board stage for gigantic information examination. Due to this, Hadoop rose in the 2000s. Due to Hadoop's ability to process and store-wide ranges of information, it encourages organizations to set up information lakes behaving like sweeping repositories before approaching floods of data. In an HDFS information lake, raw data has often stored the way it is, which will lead researchers and different examiners to the collections of the complete information. For specific applications, this raw data can then be sifted and arranged by examination or IT groups.

5.1.3 Hadoop and Virtualization

Notwithstanding the business, organization size, or geographic area, there are two inquiries that apply to all Big Data methodologies and undertakings. One of the examinations is to what extent this take will. Now, the full expense of ownership is right there in the Big Data space. So is an excellent opportunity to esteem: Hadoop and related Big Data instruments are excessively unpredictable and take too long even to consider deploying. Furthermore, presently, it is not merely Hadoop—at BlueData, it is observed that there is an enormous spike in enthusiasm for sending Spark. These equivalent inquiries apply to Spark, as well; it's only prior to the appropriation cycle.

The reason why Hadoop people group has not grasped virtualization is worries about I/O execution made virtualization a forbidden subject when Hadoop was first presented ten years back. However, various investigations and execution tests have since shown that virtualization is a feasible (and appealing) alternative for Hadoop. Furthermore, with the quick reception and prevalence of holder advancements like Docker, there are presently lightweight ways to deal with virtualization that further limit the I/O execution sway for Big Data outstanding tasks at hand like Hadoop and Spark.

Currently, it is recognized that the devoted exposed metal server way to deal with conveying Hadoop isn't just obsolete—it's additionally moderate and wasteful. Intel and BlueData have collaborated to make it simpler and more financially savvy for ventures to embrace Hadoop and Spark, utilizing the intensity of virtualization and holder innovation, accomplishment of noteworthy decreases in the TCO for Big Data venture. It is possible to turn up virtual Hadoop or Spark bunches in minutes (preferably the weeks or months it might take to fabricate a physical group). Despite everything one has accomplished, the presentation one utilized to with exposed metal.

5.1.4   What is OpenNebula?

OpenNebula coordinates stockpiling, organize, virtualization, checking, and security innovations to convey multi-level administrations as virtual machines on circulated frameworks, consolidating the two server farm assets and remote cloud assets, as per designation strategies. As indicated by the 2010 report published by the European Commission— just a few significant research devoted to the cloud has been started, and most remarkable amid them is probably OpenNebula. The toolbox incorporates highlights for joining, the board, adaptability, security, and bookkeeping. It additionally guarantees institutionalization, interoperability and versatility, furnishing cloud clients and heads with a decision of a few cloud interfaces (vCloud, OGF Open Cloud Computing Interface and Amazon EC2 Query) & hypervisors (VMware, Xen and KVM), and will be able to suit various equipment & programming mixes in a data center [2].

OpenNebula is broadly utilized by an assortment of businesses, including internet services, media transmission, data innovation administrations, supercomputing, examine labs and universal research ventures. The OpenNebula Application is likewise utilized as a cloud engine by various other cloud solutions. OpenNebula has developed primarily since opening up to the world and now has numerous eminent clients from an assortment of businesses. The OpenNebula Application is likewise used universally for research and related areas. Research groups all over the world utilize OpenNebula to test the potential threats in the utilization & arrangement of enormous sized venture cloud and server farms [2].

5.2   Literature Survey

5.2.1   Performance Analysis of Hadoop

OpenVZ (Open Virtuozzo—Container engine—Operating system-level virtualization) and KVM (Kernel-based VM—full virtualization for Linux kernel—Type 1 hypervisor) are some of the widely used virtualization platforms. Hadoop can be deployed on top of OpenNebula, which is a cloud platform based on the IaaS model, which can be implemented on top of OpenVZ or KVM. When the performance of each is surveyed and checked, it is found that performance of OpenVZ is better while CPU or IO reading and performance KVM shows better during I/O writing [2]. Performance optimization of the Hadoop cluster can be done so by carefully examining and evaluating the status of the implementation, the course along which the leading research will be, also any already present issues in its platform for the processing and evaluation of data [1].

While running Hadoop on three different types of virtual machines, performance and resource utilization have been compared using a VM monitoring tool. This tool checks the task trackers and tests the efficiency of the system when the same amount of memory is allocated to a different number of total nodes. In terms of performance and stability, it is observed that XEN ranks the highest. Live reports delivered by virtual machine monitors give information on the different stages of MapReduce and resource utilization. This way, an adaptive scheduling algorithm can be designed [3].

For the improvement of the level of performance of Hadoop from the parameter of job level of efficiency at a maximum level. To do so, firstly, the inspection of the job and the technique of execution of tasks in the MapReduce framework is to be done so as to unveil two significant drawbacks to job execution performance [4]. Then, various optimization methods have to be examined. First, optimizing the clean-up and set-up tasks of a MapReduce job. Second, introducing an instant messaging communication mechanism. And third, implementing SHadoop, a compatible and optimized version of Hadoop that decreases the execution time of MapReduce jobs, especially small jobs [5]. When Linux VServer, OpenVZ and Linux Containers, that is, container-based systems are contrasted in terms of performance and manageability, all containers get to the point of near-native execution for workloads of MapReduce and add and make a contribution with various management abilities, be it the performance isolation and execution, live migration, or checkpoint.

Yet, LXC gives the ultimate outcome. Mesos and YARN systems help from utilizing a container-based system to have higher and granular resource sharing between programming frameworks like Hadoop [6]. A hypervisor-based virtual cluster showcases more I/O performance overhead (Example: KVM, vSphere, XEN). So, a container-based cluster is used as they give low-performance costs and give a near-native performance [7]. Hadoop performance optimization is a very profoundly examined topic because of its ability of distributed storage of big data sets and its processing. Linux system's RPC and the service rpcbind is used to improve Hadoop cluster performance. This is done by implementing many benchmarks of Hadoop on a multi-node cluster of Hadoop and analyzing the result and its performance. The entire time passed when service rpcbind is turned on is much lesser, and thus, using it while building a cluster of Hadoop would be useful and would improve the performance [8].

When Hadoop is implemented physically, performance is significantly better than virtual implementation; If the services are separated, the magnitude of degradation of execution is based on the ratio of data to compute; Consumption of power is specific to execution and application, and it corresponds to application completion progress [9].

There are few problems that are responsible for the performance and implementation of Hadoop in clusters that are heterogeneous, and thus there are various guidelines that help understand how to overcome these bottlenecks [10].

5.2.2   Evaluating Map Reduce on Virtual Machines

Hadoop Distributed File System, HBase, distributed structured data table, and MapReduce, data processing model, are the three main parts of Hadoop. MapReduce (Figure 5.2) is a model that is utilized to deal with vast amounts of data on the distributed file system. The cloud has three main factors: On-demand unlimited data storage, Internet usage to use resources

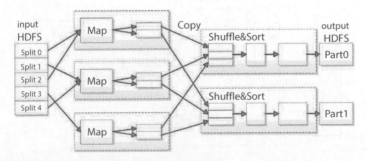

Figure 5.2 Programming model of MapReduce. Source: [20].

on the cloud, and On-demand computation power with no lock (VMs). One major bottleneck that may be projected is the usage of the internet to transfer vast amounts of data for computation. This can be avoided by adopting a data-aware approach where data and computation are co-located. This is the underlying concept of MapReduce. The map function processes a key and value pairs so as to get a standard pair of key and value. The function of reducing merges every value of intermediate keys, which are equal. Both functions are written by the customer. The run-time of MapReduce is accountable for parallelism, fault tolerance, and concurrency. Some of the conclusions drawn from implementing MapReduce on the cloud are: Permanent data storage(DFS) has to be separated from the VM's virtual memory; VM's account for better resource utilization, so it can be used only to perform computations on data stored in the physical node; VMs amid the physical node that is similar compete for I/O; Because the master node is a central point of failure and VMs are susceptible to not being successful, it is advisable to ensure the master node remains physical [11]. Implementations that are open source and of MapReduce, for example, Hadoop make use of many nodes—physical or virtual, to carry out the computation [12].

A Hadoop cluster (Figure 5.3) is made up of two components—HDFS and MapReduce. HDFS is responsible for providing a better capacity of storing and also enabling parallel processing, whereas MapReduce is responsible for the data processing, and then the output is stored back in the HDFS [13]. There are various methodologies that may be utilized with MapReduce jobs to enhance the execution by the rate of scale. Let's start with briefly explaining the listeners with MapReduce and inspire its usage for computation of for big data. Later, the focus on distinct ways to manage data, ranging from optimization and maximization of a job to physical data

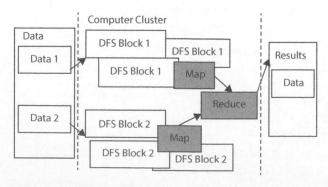

Figure 5.3 Hadoop architecture. Source: [1].

organization, for example, the layouts of data and indexes can be done. MapReduce provides its users a lot of control when it comes to how users can take the datasets as inputs and how they should be computed. People who are using it can program their queries with the help of Java instead of using SQL which eventually is more straightforward for a lot of developers and users as knowledge of databases is not required; User needs to have minimal information about Java. But, the jobs of Hadoop MapReduce are distant from databases in the processing efficiency of their queries, and hence they are better [14].

Test estimations of a few benchmarks utilizing Hadoop MapReduce to assess and think about the exhibition effect of three prominent hypervisors were carried out: a business hypervisor, Xen, and KVM. It is found that distinctions in the outstanding task at hand sort (CPU or I/O escalated), remaining task at hand size, and VM arrangement yielded significant execution contrasts among the hypervisors. In the investigation, three hypervisors were utilized to run a few MapReduce benchmarks, for example, Word Count, TestDSFIO, and TeraSort, and further approved the watched speculation using microbenchmarks. The next step is to watch the parameters that are CPU-bound, the presentation distinction amid the three hypervisors being unimportant, significant execution varieties were seen for I/O-bound benchmarks. Besides, including progressively virtual machines, the equivalent physical host debased the presentation on every one of the three hypervisors, yet results show distinctive corruption patterns among them. Solidly, the business hypervisor is 46% quicker at TestDFSIO. Whereas KVM, however, 49% more slow in the TeraSort benchmark. Moreover, expanding the remaining task at hand size for TeraSort yielded finish times for CVM that were multiple times that of Xen and KVM [15].

MapReduce programming model contributes itself significantly when talked about various analyses and jobs that are data-intensive, keeping in mind its capability to extend and hold many machines to process the data parallelly. It is argued that some MapReduce-based analytics are specifically synergistic when it comes to the model:pay-as-you-go, of a platform of a cloud. But the vital issue surfacing the end-users in this environment is the potential to provide MapReduce to reduce the cost that occurred, and finding the optimal performance while doing so. Importance of favorably provisioning a MapReduce job and exhibiting that the already existing approaches can result in not very optimal provisioning. A preliminary plan that enhances MapReduce stipulated by examining and contrasting the use of resources of the implementation and also a database of identical use of resource signatures of other applications are suggested [16].

5.2.3   Virtualizing Hadoop Containers

Containers are associated with operating system-level virtualization as it allows and shares the kernel of the host. Like, container-based virtualizations are OpenVZ and LXC. It is observed that OpenVZ is more stable and gives a faster runtime. Syslog priority parser benchmarks are almost equal for both OpenVZ and LXC [7].

Linux containers (Figure 5.4) can be used to carry out cluster-level parallelism and to overcome performance issues arising in VMs. These containers don't allow their kernel to run on to the host OS. Containers can be created and deleted based on machine overutilization or underutilization dynamically. This is called the auto-scaling. V-Hadoop creates a layer of abstraction on top of the physical resources due to which the cluster can be easily scaled up or out (elastic cluster). Hadoop performs only slightly better than V-Hadoop as V-Hadoop offers a considerable advantage in parallelization and massive I/O jobs. Some popular containers are Linux containers and Docker [12].

Docker is a container engine which can be used to co-host multiple applications along with enough isolation. It is a light-weight alternative to hypervisor-based technologies like KVM and XEN. In a container engine, various operating systems need not be installed for different containers as opposed to hypervisor-based virtualization. In a container engine, some challenges are due to Resource sharing being very high; Concurrency being

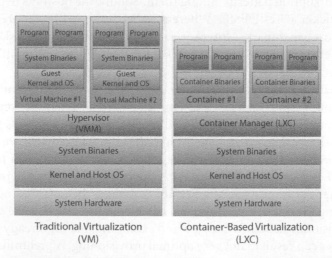

Figure 5.4   Container-based virtualization (right); program stack-Hypervisor-based virtualization (left). Source: [12].

dependent on the host-OS; Isolation being more relaxed; Dependability is lower [17]. A virtual Hadoop is developed that scales the required assets for computation in order to fulfil real-time needs. Also, the method of asset interference and assignment and auto-scaling is used to allot resources when needed based on profile data and application models. Docker containers can also be used to allow mechanisms such as auto-scaling in which a container contains a node of Hadoop and has the potential to hold computing engines that are heterogeneous in nature [18].

Installing link collection with the help of the IEEE 802.3ad and LXC (Linux Containers) cloud instances help tackle the issue of making network execution better in cloud instances that are container-based by running a set of experiments to measure throughput, latency and bandwidth utilization to evaluate its efficiency.

The results prove that with the deployment approach used, other network-intensive applications can use the approach and showed LXC has domestic network performance, and previous hypervisors have various drawbacks [19].

5.2.4   Optimization of Hadoop Cluster Using Cloud Platform

Hadoop clusters, when running on virtual machines, can be optimized in various ways. CloudStack is one such method used to create virtual clusters. It is a platform on the cloud that is open source, which makes use of hypervisors like VMWare vSphere, KVM, etc. The same hostname is given to nodes that are created using the same host. This problem is solved by implementing an algorithm. Though there are a lot of advantages to deploying Hadoop in a virtual environment like better resource utilization, easy management, etc., a virtual cluster can exhibit low performance [20].

In a Hadoop cluster, one master node (runs the name node daemon) is present, which allocates jobs to various slave nodes (runs all other daemons) [13]. A physical cluster has many disadvantages associated with it, like reduced resource utilization, complicated management, etc. Cloud platforms in which Hadoop is deployed usually have virtual clusters along with a remotely attached storage. These clusters may be geographically spread out, and when some data is required by a VM, it has to be moved to achieve data locality. Bio-inspired algorithms are used for optimizing the provision of nearby clusters and placement of VMs. This way, jobs can be completed faster as the network distance between storage and virtual cluster are reduced. This algorithm can be implemented using open source cloud platforms like OpenStack [21].

A virtual cluster can be created with the master node on a physical machine and the slave nodes on virtual machines because the master node requires higher computation power. Virtual machines in which Hadoop is configured can be cloned to efficiently create additional nodes in the cluster [22].

5.2.5   Heterogeneous Clusters in Cloud Computing

Volumes of data that has to be processed by cloud services are growing incomparably faster than computing power. This growth requires various emerging plans for analyzing and managing information. Handling tremendous volumes of data has two requirements: 1) Low-priced and dependable storage, and 2) Better tools for examining and analyzing structured and unstructured data. Both the mentioned problems can be addressed by using an open-source platform called Hadoop. Hadoop's achievement in heterogeneous clusters is lacking, where the nodes have dissimilar computing capacity [10].

As mentioned, various issues hinder the performance and implementation of Hadoop in clusters, which are heterogeneous, and thus many guidelines that help understand how to overcome such bottlenecks. Cloud computing these days is the best approach to distributed and parallel computing done on big data. Some of the proprietary cloud platforms available are Microsoft Hyper-V Cloud, VMWare vCloud, Citrix open cloud, etc. There are also open-source cloud platforms that are being used like eucalyptus, cloud stack, and open nebula. One example of parallel and distributed computing is the MapReduce framework, and it can be implemented by using Hadoop. There are some disadvantages of using the cloud, which can be overcome by using Hadoop. Eucalyptus is a cloud management system that is free and open-source. It is based on IaaS deployment and can be used as a public, private, or hybrid cloud. The API for eucalyptus and AWS is the same, as a result of which, applications developed for AWS can be run on eucalyptus. Eucalyptus has instances called EMI (Eucalyptus machine image) running on it. When it is started, the EMI contacts its components to configure the system based on the configuration files [23].

The structure and execution of a novel circulated layered store framework based on the Hadoop Distributed File System, also known as the HDFS-based Distributed Cache System (HDCache). This framework comprises of numerous reserve administrations and a customer library. The store administrations are structured with three access layers—a depiction of the neighborhood circle, an in-memory reserve, and the real plate seen as given by HDFS. Documents that are retrieved from HDFS are stacked and reserved in the mutual memory, which can be obtained by a customer library in a straightforward manner. Applications which are incorporated with a customer library can reach out to a store administration at any time. Store administrations are sorted out in a P2P fashion utilizing a disseminated hash table. Each record stored has three imitations in various store administration hubs so as to improve heartiness and reduces the remaining task at hand. Trial results demonstrate that the novel reserve framework can store documents that have a wide variety in their sizes and has the entrance execution in milliseconds in profoundly simultaneous situations [24]. The efficiency of Virtual Hadoop is examined and determined, making it easier to adopt heterogeneous computing for systematic big data processing [18].

5.2.6   Performance Analysis and Optimization in Hadoop

In order to have the ability to process massive datasets, Hadoop emphasizes more on increased throughput of computation, rather than on the performance of job execution. This emphasis causes a problem while executing small jobs. To tackle this, three significant optimizations are made: 1. Optimize setup and cleanup tasks to reduce time cost during initialization and termination of a job. 2. Using push-model instead of the pull-up model in task assignment. 3. Using instant message communication instead of heartbeat based communication. This increases the speed of execution of jobs by 23% [25].

Real parallel machine learning algorithms and a series of Hadoop benchmarks can be run in order to assess the performance of scalability, which includes a scale-up method and scale-out method [26]. Cloud platforms have helped improved resource allocation, but it causes performance degradations due to their virtualization layer [19]. Experimental results show that a wide range of sizes of files can be cached, and the performance of access can be measured in milliseconds in environments that are incredibly concurrent [27].

5.2.7   Virtual Technologies

KVM and XEN are virtualization technologies that provide workload consolidation and the required isolation. There are some overheads when it comes to virtualization platforms because the guest's kernel is run on top of it. Due to this, microservice architectures like the Linux docker platform are becoming popular. Docker is a container engine which can be used to co-host multiple applications along with enough isolation. It is a light-weight alternative to hypervisor-based technologies like KVM and XEN [17].

OpenNebula can be set up on KVM, OpenVZ, Xen, VMWare vCluster, vSphere, and also directly on VMWare workstation. Some container technologies are OpenVZ, LXC, and Docker.

5.2.8   Scheduling

Scheduling in Hadoop MapReduce in Cloud Environments: The default scheduling algorithm used in Hadoop processes is the first-in-first-out FIFO scheduling algorithm. Apart from this, other need-based schedulers are used too. Various networks use different scheduling algorithms based on their needs. Each of the scheduling algorithms considers the performance of hardware components like CPU, Memory, Job due dates, I/O, and so forth [28].

5.2.9   Scheduling of Hadoop VMs

Two types are schedulers are usually used- one scheduler in the virtualization layer, and the other in the Hadoop framework to order incoming tasks effectively. The schedulers so used form the Minimal Interference Maximal Productivity system (MIMP). The focus is on the Map function of Map Reduce because it can be parallelized to a greater extent. The Xen CPU scheduler and the Hadoop Job scheduler are modified to understand how available resources affect the completion time of a task. MIMP can get to more deadlines than an Earliest Deadline First Scheduling algorithm. This reduces the time required to complete execution by several hours [29].

Job scheduling based on Node Health Degree (named FS-HD) can be used for optimizing the already existing scheduling algorithms, and it overcomes problems faced in the Fair scheduler strategy. There is an increase in throughput, better resource load balance, and low failure rate, thus proving this algorithm to be effective [30].

A virtual cluster is advised to be created with a physical machine as a master node and virtual machine as slave nodes because the master node requires higher computation power. Virtual machines in which Hadoop is configured can be cloned to efficiently create additional nodes in the cluster. By using the capacity scheduler, which assigns tasks based on RAM or Virtual Memory usage, virtual machines can be automatically cloned if there is a need for more memory as opposed to the default fair scheduler [22].

Different scheduling algorithms like capacity scheduling, fair scheduling, and FIFO scheduling are compared based on CPU utilization, physical, and virtual memory utilization. The Youtube dataset is used to carry out the comparison, and it is observed that capacity scheduling is the most efficient when compared to fair and FIFO schedule based on the abovementioned parameters in a multi-node cluster [13].

5.3   Discussion

The three vital components that makeup HDFS (Figure 5.5) are Name-Node, Data-Node, and Secondary Name-Node. HDFS makes use of a Master-Slave architecture where the NameNode is the master node to ensure that the cluster (storage). The DataNode is a slave node adding up to all the nodes in a Hadoop cluster. Hadoop is an open-source implementation of MapReduce, which makes use of many nodes—physical or virtual, to carry out computation. Small businesses may not have enough capital for many physical nodes and are hesitant towards using virtual nodes in the cloud because of security and privacy issues. Virtual machines set up on

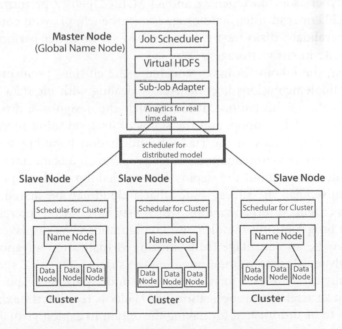

Figure 5.5 Hadoop multi-node cluster architecture. Source: [13].

physical nodes considerably reduce the cost but have a significant over-head because the virtual machines are present over a hypervisor, which means that the guest operating system's kernel is run over the host oper-ating system.

Virtualizing Hadoop is a prime factor that removes the catastrophic dam-age that can occur on the failure of a node in the cluster. This is achieved because the time to set up and get a VM running is around 20 minutes. These advantages can be widened by deploying Hadoop on the cloud, which would enable remote access to computation and data.

As a result of the extensive literature survey which was performed, we have come to the conclusion that Hadoop is an emerging platform that is taking over big data processing technology, and it would be very beneficial to expand our knowledge in Hadoop.

5.4   Conclusion

As Hadoop is an open-source implementation of a distributed computing framework, it gains momentum in the scholarly community industry. By considering the virtualized Hadoop implementations on various virtual-ization Hypervisors like OpenVZ and KVM, the OpenVZ performs better during CPU or read-intensive storage I/O (mrbench, pi, word count, ter-asort, teravalidate, dfsio test) whereas KVM shows better performances during write-intensive storage I/O.

Further, the literature survey concludes the efficient performance of Hadoop implementations is concurrently dealing with big data chunks together with few limitations. It also depicts the design of a distributed computing model-Hadoop, and the status of its application investigates already existing issues of the Hadoop information handling stage and provides a few recommendations of Hadoop bunch advancement. Also, it elucidates more about the deployment of Hadoop in cloud platforms like OpenNebula. The survey states that a cloud can be shared among numerous clients or organizations, which may have various prerequisites as far as programming bundles and configurations. As displayed, such stages may be an advantage from utilizing virtualization advancements to give advanced custom situations and asset sharing. OpenVZ and KVM are broadly used answers for virtualization under particular approxima-tions, and an asset-based application, like Hadoop, requires the exhibition overhead to be diminished for having the option to exploit virtualization frameworks.

References

1. Lu, H., Hai-Shan, C., Ting-Ting, H., Research on Hadoop cloud computing model and its applications, in: *2012 Third International Conference on Networking and Distributed Computing*, pp. 59–63, 2012.
2. Vasconcelos, P.R.M. and de Araújo Freitas, G.A., Performance analysis of Hadoop MapReduce on an OpenNebula cloud with KVM and OpenVZ virtualizations, in: *The 9th International Conference for Internet Technology and Secured Transactions (ICITST-2014)*, pp. 471–476, 2014.
3. Yang, Y., Long, X., Dou, X., Wen, C., Impacts of virtualization technologies on Hadoop, in: *2013 Third International Conference on Intelligent System Design and Engineering Applications*, pp. 846–849, 2013.
4. Gu, R. *et al.*, SHadoop: Improving MapReduce performance by optimizing job execution mechanism in Hadoop clusters. *J. Parallel Distrib. Comput.*, 74, 3, 2166–2179, 2014.
5. Zhang, H., Huang, H., Wang, L., Mrapid: An efficient short job optimizer on Hadoop, in: *2017 IEEE International Parallel and Distributed Processing Symposium (IPDPS)*, pp. 459–468, 2017.
6. Xavier, M.G., Neves, M.V., De Rose, C.A.F., A performance comparison of container-based virtualization systems for MapReduce clusters, in: *2014 22nd Euromicro International Conference on Parallel, Distributed, and Network-Based Processing*, pp. 299–306, 2014.
7. Rizki, R., Rakhmatsyah, A., Nugroho, M.A., Performance analysis of container-based Hadoop cluster: OpenVZ and LXC, in: *2016 4th International Conference on Information and Communication Technology (ICoICT)*, pp. 1–4, 2016.
8. Ahmed, H., Ismail, M.A., Hyder, M.F., Performance optimization of Hadoop cluster using Linux services, in: *17th IEEE International Multi-Topic Conference 2014*, pp. 167–172, 2014.
9. Feller, E., Ramakrishnan, L., Morin, C., Performance and energy efficiency of big data applications in cloud environments: A Hadoop case study. *J. Parallel Distrib. Comput.*, 79, 80–89, 2015.
10. Thirumala Rao, B., Sridevi, N.V., Krishna Reddy, V., Reddy, L.S.S., Performance issues of heterogeneous Hadoop clusters in cloud computing, *GJCST*, 12, 8, pp. 1–6, 2011.
11. Ibrahim, S., Jin, H., Lu, L., Qi, L., Wu, S., Shi, X., Evaluating MapReduce on virtual machines: The Hadoop case. *IEEE International Conference on Cloud Computing*, pp. 519–528, 2009.
12. Radhakrishnan, S., Muscedere, B.J., Daudjee, K., V-Hadoop: Virtualized Hadoop Using Containers, in: *2016 IEEE 15th International Symposium on Network Computing and Applications (NCA)*, pp. 237–241, 2016.
13. Dhulavvagol, P.M., Totad, S.G., Sourabh, S., Performance Analysis of Job Scheduling Algorithms on Hadoop Multi-cluster Environment, in: *Emerging*

Research in Electronics, Computer Science and Technology, Springer, pp. 457–470, 2019.

14. Dittrich, J. and Quiané-Ruiz, J.-A., Efficient big data processing in Hadoop MapReduce. *Proc. VLDB Endow.*, 5, 12, 2014–2015, 2012.
15. Li, J., Wang, Q., Jayasinghe, D., Park, J., Zhu, T., Pu, C., Performance overhead among three hypervisors: An experimental study using Hadoop benchmarks, in: *2013 IEEE International Congress on Big Data*, pp. 9–16, 2013.
16. Kambatla, K., Pathak, A., Pucha, H., Towards Optimizing Hadoop Provisioning in the Cloud. *HotCloud*, 9, 12, 28–30, 2009.
17. Garg, S.K., Lakshmi, J., Johny, J., Migrating VM workloads to Containers: Issues and Challenges, in: *2018 IEEE 11th International Conference on Cloud Computing (CLOUD)*, pp. 778–785, 2018.
18. Chen, Y.-W., Hung, S.-H., Tu, C.-H., Yeh, C.W., Virtual Hadoop: Mapreduce over docker containers with an auto-scaling mechanism for heterogeneous environments, in: *Proceedings of the International Conference on Research in Adaptive and Convergent Systems*, pp. 201–206, 2016.
19. Rista, C., Griebler, D., Maron, C.A.F., Fernandes, L.G., Improving the network performance of a container-based cloud environment for Hadoop systems, in: *2017 International Conference on High-Performance Computing & Simulation (HPCS)*, pp. 619–626, 2017.
20. Xu, G., Xu, F., Ma, H., Deploying and researching Hadoop in virtual machines, in: *2012 IEEE International Conference on Automation and Logistics*, pp. 395–399, 2012.
21. Thaha, A.F., Singh, M., Amin, A.H.M., Ahmad, N.M., Kannan, S., Hadoop in OpenStack: Data-location-aware cluster provisioning, in: *2014 4th World Congress on Information and Communication Technologies (WICT 2014)*, pp. 296–301, 2014.
22. Raj, A., Kaur, K., Dutta, U., Sandeep, V.V., Rao, S., Enhancement of Hadoop clusters with virtualization using the capacity scheduler, in: *2012 Third International Conference on Services in Emerging Markets*, pp. 50–57, 2012.
23. Mangtani, N. and Rathi, J.B., A Map-Reduce Implementation on Open Source Platform: EUCALYPTUS. *Int. J. Comput. Appl.*, 1, 30–34, 2012.
24. Xie, J. *et al.*, Improving MapReduce performance through data placement in heterogeneous Hadoop clusters, in: *2010 IEEE International Symposium on Parallel & Distributed Processing, Workshops and Ph.D. Forum (IPDPSW)*, pp. 1–9, 2010.
25. Yan, J., Yang, X., Gu, R., Yuan, C., Huang, Y., Performance optimization for short MapReduce job execution in Hadoop, in: *2012 Second International Conference on Cloud and Green Computing*, pp. 688–694, 2012.
26. He, Y., Jiang, X., Wu, Z., Ye, K., Chen, Z., Scalability analysis and improvement of Hadoop virtual cluster with cost consideration, in: *2014 IEEE 7th International Conference on Cloud Computing*, pp. 594–601, 2014.

27. Zhang, J., Wu, G., Hu, X., Wu, X., A distributed cache for Hadoop distributed file system in real-time cloud services, in: *Proceedings of the 2012 ACM/IEEE 13th International Conference on Grid Computing*, pp. 12–21, 2012.

28. Rao, B.T. and Reddy, L.S.S., Survey on improved scheduling in Hadoop MapReduce in cloud environments, *Int. J. Comp. App.*, 34, 9, 29–33, 2012.

29. Zhang, W., Rajasekaran, S., Wood, T., Zhu, M., Mimp: Deadline and interference aware scheduling of Hadoop virtual machines, in: *2014 14th IEEE/ACM International Symposium on Cluster, Cloud and Grid Computing*, pp. 394–403, 2014.

30. Xia, Y., Wang, L., Zhao, Q., Zhang, G., Research on job scheduling algorithm in Hadoop. *J. Comput. Inf. Syst.*, 7, 16, 5769–5775, 2011.

Transmission Line Inspection Using Unmanned Aerial Vehicle

A. Mahaboob Subahani, M. Kathiresh* and S. Sanjeev

Department of EEE, PSG College of Technology Coimbatore, India

Abstract

Power transmission line inspection is an essential task carried out by power generating units. The lines are exposed to the elements which increase the rate of deterioration of small faults and when not repaired in a time-efficient manner, they can become a serious problem. Current methods for inspection are labor intensive, expensive, tedious and error prone for humans to perform. A possible solution is an Unmanned Aerial Vehicle (UAV) to perform the dull, dirty and dangerous task of power line inspections. This chapter elucidates the design and implementation of an UAV that inspects the transmission lines to detect any fault instantly. A Quad copter is chosen as the UAV form factor as its building cost is less compared to other UAV forms and it gives more flight time. This particular design uses four identical rotors mounted symmetrically; the result is a very stable flight platform. The Quadcopter has an on-board flight controller which runs complex algorithms to keep the UAV stable and resistant to wind drifts. The UAV is also packed with Global Positioning System (GPS), Inertial Measurement Unit (IMU) Sensors, Couple of Radios, Power Electronic Converters, Battery, Brushless Direct Current (BLDC) Motors, Camera and so on. These electronic devices and algorithms make the UAV to go autonomously in the programmed path. Failsafe algorithms are also employed in the UAV to protect the system in case of any errors such as loss of signals or low battery where it automatically lands safe.

Keywords: Power transmission line inspection, Unmanned Aerial Vehicle, Quadcopter, Global Positioning System, Inertial Measurement Unit

Corresponding author: kathiresh.skc@gmail.com

G. R. Kanagachidambaresan (ed.) Role of Edge Analytics in Sustainable Smart City Development: Challenges and Solutions, (105–126) © 2020 Scrivener Publishing LLC

6.1   Introduction

Transmission lines are power-carrying conductors that distribute electricity to every part of the world. They are located over various places and suspended over long distance. Fault occurred in the transmission lines causes blackout in the distributed area. The fault has to be identified and fixed as soon as possible. The location of transmission lines in remote areas and its distance limits the mankind to identify fault quickly. Such situations encourage the development of special machines which fulfil the purpose.

6.1.1   Unmanned Aerial Vehicle

Unmanned Aerial Vehicle (UAV) is a manless aerial vehicle which is operated manually or autonomously. They are controlled manually in ground station by means of radio transmitter and receiver. The UAV may be in any form such as a Plane, Helicopter, MultiCopter, and Glider [1, 2]. The UAV Platform chosen is a Quadcopter. A Quadcopter consists of 4 Brushless motors, Accelerometers, Gyroscope, GPS, Flight controller, Radio receiver, Camera, and Telemetry systems. The Quadcopter's essence is the thrusters which are made by propeller in combination with brushless motors. By varying the speed of individual motors, the controls such as hover, tilt, pan, land, rotate are functioned.

6.1.2   Quadcopter

A Quadcopter, also called a Quadrotor Helicopter or Quadrocopter, is a multi-rotor that is lifted and propelled by four rotors. Quadcopters are classified as rotorcraft, as opposed to fixed-wing aircraft, because their lift is generated by a set of rotors (vertically oriented propellers).Quadcopters generally use two pairs of identical fixed pitched propellers; two clockwise (CW) and two counter-clockwise (CCW). These use independent variation of the speed of each rotor to achieve control. By changing the speed of each rotor, it is possible to specifically generate a desired total thrust to locate for the center of thrust both laterally and longitudinally and to create a desired total torque, or turning force. Quadcopters differ from conventional helicopters which use rotors that are able to vary the pitch of their blades dynamically as they move around the rotor hub. In the early days of flight, Quadcopters (then referred to as 'Quadrotors') were seen as possible solutions to some of the persistent problems in vertical flight; torque-induced control issues (as well as efficiency issues originating from the tail rotor, which generates no useful lift) can be eliminated by counter-rotation and the relatively short blades are much easier to construct. A number of manned designs appeared in the 1920s and 1930s. These vehicles were among the first successful heavier-than-air vertical take-off and landing (VTOL) vehicles. However, early prototypes suffered from poor performance, and latter prototypes required too much pilot work load, due to poor stability augmentation and limited control authority.

In the late 2000s, advances in electronics allowed the production of cheap lightweight flight controllers, accelerometers (IMU), global positioning system and cameras. This resulted in a rapid proliferation of small, cheap consumer Quadcopters along with other multi rotor designs. Quadcopter designs also became popular in unmanned aerial vehicle (UAV or drone) research. With their small size and maneuverability, these Quadcopters can be flown indoors as well as outdoors.

At a small size, Quadcopters are cheaper and more durable than conventional helicopters due to their mechanical simplicity. Their smaller blades are also advantageous because they possess less kinetic energy, reducing their ability to cause damage. For small-scale Quadcopters, this makes the vehicles safer for close interaction. It is also possible to fit Quadcopters with guards that enclose the rotors, further reducing the potential for damage. However, as size increases, fixed propeller Quadcopters develop disadvantages over conventional helicopters. Increasing blade size increases their momentum. This means that changes in blade speed take longer, which negatively impacts control. At the same time, increasing blade size improves efficiency as it takes less energy to generate thrust by moving a large mass of air at a slow speed than by moving a small mass of air at high speed. Therefore, increasing efficiency comes at the cost of control. Helicopters do not experience this problem as increasing the size of the rotor disk does not significantly impact the ability to control blade pitch. Due to their ease of construction and control, Quadcopter aircraft are frequently used as amateur model aircraft projects.

6.2 Literature Survey

Chuang Deng *et al.* [3] have proposed a multi-platform unmanned aerial vehicle (UAV) system along with multi-model communication for efficient power line inspection. This work showed that higher efficiency can be achieved for multi-UAVs by cooperative inspection. Alexandros Zormpas *et al.* [4] proposed robust and cost effective novel methodologies for power transmission line inspection using UAVs. The proposed methodologies were tested in real-world cases with the image background in each case to be characterized of non-uniform texture. This method of transmission line inspection could result in accurate detection of cable faults.

Golightly and Dewi Jones [5] have presented robotic vehicle to inspect overhead power lines based on an artificial-vision system good control of the position and attitude of the vehicle. They also described a laboratory test rig which incorporates a dynamic model for a small, ducted-fan rotor-craft so that the response of the vehicle to wind gusts can be emulated.

Transmission line localities are topography complex. Natural conditions and artificial patrol way need to spend a lot of manpower, which is inefficient. Thus, transmission line inspection based on Unmanned Aerial Vehicle (UAV) has been attracting the attention of relevant researchers since produced. This article has reviewed the development of UAV power patrol process, explored its advantages, and realized the intelligent rapid mission planning through the programming.

The proposed system in this chapter, diagnoses faults in transmission lines, notifies the user of any abnormal condition, indicates the location of the fault occurrence. According to the user requirement, it is programmed in a way that it adopts with the path that the user desires. It has a GPS based autonomous navigation system that helps to travel along the transmission line. The system mainly concentrates on the following applications such as:

1. To continuously monitor the transmission line for any faults
2. To return to the launch if any emergency or any failure condition encountered during the flight
3. To work in a full autonomous mode.

6.3   System Architecture

The system consists of four major portions:

- Sensor part
- Processing Unit
- User Interface
- Propulsion System.

Sensors are fitted in various locations where center of gravity acts in the UAV. Various sensors such as Accelerometer, Gyroscope are used to stabilize the UAV and sensors such as Magnetometer, Barometer and GPS give the current location of the UAV. The processing unit continuously monitors all the data from the sensors and stabilizes the UAV. User interface

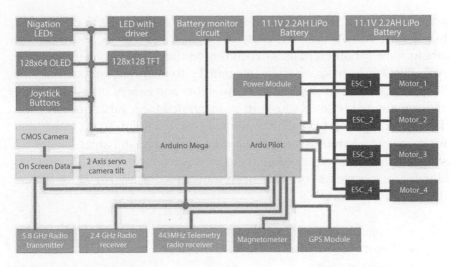

Figure 6.1 Block diagram of the proposed system.

is handled by the processor which reads data from wireless modules and controls the drone. The propulsion system is developed by four thrusters which are driven by the processors [6]. Figure 6.1 shows the block diagram of proposed system.

6.4   ArduPilot

A flight controller is a microcontroller along with IMU (Inertial Measurement Unit). IMU include Accelerometer and Gyroscope. To determine the altitude, a Barometer is used. An EEPROM (Electrically Erasable Programmable Read Only Memory) is attached in order to save the flight data. For flight controller, ArduPilot is chosen.

ArduPilot is an open source Unmanned Aerial Vehicle (UAV) platform, able to control autonomous MultiCopters, fixed-wing aircraft, traditional helicopters and ground rovers. It is based on the Arduino open-source electronics prototyping platform. The first ArduPilot version was based on a thermopile, which relies on determining the location of the horizon relative to the aircraft by measuring the difference in temperature between the sky and the ground. Later, the system was improved to replace thermopiles with an IMU using a combination of accelerometers, gyroscope, and magnetometers.

The customizability of ArduPilot makes it very popular in the DIY (Do It Yourself) field. This allows for a multitude of uses such as MultiCopter and fixed plane drones. This customizability also allows a variety of additional parts to be used by the use of different connectors and transmitters to allow for different uses depending on the operator preferences. The ArduPilot has been successfully integrated into many airplanes such as the Star, Easy, and the Bixler. The customizability and ease of installation have allowed the ArduPilot platform to be integrated for a variety of missions. The use of Mission planner has allowed the ArduPilot board to be used for mapping missions, search and rescue, and surveying areas. Figure 6.2 shows the image of ArduPilot. The open source format of ArduPilot has allowed for simple use of many open source platforms. The following are the salient features,

- Programmable 3D way points
- Return to launch
- In-flight reset
- Fully programmable actions at waypoints
- Fly by Wire mode
- Optimization of 3 or 4 channel airplanes.
- Flight Simulations.

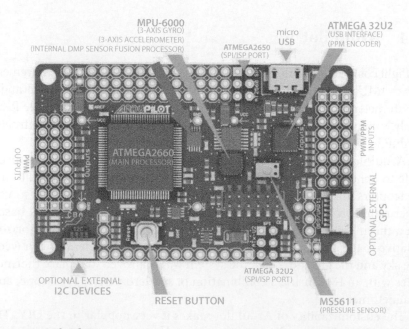

Figure 6.2 ArduPilot.

6.5 Arduino Mega

The Mega 2560 is a microcontroller board based on the ATmega2560. It has 54 digital input/output pins out (of which 15 can be used as Pulse Width Modulation (PWM) outputs), 16 analog inputs, 4 Universal Asynchronous Receiver Transmitter (UART) (hardware serial ports), a 16 MHz crystal oscillator, a USB connection, a power jack, an ICSP (In-Circuit Serial programming) header, and a reset button. It contains everything needed to support the microcontroller. The Mega 2560 board is compatible with most shields designed for the Uno and the former boards Duemilanove or Diecimila. Figure 6.3 shows the image of Arduino Mega.

6.6 Brushless DC Motor

Brushless DC electric motor (BLDC motors, BL motors) also known as electronically commutated motors are synchronous motors that are powered by a DC electric source via an integrated inverter/switching power supply, which produces an AC electric signal to drive the motor. Brushless motors offer several advantages over brushed DC motors, including high torque to weight ratio, more torque per watt (increased efficiency), increased reliability, reduced noise, longer lifetime (no brush and commutator erosion), elimination of ionizing sparks from the commutator, and overall reduction of electromagnetic interference(EMI). With no windings on the rotor, they are not subjected to centrifugal forces, and because the windings are supported by the housing, they can be cooled by conduction, requiring no airflow inside the motor for cooling. This in turn means that the motor's

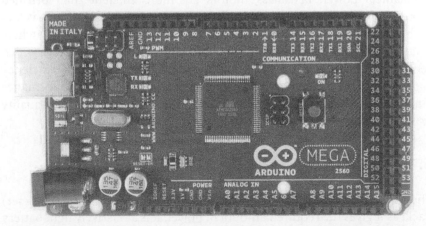

Figure 6.3 Arduino Mega.

Figure 6.4 BLDC motor.

internals can be entirely enclosed and protected from dirt or other foreign matter. Figure 6.4 shows the image of a BLDC motor.

Brushless DC motor commutation may be implemented in software using a microcontroller or microprocessor computer, or may alternatively be implemented in analog hardware, or in digital firmware using an Field Programmable Gate Array (FPGA). Commutation with electronics instead of brushes allows for greater flexibility and capabilities not available with brushed DC motors, including speed limiting, "micro stepped" operation for slow and/or fine motion control, and a holding torque when stationary.

The maximum power that can be applied to a brushless motor is limited almost exclusively by heat; too much heat weakens the magnets and may damage the winding's insulation. When converting electricity into mechanical power, brushless motors are more efficient than brushed motors. This improvement is largely due to the brushless motor's velocity being determined by the frequency at which the electricity is switched, not the voltage. Additional gains are due to the absence of brushes, which reduces mechanical energy loss due to friction. The enhanced efficiency is greatest in the no-load and low-load region of the motor's performance curve. Under high mechanical loads, brushless motors and high-quality brushed motors are comparable in efficiency.

6.7 Battery

The battery used is the Turnigy 2200 mAh 3S 25 C LiPo (Lithium Polymer) Pack, as it gives the required amount of power. It is a relatively light battery

Figure 6.5 Battery.

for the power it provides, and it is cost effective. It discharges 25 C and has a capacity of 2,200 mAh. The battery is composed of 3 cells. Each cell has a maximum voltage of 3.7 V, which gives 11.1 V for the entire battery. Figure 6.5 shows the image of LiPo battery.

6.8   CMOS Camera

A digital still or video camera that uses a CMOS based image sensor chip rather than a CCD to record the picture. The CMOS image sensors enable the integration of all required camera circuits onto the same chip, making them well suited for cameras in smart phones and tablets. Initially, they are used in less expensive devices. Now the quality of CMOS sensors has improved steadily. So, they have been incorporated into professional cameras. Figure 6.6 shows the image of CMOS camera.

6.9   Electronic Speed Control

An Electronic Speed Control (ESC) is an electronic circuit with the purpose to vary an electric motor's speed, its direction and possibly also to act as a dynamic brake. ESCs are often used in electrically powered radio controlled models, with the variety most often used for brushless motors

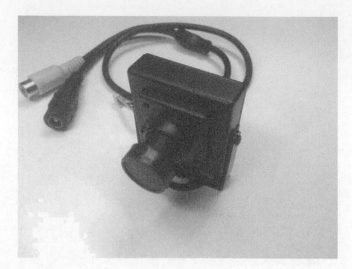

Figure 6.6 CMOS camera.

essentially providing an electronically generated three-phase electric power low voltage source of energy for the motor. Figure 6.7 shows the image of ESC.

An ESC can be a stand-alone unit which plugs into the receiver's throttle control channel or incorporated into the receiver itself, as is the case in most toy-grade R/C vehicles. Some R/C manufacturers that install proprietary hobby-grade electronics in their entry-level vehicles, vessels or aircraft use onboard electronics that combine the two on a single circuit board.

Figure 6.7 Electronic Speed Control.

Regardless of the type used, an ESC interprets control information not as mechanical motion as would be the case of a servo, but rather in a way that varies the switching rate of a network of field effect transistors, or FETs. The rapid switching of the transistors is what causes the motor itself to emit its characteristic high-pitched whine, especially noticeable at lower speeds. It also allows much smoother and more precise variation of motor speed in a far more efficient manner than the mechanical type with a resistive coil and moving arm once in common use.

Most modern ESCs incorporate a battery eliminator circuit (or BEC) to regulate voltage for the receiver, removing the need for separate receiver batteries. BECs are usually either linear or switched mode voltage regulators in the broader sense are PWM controllers for electric motors. The ESC generally accepts a nominal 50 Hz PWM servo input signal whose pulse width varies from 1 ms to 2 ms. When supplied with a 1 ms width pulse at 50 Hz, the ESC responds by turning off the DC motor attached to its output. A 1.5 ms pulse-width input signal drives the motor at approximately half-speed. When presented with 2.0 ms input signal, the motor runs at full speed.

Most modern ESC contains a microcontroller interpreting the input signal and appropriately controlling the motor using a built-in program, or firmware. In some cases it is possible to change the factory built-in firmware for an alternate, publicly available, open source firmware. This is done generally to adapt the ESC to a particular application. Some ESCs are factory built with the capability of user upgradable firmware. Others require soldering to connect a programmer.

6.10   Power Module

A power module or power electronic module provides the physical containment for several power components, usually power semiconductor devices. These power semiconductors (so-called dies) are typically soldered or sintered on a power electronic substrate that carries the power semiconductors, provides electrical and thermal contact and electrical insulation where needed. Compared to discrete power semiconductors in plastic housings as TO-247 or TO-220, power packages provide a higher power density and are in many cases more reliable. Figure 6.8 shows the image of power module.

Besides modules that contain a single power electronic switch (as MOSFET, IGBT, BJT, Thyristor, GTO or JFET) or diode, classical power modules contain multiple semiconductor dies that are connected to form

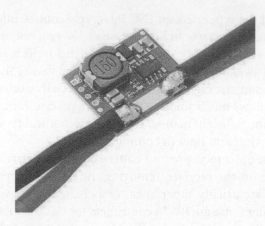

Figure 6.8 Power module.

an electrical circuit of a certain structure, called topology. Examples of broadly available topologies implemented in modules are:

- Switch (MOSFET, IGBT), with anti-parallel Diode;
- Bridge rectifier containing 4 (1-phase) or 6 (3-phase) diodes
- Half Bridge (inverter leg, with two switches and their corresponding anti-parallel diodes) three phases inverter (six switches and the corresponding anti-parallel diodes).

6.11 Display Shield

Display shield is connected to display the data such as battery voltage, its independent cell voltage, GPS coordinate data and other parameters. The system uses graphic LCD with resolution of 84 × 48 pixels. The display shield can be easily seated on Arduino without external wires and jumpers. The display uses PCD8544 controller chip which uses SPI communication to interface with Arduino. Figure 6.9 shows the image of display shield.

6.12 Navigational LEDS

Navigational LEDs are very useful during low light flights and to find the orientation of the drone. The LEDs used are advanced technology as only one wire communication is required to control all the LEDs used in the system. The communication is based on bit banging algorithm where LEDs

Figure 6.9 Display shield.

are connected in daisy chain manner. The LEDs are very bright and can produce any color. So, if orientation of UAV is changed then color pattern also changed accordingly. The LEDs used are WS2812 chip based. Figure 6.10 shows the image of navigational LEDs.

Mission Planner is a ground control station for Plane, Copter and Rover. It is compatible with Windows only. Mission Planner can be used as a configuration utility or as a dynamic control supplement for the autonomous vehicle. Mission Planner can be used for many applications. It could be used for loading the firmware for ArduPilot. The setup, configure and tune vehicle for optimum performance can be obtained. Plan, save and load autonomous missions into autopilot with simple point-and-click way-point entry on Google or other maps. It can also be used for download and analyzing mission logs created by ArduPilot.

Figure 6.10 Navigational LEDs.

6.13   Role of Sensors in the Proposed System

UAV stabilization is implemented with Inertial Measurement Unit (IMU). The IMU consists of set of sensors that measure the stability and position of the UAV [7, 8]. The Accelerometer and Gyroscope is used for implementation of stability whereas Barometer, Magnetometer and GPS help to determine the location of the UAV.

6.13.1   Accelerometer and Gyroscope

The MPU devices provide the world's first integrated 6-axis motion processor solution that eliminates the package-level gyroscope and accelerometer cross-axis misalignment associated with discrete solutions. The devices combine a 3-axis gyroscope and a 3-axis accelerometer on the same silicon die together with an onboard Digital Motion Processor (DMP) capable of processing complex 9-axis sensor fusion algorithms using the field-proven and proprietary MotionFusion engine. The MPU-6000 and MPU-6050's integrated 9-axis MotionFusion algorithms access external magnetometers or other sensors through an auxiliary master I²C bus, allowing the devices to gather a full set of sensor data without intervention from the system processor. The devices are offered in the same $4 \times 4 \times 0.9$ mm QFN footprint and pin out as the current MPU-3000 family of integrated 3-axis gyroscopes, providing a simple upgrade path and facilitating placement on already space constrained circuit boards. For precision tracking of both fast and slow motions, the MPU-60X0 features a user-programmable gyroscope full-scale range of ±250, ±500, ±1,000, and ±2,000/s (dps). The parts also have a user programmable accelerometer full-scale range of ±2 g, ±4 g, ±8 g, and ±16 g. These parts are identical to each other with two exceptions. The MPU-6050 supports I²C communications at up to 400 kHz and has a VLOGIC pin that defines its interface voltage levels; the MPU-6000 supports SPI at up to 20 MHz in addition to I²C, and has a single supply pin, VDD, which is both the device's logic reference supply and the analog supply for the part.

6.13.2   Magnetometer

The Honeywell HMC5883 is a surface mount multi-chip module designed for low field magnetic sensing with a digital interface for applications such as low cost compassing and magnetometer. The HMC5883 includes our state of the art, high-resolution HMC118X series magneto-resistive sensors plus Honeywell developed ASIC containing amplification, automatic degaussing strap drivers, offset cancellation, 12-bit ADC that enables 1° to 2° compass heading accuracy. The I²C serial bus allows for easy interface. The HMC5883 is a 3.0 × 3.0 × 0.9mm surface mount 16-pin Leadless Chip Carrier (LCC). Applications for the HMC5883 include Mobile Phones, Net books, Consumer Electronics, Auto Navigation Systems, and Personal Navigation Devices. The HMC5883 utilizes Honeywell's Anisotropic Magneto Resistive (AMR) technology that provides advantages over other magnetic sensor technologies. These anisotropic, directional sensors feature precision in-axis sensitivity and linearity, solid-state construction with very low cross-axis sensitivity designed to measure both direction and magnitude of Earth's magnetic fields, from milli-gauss to 8 gauss. Honeywell's Magnetic Sensors are among the most sensitive and reliable low-field sensors in the industry.

6.13.3   Barometric Pressure Sensor

The MS5611-01BA is a new generation of high resolution altimeter sensors from MEAS Switzerland with SPI and I²C bus interface. This Barometric Pressure Sensor is optimized for Altimeters and Variometers with an altitude resolution of 10 cm. The sensor module includes a high linearity pressure sensor and an ultralow power 24-bit ADC with internal factory calibrated coefficients. It provides a precise digital 24-bit pressure and temperature value and different operation modes that allow the user to optimize for conversion speed and current consumption. A high resolution temperature output allows the implementation of an altimeter/thermometer function without any additional sensor. The MS5611-01BA can be interfaced to any microcontroller. The communication protocol is simple, without the need of programming internal registers in the device. Small dimensions of only 5.0 mm × 3.0 mm and a height of only 1.0 mm allow for integration in mobile devices. This new sensor module generation is based on leading MEMS technology and latest benefits from MEAS Switzerland proven experience and know-how in high volume manufacturing of altimeter modules, which have been widely used for over a decade. The sensing principle employed leads to very low hysteresis and high stability of both pressure and temperature signal.

6.13.4   Global Positioning System

The NEO-7 series of standalone GNSS modules benefit from the exceptional performance of the u-blox 7 GNSS (GPS, GLONASS, QZSS and SBAS) engine. The NEO-7 series delivers high sensitivity and minimal acquisition times in the industry-proven NEO form factor. The NEO-7 series provides maximum sensitivity while maintaining low system power. The NEO-7M is optimized for cost sensitive applications, while NEO-7N provides best performance and easy RF integration. The NEO form factor allows easy migration from previous NEO generations. Sophisticated RF-architecture and interference suppression ensure maximum performance even in GNSS-hostile environments. The NEO-7 series combines a high level of integration capability with flexible connectivity options in a miniature package. This makes it perfectly suited for industrial applications with strict size and cost requirements. The I^{2}C compatible DDC interface provides connectivity and enables synergies with u-blox SARA, LEON and LISA cellular modules. u-blox 7 modules use GNSS chips qualified according to AEC-Q100 and are manufactured in ISO/TS 16949 certified sites. Qualification tests are performed as stipulated in the ISO16750 standard: "Road vehicles—Environmental conditions and testing for electrical and electronic equipment".

6.14   Wireless Communication

The proposed design has three set of wireless communication modules.

- Radio Controller
- Telemetry Radio
- Wireless Camera.

The Telemetry radio provides bidirectional communication whereas radio controller and wireless camera follow one-way communication. Radio controller transmits control signals. Wireless camera transmitter transmits live video feedback to ground station and Telemetry radio establishes link between the ground station and the UAV which shares data of sensors and other parameters [9, 10].

6.15   Radio Controller

Radio controller is a wireless remote controller to operate the drone manually. The Radio controller chosen is capable of controlling all types of model aircrafts and helicopters. Transmitter is modified by flashing the custom firmware with stock firmware. The custom firmware allows us to utilize every input to the transmitter by assigning it to output. The design needs custom controls to operate the drone such as changing its mode, emergency disarm and return to home functions. The transmitter used is capable of transmitting nine channel independent signals. Stock transmitter and receiver modules are replaced with advanced modules in order to achieve long range flights and adding failsafe functionality. The current configuration can operate drone about range of 2.5 km. The frequency of the radio is 2.4 GHz which is selected to avoid interferences with the other radio frequencies.

6.16   Telemetry Radio

Telemetry radio is a ZigBEE based transceiver system establishes wireless communication between drone and ground station. The radios are connected to ground station software on computer via a USB port and connected to drone via a serial port. The operating frequency of radio is 433 MHz. This frequency is selected because it is accepted by Indian Government. The data is transmitted and received simultaneously between drone and ground station. The same radio is used to connect drone and smart phone. One of the modules consists of USB to TTL logic converter chip to connect to COM ports in a computer. The obtained range is 500 m with current modules.

6.17   Camera Transmitter

The camera transmitter is used to transmit live video feedback to ground station. The user can operate the drone by seeing the FPV in the ground station. The camera modules we used are capable of transmitting range of 2 km. By using circular polarized antenna we obtained 1.5 km range. The module works in a frequency of 5.8 GHz which is selected to eliminate interference from radio controller signal and telemetry radio signal. The ground station uses video capture device connected to computer to receive video signals from the receiver.

6.18   Results and Discussion

Figure 6.11 shows the top view of the UAV. This view clearly shows the arrangement of components on the frame. The ArduPilot flight controller board is mounted on the frame where centre of gravity is aligned.

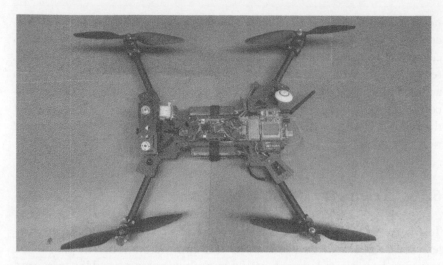

Figure 6.11 Top view of UAV.

Figure 6.12 Front view of UAV.

The batteries are mounted on either side in order to balance the frame using Velcro strap which is very helpful in swapping batteries quickly. The GPS and magnetometer are mounted on front side of the UAV. The backside of UAV is equipped with Arduino Mega with LCD shield connected for displaying battery current, GPS location and some other details.

The radio controller receiver module and wireless telemetry module are also mounted on either sides of Arduino Mega.

Figure 6.12 shows the front view of the UAV. The camera is placed at the centre of UAV which sends live video feedback to ground station. The front motors along with propellers are mounted on either side of the carbon fiber boom with equal distance from the center.

Figure 6.13 Side view of UAV.

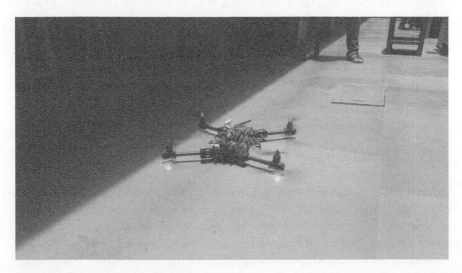

Figure 6.14 Isometric view of UAV.

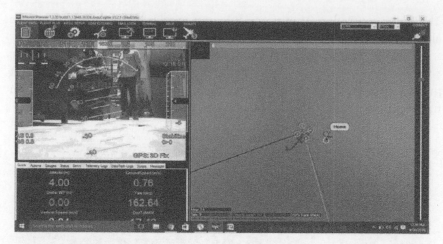

Figure 6.15 Screenshot of Mission Planner with UAV located.

Figure 6.13 clearly shows the side view and wiring harness of the UAV. The backside of the UAV is fitted with shock absorbing bushes which help to absorb the shock while landing. The back plate is fitted with power distribution boards, four ESCs, DC-DC power module and camera transmitter.

Figure 6.14 clearly shows the isometric view of the UAV in which, the whole setup is visible with the propellers spinning. The Quadcopter is in ARMED mode and it is waiting for command to take-off. Figure 6.15 shows the screen shot of the Mission planner software tool which is connected to UAV via telemetry. It shows the camera viewfinder along with map that has the location of Quadcopter. The data shown in software tool displays current altitude, speed, etc. It also shows an on-screen display on viewfinder which also shows some data of GPS, Modes, RSSI and Directions.

6.19 Conclusion

Interest in Unmanned Aerial Vehicles is growing worldwide and several efforts are underway to integrate UAV operations routinely and safely into civil airspace. Currently, UAV operations are confined to special-use in airspace and are limited in their access sometimes, for safety reasons, by a restrictive authorization process. To inspect the transmission lines being the main aim, also identify any kind of faults and the attempt for that is done through a constructive model of an UAV. It is developed with some software that help in its operation to perform the task.

The idea of inspecting transmission lines for faults in remote areas where human effort can be reduced and the risk levels can be minimized. The design of the drone for this purpose is completed. It can be operated on automatic basis also. The GPS has been interfaced and the drone flies according to the directions given. Then, the CMOS camera is attached to the drone through which live video stream can be obtained and fault can be identified.

References

1. Wang, B., Chen, X., Wang, Q., Liu, L., Zhang, H., Li, B., Power line inspection with a flying robot. *2010 1st International Conference on Applied Robotics for the Power Industry*, Montreal, QC, pp. 1–6, 2010.
2. Larrauri, J.I., Sorrosal, G., González, M., Automatic system for overhead power line inspection using an Unmanned Aerial Vehicle—RELIFO project. *2013 International Conference on Unmanned Aircraft Systems (ICUAS)*, Atlanta, GA, pp. 244–252, 2013.
3. Deng, C., Wang, S., Huang, Z., Tan, Z., Liu, J., Unmanned Aerial Vehicles for Power Line Inspection: A Cooperative Way in Platforms and Communications. *J. Commun.*, 9, 687–692, 2014.
4. Zormpas, A., Moirogiorgou, K., Kalaitzakis, K., Plokamakis, G.A., Partsinevelos, P., Giakos, G. C., Zervakis, M.E., Power Transmission Lines Inspection using Properly Equipped Unmanned Aerial Vehicle (UAV). *2018 IEEE International Conference on Imaging Systems and Techniques (IST)*, Krakow, pp. 1–5, 2018.
5. Golightly, I., Jones, D., Visual control of an unmanned aerial vehicle for power line inspection. *ICAR '05. Proceedings, 12th International Conference on Advanced Robotics, 2005*, Seattle, WA, pp. 288–295, 2005.
6. Pagnano, A., Höpf, M., Teti, R., A Roadmap for Automated Power Line Inspection. Maintenance and Repair. *Procedia CIRP*, vol. 12, pp. 234–239, 2013.
7. Menendez, O.A., Perez, M., Cheein, F.A.A., Vision based inspection of transmission lines using unmanned aerial vehicles. *2016 IEEE International Conference on Multisensor Fusion and Integration for Intelligent Systems (MFI)*, Baden-Baden, pp. 412–417, 2016.
8. Zimmermann Homma, R., Cosentino, A., Szymanski, C., Autonomous inspection in transmission and distribution power lines—methodology for image acquisition by means of unmanned aircraft system and its treatment and storage. *CIRED—Open Access Proc. J.*, 2017, 1, 965–967, 10 2017.

9. Homma, R.Z., Szymanski, C., Faraco, R.A., Information and communication architecture for transmission power line inspections using unmanned aircraft system. *CIRED—Open Access Proc. J.*, 2017, 1, 238–241, 10 2017.
10. Bai, L., Guvenc, I., Yu, Q., Zhang, W., Guest Editorial Special Issue on Unmanned Aerial Vehicles Over Internet of Things. *IEEE Internet Things J.*, 6, 2, 1636–1639, April 2019.

7

Smart City Infrastructure Management System Using IoT

S. Ramamoorthy[1], M. Kowsigan[2]*,
P. Balasubramanie[3] and P. John Paul[4]

*[1]Department of Computer Science and Engineering, SRM
Institute of Science and Technology, Kattankulathur, India*
*[2]Department of Computer Science and Engineering, SRM
Institute of Science and Technology, Kattankulathur, India*
*[3]Department of Computer Technology, Kongu Engineering College,
Erode, India*
*[4]Department of Computer Science and Engineering, SRM
Institute of Science and Technology, Kattankulathur, India*

Abstract

The development of smart cities involves adoption of advanced Information and Communication Technologies (ICT) in the process of enhancing the performance of the urban services. The major objective of the smart city is to reduce the resource, energy consumptions and overall cost. The models also ensure that individual privacy and safety on the data today activities across the city. The Internet of Things (IoT) is the major enabling technology in the background of smart city development in the urban location. An efficient way of placing and integrating the smart intelligent sensors on the predominant locations of the city and capture the data for analysis and decision making process. The sensors embedded as a part of object which can sense and transmit the data to the reporting end. The centralized server with customized software can be able to analyze the data received from the intelligent servers to predict and initiate the real time actions accordingly [3].

Keywords: Intelligent servers, smart intelligent servers, information and communication technologies

Corresponding author: mkowsigan@gmail.com

G. R. Kanagachidambaresan (ed.) Role of Edge Analytics in Sustainable Smart City Development: Challenges and Solutions, (127–138) © 2020 Scrivener Publishing LLC

7.1   Introduction

Infrastructure with low-cost intelligent sensors and Wi-fi enabled wireless communications networks create the atmosphere of continuous monitoring of the object. The data sensed by these sensors are processed in real-time to ensure the timely response. The major drivers in the process of IoT applications in smart cities include cost, performance, efficiency and resource minimization.

The wide applications of IoT on the Smart city development include:

- Smart water resource management system can sense flow rates, tank pressure and water levels. The IoT-based smart sensors fixed on the locations of reservoir and water storage Dams can automatically make the decision over the excessive water flow management and flood alerts to the public living near to this locations. This model provides the safety solution to the government as well as public to avoid severe loss of human life. The Smart Flood and disaster management can be treated effectively using IoT based smart applications.
- The Traffic Congestion issues can be effectively addressed by using IoT-based smart traffic control management system to track the real-time traffic flow and route the transit into less traffic locations.
- Smart Public safety system capture the real time crowd data through surveillance camera and processed using video analytics to identify the crime details in the open public locations.
- Smart Energy management system implements the smart street light with inbuilt intelligent sensor for automatic light control, power charging, etc. [2].
- The smart parking system with GPS tracking assists the driver to easily locate the empty space to park the vehicle with least time to search the location.
- The smart life care measures are achieved through IoT-based health care emergency vehicle to automate the process by connecting the emergency vehicle with the hospital and doctors in the real-time to save the human life.
- The smart home automation system with IOT-based sensor detects and alerts the individual to improve their life styles.

The proposed research article will discuss about the real-time challenges related to the development of smart cities using IoT. The IoT-based smart cities open the number of research challenges which includes sensor security, limited power, secure wireless communication and uninterrupted network connectivity, etc.

7.2   Major Challenges in IoT-Based Technology

- Peer to Peer communication security
- Limited Battery power
- Fault tolerance nature of the Sensor
- Lack of standard interface connectivity
- Automated Data storage
- Coordination of multiple sensors
- Collaborative decision making
- Smart Data collection and repository.

7.2.1   Peer to Peer Communication Security

The major challenge on the IoT infrastructure is to protect the end to end communication between the sensor device and server. The sensor which is placed on the field to sense and transfer the data to the server is facing a number of security threats. The attackers try to breach the security mechanism and gain the knowledge about the sensitive data shared among the peer ends.

The security attacks related to the peer to peer communications are listed out below:

- Intrusion detection attack
- Masqurader
- Man in the Middle attack
- Traffic Analysis
- Distributed Denial of Service (DDoS)
- Security and Privacy attack on the Data.

The communication network established to share the data must ensure the security mechanism to avoid the data leakage on the network.

Masqurader

One entity pretends to be an entity to monitor and collect the data from the sender side. This type of attacks introduces the new responder for given source to gain the conversation information between the target ends.

Man in the Middle Attack

The attack intercepts the message which is exchanged between the two peer ends. The actual content of the message altered according to their wish. The message has to be protected with strong security algorithm to avoid this type of attacks and data leakage.

Traffic Analysis

Monitor and understand the data format while it is in process by the attackers. The stream of data formats are analyzed through breached network entity. The lack of security enforcement leads to this type of traffic analysis attack.

Distributed Denial of Service (DDoS)

Overload the particular network communication channel to restrict the data exchange between the peer ends fall under the Distributed Denial of Service (DDoS). This type of services makes the network unavailable for the authenticated user for the routine communication between the target ends. The inclusion of secure Tunneling and Virtual Private Network (VPN), etc., avoid this type of security breaches.

Security and Privacy Attack on the Data

The sensitive data leakage is a major issue in any open interface device. The government and confidential data leakage lead into number of challenges. The data leakage by the authorized used becomes the more challenging part as compared to the attacker.

7.2.2   Objective of Smart Infrastructure

The major objective of the smart city infrastructure is to improvise the development of physical, institutional, social and economic infrastructure (Figure 7.1). The development focuses on the people's lifestyle living in the remote villages. Every citizen in the country must be provided with core infrastructure and advanced environmental, health care solutions through smart applications [1].

The implementation objectives of the Smart City:

Ensure sufficient water availability
Clean environment
Uninterrupted and adequate power supply

Figure 7.1 Smart Infrastructure solutions.

Sanitation and waste management
Improvised urban development and transportation [8]
Advanced health care systems
Adequate houses for everyone
Digitalization and high performance connectivity
Improvised E-governance application
Health and education systems [5].

7.3   Internet of Things (IoT)

The Internet of Things (IoT) acts as a backbone for the development of core smart city infrastructure (Figure 7.1). The sensors and actuators embedded as a part of the object perform the continuous monitoring and data transfer operations. The smart devices also help the user to set up automated alerts and notifications regarding the event to perform. The interaction among this smart object improves the quality of the collaborative smart infrastructure management [4].

7.3.1   Key Components of Components of IoT

The list of following key components supports the various activities in the smart city management using IoT:

- Network Gateway
- Data Analytics

- Connectivity of Devices
- Cloud Computing Technology
- User Interface
- Database Systems
- System Automation
- Infrastructure Development.

7.3.1.1 Network Gateway

The Gateway monitors the data traffic flow across the protocol and communication network. The End-to-End communication networks provide the maximum security features for the data exchanged between the sensors and the communication devices. The numbers of standard protocols are deployed to monitor the data flow to ensure the security of the network devices. The network gateway also preprocesses the sensor data before it transferred to the next level and performs the basic configuration like TCP/IP data format.

The standard IoT Network Protocols are classified based on Network and Data related functionalities listed out as follows:

1. IoT Network Protocols
   - HTTP (HyperText Transfer Protocol)
   - LoRaWan (Long Range Wide Area Network)
   - Bluetooth
   - ZigBee
2. IoT Data Protocols
   - Message Queue Telemetry Transport (MQTT)
   - Constrained Application Protocol (CoAP)
   - Advanced Message Queuing Protocol (AMQP)
   - Machine-to-Machine (M2M) Communication Protocol
   - Extensible Messaging and Presence Protocol (XMPP)

7.3.1.2 HTTP (HyperText Transfer Protocol)

The HTTP protocol lays the foundation for the general communication across the network devices on the web. This is the common protocol used in number of IoT-based application to exchange the huge volume of data across the network devices. However the protocol is not preferred in most of the applications because of its cost, energy consumption and more constraints.

7.3.1.3   LoRaWan (Long Range Wide Area Network)

One of the most preferred protocols for the smart city infrastructure is due to its low power and memory consumption. The major advantage of this protocol detects the low signal below the noise level. The smart street light becomes the real time application for this protocol. The street light bulb connected with the LoRaWan gateway automatically controls the intensity of the bulb to reduce the power consumption.

7.3.1.4   Bluetooth

It's a short range communication protocol for wireless transmission. The protocol connected with the network gateway performs the short range communication across the network devices. It's a short range, low-power and low-cost wireless communication device. It reduces the power consumption of the IoT devices communicating under the smart city infrastructure.

Smart wearable devices and mobile phones are used this type of protocol for the intelligent short range communication. Most preferred protocol on the smart infrastructure development model.

7.3.1.5   ZigBee

Smart short range wireless protocol allows smart objects work together. The protocol mostly used under the low rate data transfers application within the short range communication. Street light and electric meters in urban areas make use of this protocol for communication. The smart home management system uses this zigbee protocol along with the security features.

7.3.2   IoT Data Protocols

IoT data protocols are used to connect low power IoT devices which are deployed under the smart city infrastructure.

7.3.2.1   Message Queue Telemetry Transport (MQTT)

MQTT protocol collects the data from the multiple sensors communicating under the smart infrastructure and supports the device monitoring. Mainly used in the application like car sensors, fire alarm and message based application.

7.3.2.2   Constrained Application Protocol (CoAP)

The protocol mainly used to exchange data between client and server using HTTP protocol. Only on limited electronic gadgets with certain constraints data exchange can be performed. The CoAP mainly used in Mobile automation and microcontroller based devices.

7.3.2.3   Advanced Message Queuing Protocol (AMQP)

Message-oriented protocol mainly used to support routing and queuing based operations on network. It enables secure data exchange between the sensors connected in the network and cloud storage. AQMP protocol mainly used in the banking applications to trace the message delivery on the peer end [10, 11].

7.3.2.4   Data Analytics

The data collected from the various IoT-based smart sensors fixed on the smart infrastructure pushed to the cloud storage space. The data collected in this form are analyzed to perform various response activities.

The response for the given condition triggered through any electronic gadgets like mobile phones. The data analytics algorithms are applied over this type data for the instant Decision making process. The data must be analyzed and responded in real time applications. Huge volume of data generated by the sensors deployed on the field of smart city infrastructure. The efficient data analysis algorithms are required to analyze this type of data.

The general process of Data Analysis given as follows:

- Huge volume of data creation
- Analysis over data collection
- Framing business application strategies
- Obtain the knowledge for the analysis
- Unstructured data.

List of Data Analytics operations as follows:

- Analyze the data
- Obtain the knowledge
- Application of business intelligence
- Promote the product or service
- Improved performance.

The data must be analyzed and responded in real-time applications. Huge volume of data generated by the sensors deployed on the field of smart city infrastructure. The efficient data analysis algorithms are required to analyze this type of data.

Types of Analytics Models

- Database Analytics—In database Analytics example SQL, MADLIB, etc.
- Text Analytics—Natural Language Processing (NLP)
- Sentimental Analytics—Reviews & Feedback
- Click Stream Analytics—Web based Selections
- Time Series Analytics—Forecasting
- Predictive analytics—Business Intelligence
- Live Stream analytics—Streaming Data
- Multimedia Analytics—Text, Audio & video.

7.4   Machine Learning-Based Smart Decision-Making Process

The sensors involved in the process of sense the environment must be capable to take the decision by themselves. The smart intelligence must be incorporated along with the sensor to take the decision when its required instantly. The Machine Learning algorithms under the Artificial Intelligence provide the opportunity to implement such a intelligent sensors to make the decision by itself under the critical situations [9].

The application of machine learning concepts to implement smart intelligence sensor involve the following activities:

- Data collection
- Data preprocessing
- Classification and clustering process
- Model generation
- Evaluation and testing
- Decision-making process
- Application of decision outcomes.

The sensors must also be capable to carry out the above activities as a part of monitoring and sensing the object. The sensor may also offload this process and take its final decision to respond the given acitivity. The sensors must be empowered with high level battery power to carry out the process of smart data analysis [6].

The Data collected by the sensor is used to perform the data analysis process. During preprocessing stage the incorrect and noisy error values are removed from the data. The preprocessed data has to be classified and clustered according to the nature of target evaluation model. Number of classification and clustering algorithms are available to perform the classification process. Once the data classified, the decision making model can be created for analysis. The model has to be tested with the random test data to find the accuracy of the new analysis model. The IoT based sensor can make use of this decision to perform instant decision under the critical situation.

7.5   Cloud Computing

Cloud Computing Services occupies the wide range of space in the field of Information Technology (IT). The Cloud Services support any IT operations to complete the process with minimal infrastructure requirement with greater reduced cost. The Total expenditure required to enable the IT model will be converted into an Operational model which requires only the operational level cost. The elimination of high investment and uninterrupted automated services through highly available network bandwidth attract more technologies towards this cloud services. The cloud computing technology allows the end user to create, deploy and provision the computing resources like server, storage and network, etc., from the remote location at anytime. The cloud security is the one of the major challenge need to be addressed in an effective way to ensure the hassle free environment for the cloud user. The open public network space, open interface and multiuser shared cloud storage space will lead to the user and service level security challenges. The enhanced secure communication channel establishment and isolated user storage environment will ensure the security measures against the vulnerable attacks over the cloud service platform.

Cloud Deployment Models

- Public Cloud
- Private Cloud
- Hybrid Cloud
- Community Cloud.

Smart mobile phone application with digital data dominates the entire virtual world of IT Technology. The data generated through multiple sources start from the satellite images to virtual communities like Facebook, Whatsapp, Youtube, etc. The vast amount of this digital data need to be stored, processed and reused for the next level of information analysis process. This processed information are used as an input for the next higher level of predictions to achieve the greater decision making process. The model ultimately require enormous amount of storage space where the continuous flow of data need to be accommodated for the process of refinement and analysis. The insufficient and short of computing resources end up with incomplete solutions for any application process. The cloud computing model replaces this insufficient resource model with the infinite resource utilization model to ensure the availability of business service operations. The lesser cost and greater flexibility of this particular technology attracts enormous amount of IT operations towards cloud technology. The greater witness for the strength of this technology is real-time exposure in day today activity like usage of Gmail, Facebook, GDrive, Twitter applications etc., in regular aspects. The Amazon EC2 from the public cloud service provider offer the complete stack of computing resources as a service to its end users [7].

Securing the user data and protecting the unstable public network from the end to end user service delivery model requires the high capability security algorithms. The classical Cryptographic algorithms are provided the basic level of foundations to ensure the security at primary aspect. The greater level of enhancement is required to complete this enormous amount of service level attacks in the cloud network model.

Cloud Service Models

- Infrastructure as a Service (IaaS)
- Platform as a Service (PaaS)
- Software as a Service (SaaS)
- Security as a Service (SecaaS)
- Storage as a Service (SaaS).

The Chapter mainly focused on smart infrastructure management using Internet of Things (IoT). The major issues faced in the real-time scenario to establish the smart infrastructure under the smart city is addressed. The various security threats and levels of attacks are classified with the standard IoT-based devices.

References

1. Saba, D., Sahli, Y., Berbaoui, B., Maouedj, R., Towards Smart Cities: Challenges, Components, and Architectures, in: *Toward Social Internet of Things (SIoT): Enabling Technologies, Architectures and Applications*, pp. 249–286, Springer, Bouzereah, 2020.

2. Nižetić, S., Djilali, N., Papadopoulos, A., Rodrigues, J.J.P.C., Smart technologies for promotion of energy efficiency, utilization of sustainable resources and waste management. *J. Clean. Prod.*, 231, 565–591, 2019.

3. Miorandi, D., Sicari, S., De Pellegrini, F., Chlamtac, I., Internet of things: Vision, applications and research challenges. *Ad Hoc Netw.*, 10, 7, 1497–1516, 2012. Sep 30.

4. Zanella, A., Bui, N., Castellani, A., Vangelista, L., Zorzi, M., Internet of things for smart cities. *IEEE IoT-J.*, 1, 1, 22–32, 2014. Feb.

5. Arasteh, H., Hosseinnezhad, V., Loia, V., Tommasetti, A., Troisi, O., Shafie-khah, M., Siano, P., IoT-based smart cities: a survey, in: *2016 IEEE 16th International Conference on Environment and Electrical Engineering (EEEIC)*, pp. 1–6, 2016.

6. Rizwan Bashir, M. and Qumer Gill, A., IoT enabled smart buildings: A systematic review. *Intelligent Systems Conference (IntelliSys) 2017*, 151–159, 2017.

7. Kaur, M.J. and Maheshwari, P., Building smart cities applications using IoT and cloud-based architectures, in: *2016 International Conference on Industrial Informatics and Computer Systems (CIICS)*, pp. 1–5, 2016, IEEE.

8. Zantalis, F., Koulouras, G., Karabetsos, S., Kandris, D., A review of machine learning and IoT in smart transportation. *Future Internet*, 11, 4, 94, 2019.

9. Salamone, F., Belussi, L., Currò, C., Danza, L., Ghellere, M., Guazzi, G., Lenzi, B., Megale, V., Meroni, I., Application of IoT and Machine Learning techniques for the assessment of thermal comfort perception. *Energy Procedia*, 148, 798–805, 2018.

10. Sethi, P. and Sarangi, S.R., Internet of things: architectures, protocols, and applications. *J. Elec. Comput. Eng.*, 1, 1–25, 2017.

11. Kowsigan, M. and Balasubramanie, P., A novel resource clustering model to develop an efficient wireless personal cloud environment. *Turk. J. Electr. Eng. Co.*, 27, 2156–2169, 2018.

8

Lightweight Cryptography Algorithms for IoT Resource-Starving Devices

S. Aruna*, G. Usha†, P. Madhavan and M.V. Ranjith Kumar

School of Computing, SRM Institute of Science & Technology, Chennai, India

Abstract

In both symmetric and asymmetric cryptography, one of the most important topics is lightweight cryptography. Many lightweight cryptographic algorithms were implemented and used in RFID tags, embedded devices, smart internet of things, mobile services, cloud data, etc. which help the society to evolve into a sustainable and secure smart city. The main aspire is to use minimum computing power devices for providing an advanced level of security. Many proposed lightweight algorithms were implemented in both hardware and software with the evaluation of important parameters of security which help the end-user to select the suitable algorithms at a particular circumstance, based on their requirements of security parameters such as authentication, confidentiality, integrity, etc. In this chapter, we introduce the authentication protocol and lightweight protocol which will help the user to safeguard the data in any practical applications such as IoT, mobile devices without any security threats.

Keywords: Cryptography, RFID, smart IoT, smart city

8.1 Introduction

In this digital world, what we are focusing on is all about the communication and connection between one end to other end via internet and network

---

*Corresponding author: arunas@srmist.edu.in
†Corresponding author: ushag@srmist.edu.in

G. R. Kanagachidambaresan (ed.) Role of Edge Analytics in Sustainable Smart City Development: Challenges and Solutions, (139–170) © 2020 Scrivener Publishing LLC

itself. In this course, we are majorly focusing on the development in our communication and network speed. But what affects us more is security. A network-based device is much popular to communicate but there are many things inside that which can be a great source to steal someone's information which are streaming and transferring over the network. So security is more important in today's network communication.

Keeping the security portion in mind, we have many algorithms to secure our data like AES, SHA, etc. But this algorithm works well in computer devices. They face lots of issues over an embedded world or IoT. Why so we will discuss later on. Basically resource-constrained devices have a bad response with the existing algorithms like SHA, AES, etc. So, to get rid of this problem, the concept of lightweight cryptography came into the market. Basically we can say it is a trade-off between lightweight and security.

8.1.1   Need of the Cryptography

According to the NIST & ISO/IEC, a definition of a device spectrum should be like:

- Conventional Cryptography
- Lightweight Cryptography

Conventional: It is basically smart phones, computer devices, servers on and on.

Lightweight Cryptography: RFID, Sensor and Embedded Systems.

In security, AES and SHA dominate all the problems on security from all the directions. Then what is the need of going with again lightweight cryptography? Well what we can see, we can protect though easily and sometimes, what we can't also we can manage to have some procedure to handle those things. But the fact is, it is not possible to handle all the things all the time. For example, take the c anase of embedded system, sensors and so on.

Why because, these devices like sensors enroll don't have:

1. Processing power with some valid reason. That can be different many times.
2. Memory capability.

In this case lightweight cryptography does some great job, as it uses:

1. Less Space
2. Less Resources to compute something

3. Power supply very less
4. End to end encryption only using single availability of block or stream.

What happens with an embedded system is that microcontroller of an 8-bit, microcontroller of a16-bit and microcontroller of a 32-bit, struggle to match with the scenario of real-time for the methods of conventional cryptography.

On another hand, devices of RFID and sensor have a limited number of gates for security [2].

So AES has been useless for embedded systems. What we see in lightweight cryptography is that we often look for much smaller blocks (less than 90 bits) and the systems which is having S-boxes less than 4 bits [3]. For the cryptography of lightweight, the main obstacles are the power requirements that are related to the GateEquivalents (GEs), and time. With the category of RFID, devices of passive, the category of RFID, devices of passive. In RFID device for power supply, the device is not using an associated battery, and somewhere the chip must derive power from the energy tied radio wave. RFID component is likely to be seriously forced into a power drain while performing cryptographic operations, with being constrained on time requirements and gates used. Even with RFID devices, an active RFID is having an associated battery that is hard to recharge, so a drain on the power must often be minimal. On another side, exposing the subsequent wave of IoT innovation owed to its intrinsic ability to connect smart 'things' in the cloud-based in an Information Technology Architecture for physical world. The fundamental success of IoT is on Data protection and privacy protection and will present novel security challenges in cryptography, credit, and management of identity [4].

8.2   Challenges on Lightweight Cryptography

Lightweight cryptography mainly concentrates on the devices, works with limited resources—what standard cryptographic algorithm has much consumed much power, more size of its implementation and so on. In lightweight cryptography, working is much simpler and faster than the cryptography that we used conventionally.

1. Challenges in Hardware Implementation:
   In hardware perspective we should always concentrate on RAM, storing of internal states clock, memory, the code size

and key states [5]. Read-only mask knowledge is used in reducing the space of key, burning the keys on devices i.e., on chips [6].

2. Challenges in Software Implementation:

In the Software perspective, implementation size, memory consumption (RAM), and the throughput are more considerable things we should keep in mind. In programming cases, they brought together FELICS—Fair Evaluation of Lightweight Cryptographic Systems [6] structure and is proposed to assess the showings of lightweight cryptography or stream cipher exhibitions in execution size [7].

3. Challenges in Design:

Certainly, maximum of the lightweight cryptographic block ciphers uses 64-bit blocks size but in AES is demanding a 128-bit size of block and the size of 128-bit key. We follow some design trends in lightweight cryptography design which are as follows:

a. block with small size and the key in small size will carry problems: CBC block cipher mode will erode faster than other modes and invites more problems when the size of block is small. When the numerous n-bit blocks encryption approaches the time $2n/2$ [8], meanwhile attacks related on key will invite more risk in the case of short key

b. In cryptography of lightweight in symmetric side, number of operations is doubled in the case of doubling in key primitive of input size in symmetric part [7]. 12 rounds are always used in the family of PHOTON, when s-box size is doubled then the number of block size is doubled. Correspondingly, in AES 256, if there is increase in block size as double then there is doubling in number of s-box and there will be increase in number of rounds.

8.3   Hashing Techniques on Lightweight Cryptography

For lightweight cryptography, hashing methods approved by ISO/IEC29192-5:2016 are to be considered as standards in the construction of Lesamanta-LW [13], SPONGENT [4, 9] and PHOTON [12], ISO/IEC standards 29192-2:2012 are followed by CLEFIA block methods and PRESENT block methods, and for stream methods the ISO/IEC standards 29192-3:2012 followed by Trivium and Encoro. In this case, two most popular hashing techniques will be discussed, one is Hashing and another one is Streaming.

Hashing:

In the world of IoT, often we will take KB as memory capacity. The hash functions of Message Digest 5, SHA-1, and the other methods used to construct hash functions will not work efficiently for the devices of IoT. So the recommendations from NIST some new suggested hashing methods for IoT such as PHOTON, Quark with different version, SPONGENT with different versions, and Lesamnta-LW. The above said hash methods are supporting the input of characters with 256 bits These approaches yield a much slighter memory footprint, and consume a goal of an input of 256 bits and it will produce very smaller footprint of memory.

Hash Function Construction:

a. Sponge
The challenge of developing hash functions for lightweight is to achieve a balance between the requirements of protection and memory. It is a common approach to generate a size output >256 bits to avoid collision; though, it is computationally expensive. The Sponge construction is widely adopted for solving this problem by the pre-image protection for the similar internal state size. Based on permutation P of 'b' bit, bit rate r and with the capacity of 'c' bits, this construction is built. M_i is the block of 'r' bit messages and Z_i is a component of the output of hash function with output of n bits. Its width determines the size of the internal state using b = r + c with output 'n'. At first, the initial state's bits set to zero. The second step is: Input message is expanded and fragmented into r-bit blocks. Design consists of two stages, i.e. phases of absorption and squeezing. The input message blocks of 'r' bits are XORed in the absorbing step with the initial 'r' bit of input state formerly the permutation function P is added. The squeezing phase begins after the processing off all blocks of message. The state's first r-bit is produced a single output block and the Permutation function P is included and User determines the number of output blocks. Because of its lightweight nature, in the sponge structure is the solitary substitute

to the traditional Merkle–Damgard mode hash function creation. The Merkel–Damgard method depends on single permutation only, then the blocks of message are pooled with the internal state with a simple XOR. In sponge construction, unlike the construction of Davies–Meyer, storage of blocks of message and intermediary values of "feed forward" are not needed.

b. Merkle–Damgard

In many hash function algorithms such as SHA1/SHA2, MD5, STITCH are the lightweight hash function processes, for example, the Merkle–Damgard architecture was adopted. It is generated based on collision-resistant compression function of one-way to create collision-resistant cryptographic hash functions. The Merkle–Damgard mode for the generation of hash function involves applying the padding function of MD-compliant to create a size of output that is twice that of a static input size because compression function cannot handle dynamic size of inputs. The hash function splits the output of the function into blocks of static size, processing the output of intermediate hash functions output with the compression function individually. A block of input is paired with output of the previous round at each time. We used a function H for compression mapping $\{0, 1\}n$ and$\{0, 1\}k$ to $\{0, 1\}n$, in the current work. A text block such as m1, m2, ..., mt, each text block is with a size of k bits are processed with Initial Vector with $\{0,1\}n$ to create a hash function H.

c. Davies–Meyer

As a compression tool, modern hash functions were used. Merkle and Damgard have given their theoretical foundations. To produce output with fixed length, taking fixed length input applies to a compression function H holds a message extract and chaining variable. The compression method Davies–Meyer feeds a key to the block cipher for each message block (m_i). It also feeds with an encoded plaintext with H_i-1 the previous hash value. Also, to derive the next level of hash output (H_i), the production of cipher texts is XORed with H_i-1previous hash value. By applying a persistent pre-specified initial value (H_0) is needed due to the nonexistence of the preceding hash value of the first round.

Hash Function Algorithms on Light Weight Cryptography:

In the mode of block cipher, we can produce hash value using lightweight hashing algorithm called PRESENT [14, 25]. The applications of PHOTON, GLUON and Spongent, have also been highlighted in the development of a dedicated lightweight sponge-based hash feature and Davies–Meyer function for compression as shown in Figure 8.1.

a. PHOTON

Guo *et al.* developed the lightweight hash function of PHOTON, as an inner unkeyed permutation, using sponge-like structure and the primitive of AES. For 64-bit collision tolerance, it produces a hash function for lightweight with 1,120 GE. The sample size is 64 to n, 128 to 256, input bit rate 'r' and output bit rate r' respectively. A PHOTON hash function can be characterized as PHOTON-block size n/input r/output r'. The size of its internal state is depending on the size of the hash output: 100 bits, 144 bits, 196 bits, 256 bits and 288 bits. P as an internal permutation is applied to elements of d2 based on internal conditions of bit. Two kinds S-box are applied in this functions, i.e. PRESENT S-box and AES S-box of 8-bit, are used.

b. Spongent

The Spongent lightweight hash functions are developed by Bogdanov with PRESENT form permutations. In terms of linear and differential properties, the S-box of 4-bit, were used in the implementation of Spongent of a serial low-area as functional logic of main, follows the design criteria of PRESENT. For each collision/(second) pre image resistance level, Spongent has 13 variants and implementation constraints. It is having very simple round function; the logic of this hash function is similar to the smallest theoretical scale. In the given hash technique, b-bit 0 is the initial value. The hash size 'n' is equivalent to strength c or 2c in all variants of Spongent. The parts of the text were XORed into the state's locations of rightmost bit. Positions of 'r' bit form as a hash output. Over the S-box of linear approximation (i.e. input and output masks involve only single bits) unbiased output. In round of PRESENT helps to minimize the effects of linear hull using linear approximation.

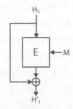

Figure 8.1 Davies–Meyer round function [24].

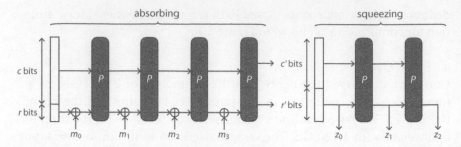

Figure 8.1a Spongent Lightweight hash functions [10].

Spongent practices the function of sponge. For sponge construction, it is a formal method to use permutation i.e., transformation of fixed length and padding rule. In Figure 8.1a shows the framework of extended sponge which is used by Photon hash family. We have not discussed much about lightweight cryptography Hash function.

c. Keecak

The implementation of lightweight supported hash function such as Keccak-f[200] and Keccak-f[400] transformations was described by Kavun and Yalcin. Version 3 of Secure Hash Algorithm are Keccak-f200 and Keccak-f400. In fact, the development of Keccak is created on the structure of the sponge. Its fundamental component is permutation of Keccak-f, which includes several formal rounds that consist of logical operations and 'b' bit permutations. The Keccak-f 'b' contains permutation selected from the set of seven given permutations, where 'b' represents the width of permutatsion {25, 50, 100, 200, 400, 800, 1,600} and the state width in the sponge construction.

d. Quark

In 2010 Aumasson developed a hash function using the method of sponge construction called Quark. It is the initial lightweight function to prove integrity i.e., hash which is designed to minimize the memory requirement, which provides on single level of security. It uses a permutation P, which is basically incorporated in stream cipher for Grain and the block ciphers of KATAN. Quark can be classified into three types: security of 64-bit called U-Quark and security of 80-bit called D-Quark and security of 112-bit called T-Quark. U-Quark provides security against all attacks at least 64-bit. U-Quark, meanwhile, takes 1,379 GE and the consumption of power approximately 2.44 μW, throughput at 100 kHz. T-Quark needs

GE as 2,296. The inward permutation P includes three nonlinear Boolean functions, i.e. f, g and h. It also contains one linear function of Boolean 'p' with process P involved. For each Quark function, all nonlinear Boolean functions are unique. The process P depends on three stages, i.e., the first stage is initialization, second stage is state update and the third stage is performance measurement.

e. Neiva

In Proposed construction using state 'a' the mode of sponge-based lightweight hash function called PRESENT. State 'b' is about 256-bit. The frequency and strength are 32-bits, 224-bits and 32 rounds respectively. Neiva's hashing is as follows, first one is padding the Message M and then splitting it into blocks with the size of 32-bits until XORed to the state of M1 that is the first message block. The revised register is divided into 16-bit words later applying on PRESENT S-box parallely and applies Feistel structure to every 64-bit. It is applied to a round constant after a left rotation of 8-bit. After modular addition, the modified register is the first round production. It continues to feed until 32 rounds in the next round. Select the utmost important 32-bit in absorbed phase of last record in the squeezing process. Then add 'f' to the modified register seven times and take out the most appropriate 32-bit each time. The seven 32 bit will be concatenated to get the 224 bit output.

f. ARMADILLO

ARMADILLO introduced by Badel *et al.*, which is used in simple multi-application. It has been developed as MAC, as well as digital signatures like PRNG and PRF. The structure followed on this method is similar to that of Merkle–Damgard. This hash function usually requires 2,923 GE. To complete one calculation (consuming 44 μW of power), a maximum of 176 clock cycles are needed. ARMADILLO2 is more robust than ARMADILLO, which is a new variant of ARMADILLO. It uses a compression function which is more compact and more secure.

g. GLUON

The GLUON feature is using Filtered Carry Shift Register—FCSR feedback. GLUON hash function is created by Berger and its co-author by using the mode of sponge construction. The GLUON using FCSR was developed using the technique of hardware stream cipher v3 of F-FCSR and the application X-FCSR-v2. It's a little heavier than PHOTON and Quark. GLUON-64's lightest example offers a 64-bit level of security and requires 2,071 GE. In the meantime, for securing 80-bits in GLUON–GLUON80, for securing 112-bits in GLUON–GLUON112 and includes 4,724 GE. A stream cipher can be used to develop the function from {0, 1} b with size of n as follows:

1. The input size of b-bit is padded to form an initial state of n-bit status length.
2. By initializing the stream cipher the output function f is generated and collected by the first b output bits.

If the stream cipher is "full", the algorithm will imitate an arbitrary function used to classify the siding in the process (twice that of the stream cipher).

GLUON will initiate a random function in the case when the stream cipher is "full" by increasing the size of memory block by doubling the stream cipher in the process.

h. PRESENT [24]

A single chaining vector of 64-bit (H_i) is modified with a message extract (M_i): H_i is calculated as E (H_i, M) or H_i from the Davies–Meyer process. In this case, PRESENT encryption is used and E 80 or 128 encryption, which will provide a high security of 64-bit. In each compression function iteration requires 64-bit chaining variable compressions and 80-bit message data. DM-PRESENT of 80 and 128 are therefore capable of making a balance between space and performance. During the implementation process, using various block cipher as the replacement of PRESENT would definitely increase the space required. Compression feature H-PRESENT-128 handles chaining variables of two 64-bits as input and one message extract of 64-bit (referred as triplet (H_i, H_{i+1}, M_i)). It then generates modified chaining variables as a pair (output) based on the following calculations: E (H_i, H_{i+1}, M_i)H_i = E (H_ic, H_{i+1}, M_i)H_i, where E corresponds to 128 of PRESENT and where c is a (fixed) non-zero constant. In chaining vector with the size of 128-bits H_1 and message-related data of 64-bits are hashed by iteration. Hirose has shown that in an ideal cipher model, an opponent of at least 2n queries is required to attain a collision without any negligible advantage. Here, 'n' is the cipher's block size. Same kind of analysis can be performed for pre-image resistance to demonstrate that it takes an adversary of at least 22n queries to define a pre-image.

Table 8.1 Lightweight Hash functions performance comparison [24].

Primitives	Construction mode-Hash Functions	Output Size-Hash	Size of Data path	Cycles per block	Throughput at 100 kHz	Power (µW)	Logic Process (µm)	GE
DM-Present-80	Davies Meyer	64	4	4,547	14.63	6.28	0.18	1,600
		64	64	45	242.42	1.23	0.18	2,213
DM-Present-128		64	4	559	229	7.49	0.18	1,886
		64	128	74	387.88	2.94	0.18	2,530
Photon-80/20/16	Sponge- like	80	4	708	2.82	1.59	0.18	865
		80	20	132	2.82	2.7	0.18	1,168
Photon-128/16/16		128	4	996	1.61	2.29	0.18	1,122
		128	24	156	15.15	3.45	0.18	1,708
Photon-160/36/36		160	4	1,332	2.70	2.74	0.18	1,396
		160	28	180	10.26	4.35	0.18	2,117
Photon-224/32/32		224	4	1,716	1.86	4.01	0.18	1,735
		224	32	204	15.69	6.5	0.18	2,786
Photon-256/32/32		256	4	996	3.21	4.55	0.18	2,177
		256	38	156	20.51	8.38	0.18	4,362

(Continued)

Table 8.1 Lightweight Hash functions performance comparison [24]. (*Continued*)

Primitives	Construction mode-Hash Functions	Output Size-Hash	Size of Data path	Cycles per block	Throughput at 100 kHz	Power (µW)	Logic Process (µm)	GE
Parallel keccak -f[1600]		256	64	24	4533	315.1	0.18	4,763
Serial keccak -f[1600]		256	64	1,200	90.66	44.9	0.18	2,079
Parallel keccak -f[400]		128	16	20	720	78.1	0.18	1,056
Serial keccak -f[400]		128	16	1,000	14.4	11.5	0.18	509
Parallel keccak -f[200]		64	8	18	400	27.6	0.18	409
Serial keccak -f[200]		64	8	900	8	5.6	0.18	252
U-Quark		128	1	544	1.47	2.44	0.18	1,379
		128	8	68	11.76	4.07	0.18	2,392
D-Quark		160	1	704	2.27	3.10	0.18	1,702
		160	8	88	18.18	4.67	0.18	2,819
T-Quark		224	1	1,024	3.13	4.35	0.18	2,296
		224	16	64	50	8.39	0.18	4,640

(*Continued*)

Table 8.1 Lightweight Hash functions performance comparison [24]. (*Continued*)

Primitives	Construction mode-Hash Functions	Output Size-Hash	Size of Data path	Cycles per block	Throughput at 100 kHz	Power (μW)	Logic Process (μm)	GE
GLUON-64		128	8	66	12.12	N/A	0.13	2,799.3
GLUON-80		160	16	50	32	N/A	0.13	4,724
Spongent-224/224/16		224	240	120	13.33	5.97	0.13	2,903
Spongent-256/256/16		256	272	140	11.43	6.62	0.13	3,281
Neiva		224	32	12,067	4.99	–	–	–
ARMADILLO	Merkel-Damgard	48	80	176	272	44	0.18	2,923
Lesamnta-LW		256	20	188.3	125.55	–	90 nm	824

i. Lesamanta-LW

Lesamnta-LW is a hash function of 256-bit for lightweight was proposed by Hirose *et al.* We claimed their level of security in primary preimage, secondary preimage and collision attacks was at least 2120 of GE. Lesamnta-LW has been developed as a domain extension constructed by the Merkle-Damgard. This uses AES as the method of compression. Lesamnta-LW's weight on 90 nm technology is 8.24 KG. Lesamnta-LW supplies 50 bytes of RAM and manages 8-bit CPUs with short messages. Performance comparison of various Lightweight hash function as shown in Table 8.1.

8.4   Applications on Lighweight Cryptography

RFID TAGS:

In our day to-day life RFID plays a main part in our daily activities and it is incorporated in various applications such as attendance system, library system, smart homes, bogus goods, pharmaceutical industry, automobile devices, etc. Often in literature it is described that RFID is used from supply chain to smart home. Still, security is a major issue and we have to concentrate more on privacy part and security part [15].

It is a lengthy process for recognizing the cryptographic techniques which is used to aid to lighten these difficulties. Though, the techniques used in cryptography are more expensive for implementation and it is not much suited for these areas. But in the recent years the above said has changed due to considerable advancement in the design of cryptography, for an example PRESENT is a new cryptographic algorithms of block cipher [3]. The advancement in symmetric cryptography which is appropriate for lightweight cryptography and there will be increasing kind of asymmetric methods which are existing and it should be implemented. In Figure 8.2 shows sample protocol for sharing the key between reader and tag.

In this decade more works are done on RFID tags in the category of cryptography of public-key. RFID concentrates more on elliptic curves. Comparison or performance measurement of ECC is not easy as the selection based on the points selected on the curve.

In ECC both security and efficiency of the algorithm is satisfiable. Although there is no implementation is not yet published on the Gate Equivalence of 5,000, which will still happen Very good for the passive RFID-tags. Many elliptical curve operations with 80-bit security level are high but with the smaller input. Limit or above Gate Equivalent 10,000 GE [2, 6, 8]. Gaubitz and their co-authors [4] have examined the efficiency of

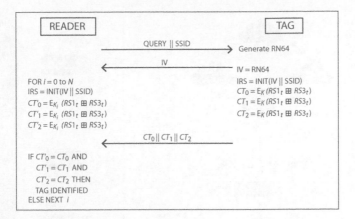

Figure 8.2 RFID in lightweight cryptography [17].

hardware of the encryption algorithm NTRU [1, 16] with the given set of parameter (N, p, q) = (16, 3, 12ated). It provides a level of security above 57 bits. Their implementation needs 2,850 Gate Equivalents, it will take clock cycles of 29,225, which is modified into 292 ms. The reply must be calculated at an exact clocking frequency as 100 kHz. In addition, it is notable that storage elements are occupied 80% of the area and the serial port is used. It means that Future improvement openings are very restricted. Oren and the co-authors generated a PID-Pubic key Identification called Vipra [21]. Their implementation of ASIC with Gate Equivalents 5,705 and the clock cycles 66,048 are required, although a proposed optimization [22]. This suggests a low field requirement of about 4,700 GE.

B. IoT Devices:

The important properties of an IoT prototype which will collect data using sensors, in the core network the entry point is considered as the edge. In the top the edge data will be processed and it is more supportive for the construction of fog, and at last data storage and data distribution is managed by cloud. A complete diagram for the security levels of IOT as shown in Figure 8.3. The complete architecture integrates the different network protocols with varied technologies i.e., Bluetooth with low energy, NFC-Near Field Communication, Wi-Fi direct-wireless fidelity ZigBee, etc. There will be marvelous merits of using IoT sensors in the environment of a smart city, in a scenario where security and privacy worries are extremely challenging in the period. By investigating the data, security level is decreased from the data level in the cloud level, i.e. data in transit has more threats [10, 11].

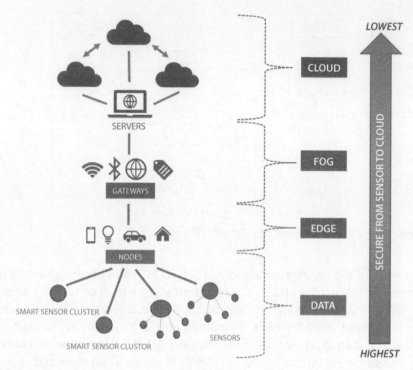

Figure 8.3 Security Level for IoT Architecture [18].

As indicated by the most recent estimations, in excess of 18 billion IoT gadgets will be associated by means of cloud platform in the year 2020, almost 57% of IoT applications on industry side [19]. In this manner, the protection of security and information insurance is battling right now to be settled. Usually, IoT devices goal is to process simple data, i.e., RFID tags, smartwatch, mobile apps, etc. Subsequently the physical appearance just as computational limits are frequently little, i.e., low RAM- Random Access Memory, small internal memory, powered battery, small data rates, etc. Thus, dissimilarity in PCs, tablets, and soon, IoT gadgets can't apportion extensive memory and handling vitality only for security capacities. That is the point at which a need of lighter rendition of ordinary cryptography emerged, which is named as LWC-lightweight cryptography [20]. This rendition hopes to execute cryptographic scheming with utilization of a couple of computational cycles giving high strength against security assaults.

The data collection from sensors can also be a focus for cyber-attacks with the IoT systems that make use of information in the real world. This is why countermeasures based on encryption are becoming increasingly important at the moment. Lightweight cryptography is a form of authentication with a small footprint and/or a low complexity of computation. This seeks to extend cryptography applications to restricted devices and is currently underway the associated international standardization and compilation of guidelines. Special attention has been paid to encrypted authentication that ensures confidentiality and honesty, and there has been a software competition called CAESAR. The lightweight block cipher is an authenticated encryption technique developed by NEC called TWINE, the next choice is CAESAR

Block Cipher—TWINE

TWINE is a Lightweight Block Cipher which is designed based on the existing lightweight cryptography of PRESENT's and it is very easy in software implementation developed by NEC. Simultaneously, its usage in little size hardware will be initiated. This uses the same environment as PRESENT, i.e. block length of a 64-bit and two forms i.e., 80 and 128-bit secret key sizes.

TWINE was picked as one of the figures to be assessed by CYRPTREC's Lightweight Cryptography WG as referenced in the abovementioned, indicating top-class accomplishment in both software and hardware. Below, we will talk about TWINE execution dependent on the Lightweight Cryptography WG's assessment results.

The block cipher algorithms performing the similar processing actions that are known as round functions. As far as hardware implementation is concerned, the circuit size per AES round is 15K gates, but 2K gates are used in TWINE, about one-seventh of AES (same as PRESENT scale). TWINE's efficiency is more than twice that of AES when the comparison is done based on circuit size. Due to parallel processing, encryption increases the circuit scale for high-speed communication functionality, but in such a case, TWINE's small-scale circuitry is also efficient.

On next side, in software implementation, AES is superior. In the case of implementation of the microprocessor, when the ROM is 1K bytes or more, it is faster than the lightweight cryptography like TWINE. Nevertheless, AES cannot be applied to 512 bytes ROM size, but TWINE can. TWINE's processing speed is 250% higher than PRESENT.

As far as security is concerned, we tested attacks on the TWINE, it is utilized in modern cryptanalysis like AES evaluation and found no problems. Several papers have been released endeavoring to attack on TWINE, but not even a single one have been able to undermine TWINE's security level to the present.

OTR—Authenticated Encryption

Generally speaking, the measure of computation required for authenticating the message is equivalent to that required for encryption, and the measure of AES-CCM/GCM calculation, NIST-suggested validated encryption, is double the sum required for encryption. Meanwhile the sum of authenticated encryption computation is greater than that for encryption, the amount of computation equal to the computation of encryption, which turn into the theoretical limit of authenticated encryption.

An authenticated encryption OCB is capable of clearing the theoretical bound, but to perform decryption it requires a function for block cipher. Then again, as is apparent in the way that AES-CCM designs the preparing of unscrambling through the technique for block cipher encryption, the size can be diminished by lessening the quantity of its composite components. OTR2 created by NEC is the world's first verified encryption which uses block cipher encryption functions exclusively to reach the theoretical limit of measurement number. OTR was nominated in the above-mentioned CAESAR verified encryption rivalry and was picked as one of 30 applicants in the first cycle (round) in 2015 and as one of 15 competitors in the second cycle (round) in 2016.

OTR's message authentication is based on data block checksum encryption and can be enforced through a single block encryption irrespective of the file size. The encryption uses a structure which is mostly followed in symmetric called the structure of 2R Feistel and can be decrypted using the reverse of encryption functions of the block cipher as in encryption. OTR's security is demonstrated based on block cipher's security. An arbitrary block cipher can be used to merge OTR. The rich implementation properties of AES can be used in conjunction with AES, and "AES-OTR" has been suggested to the CAESAR. "TWINE-OTR" combined with TWINE can further diminish the scope compared to AES-OTR.

At NEC, together with Nagoya University *et al.*, we developed authenticated CLOC/SILC encryption. Compared to little data size, CLOC/SILC has a small computational amount surplus. It was also planned to CAESAR and accepted the choice of another round (cycle). In the above, by concentrating on those developed by NEC, we presented the lightweight cryptographies pertinent to IoT's resource-constrained environment. Lightweight cryptography also comprises consideration in actual applications of the key management operations and functions. Therefore, NEC supports R&D for the realistic gratitude of a library used in lightweight cryptography through the upgrading and sharing of keys as well. We also concentrate research in the topic key exchange for the kind of public-key encryption in lightweight cryptography. In the future, as discussed above, we intend to continue contributing to stable IoT systems through work on cryptographic technologies.

C. Lightweight Cryptography on Cloud Data

Computer and storage outsourcing data to the cloud has been on the rise over the past few years. We analyze the question of using mobile devices to help write activity on outsourced data for customers. We find CP-ABE as Ciphertext Policy Attribute Encryption method as it is ideal for outsourced cloud environments to enable access control. One shortcoming of CP-ABE is that, if written operations are inserted into the system, access policy can be altered by the users defined by the data holder. We suggest a protocol for co-operative outsourced data processing that allows write operations to be performed by the authorized users without altering the data owner's policy. Our method is joined with the scheme for lightweight signature which is simple, cheap and the user cancellation mechanism was suitably built for user cancellation mechanism for processing the mobile devices. The scheme's design and thorough performance analysis suggest the suitability for actual mo-bile applications of the proposed scheme. In fact, the security analysis shows that the system's security assets are not compromised.

Major challenges are confidentiality and the security of the information in which they stock and provide admittance to cloud services. Using encryption is the universal method of addressing cloud data privacy and security. However, this exacerbates the communication and energy challenges. Therefore, efficient mechanisms to use cloud data using encryption on mobile platforms need to be developed. CP-ABE is Ciphertext-Policy Attribute-based Encryption [23], a method of encoding technique that meets the criteria for providing data stored in the cloud with encryption, privacy and access control. This system will allow data owner to define scalable keys, access policy and cipher texts management. CP-ABE's fundamental drawbacks are that users who are given write privileges will override the original read/write privileges granted by the data owner and the data owner's inability to revoke the privileges of users instantly. Furthermore, the reliability of CP-ABE in terms of interactions and energy costs when used on mobile platforms has not been discussed.

By extending CP-ABE to allow data owner to hold access privileges control by not allowing write privileged users to overwrite original access privileges and revoke privileges.

Description of Attribution Based Encoding

Attribute-based encoding mechanism is a category of public key encryption method that displays attributes or properties set of users and data. In these attributes, the user access policy is established. This access policy is developed either by the users ' private keys or in the cipher texts. A client can decrypt a cipher text if the set of attributes and the access policy are appropriately matched. The key generator specifies the forms of data, when the access policy is developed by the private key for the access of user. The information holder manages access when the access policy is written in the cipher texts. The proposed scheme extends CP-ABE Ciphertext-Policy Attribute-based Encryption [23] as the aim of this scheme is to provide control to the data owner.

1. The key generator, the setup phase, generates and stores a single PK public key and a single MK master key. Public Key (PK) in the cloud server and to produce decryption keys, and MK is stored internally.
2. The Key Producer uses MK produced in the setup process, a set of S attributes that defines a user to create a SK decryption key.
3. The data holder uses the cloud server for downloading PK (public key) in the encryption process and uses it to encrypt the sharing information. It also specifies, and contains, the data access rule, T, in the ciphertext (CT). Eventually CT+T is transferred to the cloud server by the software owner (step 4 to 5 of Figure 8.4).

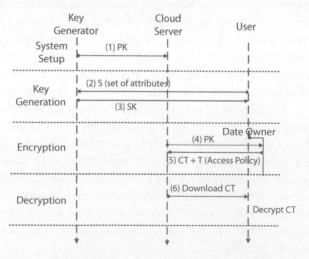

Figure 8.4 CP-ABE's operation [23].

4. Decryption stage, when and only when there is ample inter-
section between the characteristics of the access policy in
CT (ciphertext) and attributes 'S' in SK, the approved users
will decrypt CT.

In CP-ABE, the data can be decrypted by the authorized users who satisfy the constraints of access policy. There is no technique to differentiate
the readers and writers, however, and when they re-encrypt the changed
information, writers may circumvent the access policy defined by the data
holder. In Figure 8.5, the process of proposed scheme is illustrated sche-
matically. To represent the proposed scheme unique features, in which the
CP-ABE are shaded in the overlapping sections of the proposed scheme

The extended CP-ABE's main idea is

1. By Providing separate access to ciphertexts by authorized
users using GSK—Group Secret Key, GSK and Sk—Sign

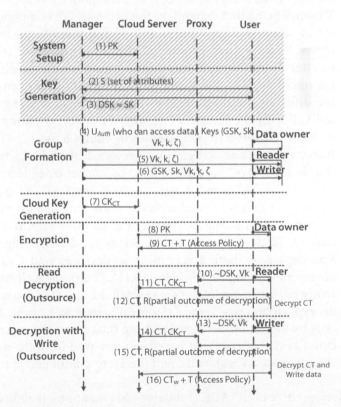

Figure 8.5 Operation scheme of extended CP-ABE [23].

Key. By broadcasting GSK and Sk between them, for writing process the data holder chooses a group of users from the collection of authorized users (step 6 of Figure 8.5). By sharing GSK and Sk with them, the data holder selects a group of users as writers from the collection of authorized users (Step 6 of Figure 8.5). Readers are able to decrypt but cannot do encryption of new data due to the absence of access to SK and GSk (Figure 8.5, step 5).

2. Prevents writers from overriding the data owner's defined access policy. Like the CP-ABE, 'T' is an access policy defined in our scheme when the data owner first encrypts information (Figure 8.5 of step 9). Then in order to prevent the writers from overwriting the access policy in successive writing operations, our proposed scheme only requires the writers to encrypt the data and join it in the new ciphertext CT. Connection policy T sets the standards to few CT elements. Writers can extract only the components of CT and T components that depend on the previous CT component for the current T component and adding them in the current CT rather than producing them. If the author tries to alter T, CT components depend on T which modifies the maximum CT components. Such modifications can be identified by the cloud server which prevents replacing an old CT with the author's CT, where the access policy of data owner is overridden (step 16 of Figure 8.5).

3. Allow readers and writers to be revoked by the information holder. Three keys are created by our scheme: decryption key, DSK (Figure 8.2, step 3), cloud key, CKCT (Figure 8.5, step 7) This is blinded with the value provided for each ciphertext of the data holder, 'k', and sections (Figure 8.5, step 4). To decrypt ciphertexts, access to ubiquity (Figure 8.5, steps 5, 6) both Decryption Session Key and CKCT are necessary (Figure 8.5, steps 10,11). Each time a client is removed, the owner of the data switches k and ζ. In order to decrypt ciphertexts, k and ζ (Figure 8.5, steps 5,6) can access only by the authorized users and can thus access the current cloud key. The users that have been removed from the network cannot access k and ζ and therefore cannot decrypt.

It addresses three of CP-ABE's fundamental limitations: inability to provide data owner power, user revocation, and mobile device functionality.

It ensures control of the prohibiting writing on data by the data from modifying the CT access policy and separating the master secret into 2 separate parts without compromising the security of the CP-ABE scheme. It implements a user revocation process without increase in the complexity by requiring data owner to create re-encoding keys to be updated only in selected CT elements, sharing a key of constant size with the administrator, and not altering the decryption side keys. This provides the capacity to outsource the computationally expensive activities to use mobile devices. An implementation proof for demonstrated the viability of the Extended CP-ABE's solution. The implementation not only demonstrated the feasibility of the Extended CP-ABE's scheme, but also showed that the Extended CP-ABE's scheme can be implemented without raising the overheads of energy consumption and interaction or decreasing efficiency. The Extended CP-ABE's scheme therefore delivers a unique way to meet the necessities of applications that is essential to have selective read access, write access without losing control of the data holder, in dynamic environment, the community composition which access the change of data, in all application scenarios on cloud.

D. Automotive Device

Vehicular Adhoc Network (VANET) is a new communication technology in wireless mode in the industry of automotive which give more scope in the research area of security in automobile. In future the goal of automotive industry is to develop a new technology for safe and effective communication they have developed the platform called ITS (Intelligent Transport Systems). In terms of features, challenges, design and implementations, vehicle networks are special. As a result, security necessities applicable to vehicle networks are more complicated relative to mobile networks and conventional wireless networks. Address developments from the lookout of cryptographic lightweight protocols and security-preserving algorithms in vehicle networks. Various vehicle network features are addressed that make the embedded protection applications as well as memory restricted are computationally difficult. The existing learning also deliberates the basic safety criteria that are important to vehicle interaction.

The latest Wireless Access in Vehicle Environments (WAVE) [25] is using the protocol DSRC to relay services of RSU. Basically short messages include critical place, speed and track data, by means of emergency info about airbag placement, crash reporting, emergency-brakes. Recent broadcast mechanism method, however, may result in congestion of network stream of traffic owed to irrelevant use of resources of networks. This problem will be solved by tracing the address of OBU and their connection to the respective RSU to effectively manage mobility. In WAVE [25] there are many recommendations regarding the control of mobility.

Chun suggested two kinds of Management systems of mobility for WAVE services, namely position estimation based mobility management (LEMM) [25] and simple mobility management (BMM) [25]. Locating systems such as GPS are used in the LEMM scheme to regulate the position of OBU in a speeding automobile, while in the BMM system, entire RSUs stay separated into changed position zones that determines the location of OBU by their MAC address. Torrent *et al.* describes a congestion management method based on distributed and equal power-control transmission and introduced a controller for message level that applies multiple hops to disseminate information about congestion to achieve global equality. Almost all techniques suggested a joint Functionality of congestion management in mythical work, with the objective of achieving unweighted equal sharing of limited channel space with all vehicles. Xu *et al.* [25] recently planned a lightweight system called as the Dynamic Fully Homorphic encryption-based Merkle Tree (FHMT) [25] is a data structure to ensure the authentication for the streaming of lightweight that can be used as a congestion mitigation technique in vehicle networks. By taking advantage of the finding the ability of FHMT [25], it changes the entire computing chore for the server which helps the client to attain almost without any downsides. These methods are important for vehicle safety requirements; however, for authentication and authorization purposes, DSRC requires cryptographic protocols that may result in network congestion. Therefore, the first option to ensure efficient security in automotive technology should be lightweight cryptographic algorithms.

Cyber attacks—Automotive

Vehicle network attacks are carried out by member nodes that have already been registered with the network and are considered intruder attacks. If an attack is carried out by an unregistered node, it is known as an intruder attack. You can also categorize these attacks as active and passive attacks. The attacker can generate new packets in an active attack to harm the network or to fabricate the genuine information, whereas the passive invader will snoop the channel and increase susceptible data. Classification of the following attacks will result in the violation of vehicular networks security services. Authentication-related attacks are carried out by unauthorized nodes will try to come into the network and trying to get the access of network rights or asserting the illegitimate power. Common kinds of attacks linked with Authentication of Vehicle are summarized as follows:

1. Sybil attack [25]:
By simulating multiple identities, in sybil attack many nodes are asserted by a single node. An invader sends numerous identity mail and at the same time declares the different positions. An invader sends numerous identity mail and at the same time declares the different positions. Sybil attacks [25] are damaging the network topology and bandwidth consumption.

2. Impersonation attack [25]:
An invader characterizes himself as an approved node in this type of attack. These attacks are intended either to expanding access to increase privileges of the network or to damage the network. Such invaders may be viable by having false attributes or theft of identity.

3. Bogus information:
Attackers can, for their own benefit, submit false or fake data to the system. For instance, an invader sending the fake information about traffic is very heavy as a result of an accident on some highway to clear the traffic. Such attack undermines the requirement authentication of vehicle networks.

4. Session hijacking:
The attacker is targeting the specific SID-Session Identifier, allocated for all the sessions which have been created newly and may expand power of particular session. An attacker got the information that only once encryption is performed on the network layer. After SID generation and SID allocation, authentication will not be verified; thus, attackers benefit from this function.

5. Replay attacks [25]:
The invader claims to be an authorized vehicle or/and RSU for capturing the sequence of packets and it will concentrate on sending the captured signal copy to another node for its own benefit. Replay attacks are seen as a challenge to the system's privacy and authenticity.

6. GPS spoofing [25]:

The GPS—Global Positioning System [25] will stores the vehicle's information such as geographic location and identity as a table of location. Such location table readings may be modified by the attacker to confuse the car. The attacker can use signal simulators to generate signals that are stronger than the actual satellite-generated signals.

Lightweight Encryption Algorithms in VANET:

Sometimes, symmetric algorithms require fewer resources for memory and tendentially playing much faster when compared to public key cryptography. There are many famous cryptographic algorithms using same key called symmetric algorithm, including block ciphers: AES—Advanced Encryption Standard [25] and DES—Data Encryption Standard [25] among many symmetric algorithm. There are also several symmetric stream ciphers exiting other than block ciphers, which prove to be even more powerful than block ciphers. For embedded applications, stream ciphers are sometimes preferred; however, block of ciphers are much better. We proposed the many kinds of symmetric cipher suitable to meet the requirements of vehicle network security as follows:

a. Blowfish [25]:

A symmetric block cipher was proposed in the year of 1993 by Bruce Schneier called Blowfish. In software we can implement the encryption methods effectively for embedded devices comfortably we can switch over to the techniques of keys with fixed length or keys with variable length in concern with speed and security. A simple and easily implemented algorithm for encryption must concentrate on efficient results and speed. Blowfish [25] is a licensed and unpatented cipher available for almost all applications free of charge. Blowfish encryption is susceptible to attack on a every kinds of keys either shared or public; thus users of Blowfish need to carefully select the category of keys. Even though it suffers from poor key attacks, there is no attack from the cipher itself on S-boxes and subkeys. If the private key is big enough, it is not possible to search for the brute-force password. It's also protected against the associated main differential attack.

b. PBAS [25]:

Proxy-Based Authentication Scheme (PBAS) is based on computing capabilities of other vehicles. PBAS will allow proxy vehicles for message authentication of other vehicles. This method helps to minimize the load of RSU. It offers an effective and standardized method for RSUs to authenticate proxy vehicular messages. Therefore, PBAS have a capability of negotiating other vehicular session keys for the sake of confidentialize sensitive information. Even after compromising some of the proxy nodes in the networks, PBAS scheme function will work without any disruption. For efficient authentication in VANET, it is an efficient protection scheme.

c. Camellia:
In 2000, Nippon Telegraph combined with Mitsubishi Electric Corporation developed a symmetrical cipher called Camellia. It has the same level of security and ability to process when it compared with AES. It is compatible with popular 8-bit and 32-bit processors, such as cryptographic hardware, embedded systems, and smart cards for both hardware and software implementation. Camellia offers high-level security for embedded systems on multiple platforms.

d. CAST:
In 1996, Carlisle and Tavares formed a symmetrical cipher called CAST. It is working as 64-bit block cipher which allows maximum key size either 128 or 256 bits. It has been approved by the Canadian government to use the Secure Communication Establishment. CAST cipher is capable of surviving linear and differential attacks on cryptanalysis.

Lightweight Protocols

The following lightweight protocols were developed on the basis of asymmetric and symmetric cryptography to improve automotive security for future and also satisfy the safety requirements of VANET as follows:

a. ARAN:
Authenticated Adhoc Network Routing (ARAN) depends on the Adhoc On Demand Distance Vector—AODV routing protocol in which the CA Third parties present signed certificates to vehicle nodes. For every new node that joins the network must submit the certificate of application to CA. All authenticated nodes are supplied with CA's public key. For safe route discovery authentication, ARAN uses time stamps for path freshness and asymmetric cryptographic technique.

b. SEAD:
Secure and Efficient Adhoc Distance—SEAD vector protocol works for encryption purposes on a one-way hash feature. This protocol protects from routing inappropriately. Destination-sequence number is used to prevent long-lived route, it will ensure the freshness of the route. To ensure the integrity of each path, the protocol applies intermediate node hashing.

c. ARIADNE:
This is demand routing protocol based on Dynamic Source Routing. Ariadne deals for symmetrical cryptographic operations very effectively. For secure communication between nodes, it uses hash function as one-way and MAC authentication. Using shared pin, authorization is completed. Broadcast authentication technology of TESLA is the origin of Ariadne protocol which uses TESLA time interval to authenticate and discover the path.

d. SAODV [25]:
In this protocol it was planned to incorporate AODV security. For securing the hop count Hash functions are used, and to ensure the validity of routes, all messages are digitally signed. This strategy, however, prevents any route response from being sent to the intermediate node even if it knows the fresh path. Using Double Signature can solve this problem, but at the cost of increasing device complexity.

e. A-SAODV [25]:
An extension of Secure adhoc On-Demand Distance Vector—SAODV protocol was proposed the features of adaptive respond decisions. Based on queue length and threshold conditions, each intermediary node will take decision to send a reply to source node.

f. OTC [25]:
Cookies are generally allocated per session for the purpose of session management. Protocol for one time cookie—OTC for securing the device from session hijacking and SID theft For each request, this protocol generates tokens and it will attach with the request by using HMAC to avoid token reuse.

g. ECDSA [25]:

The algorithm uses the Elliptical Curve digital signature (ECDS). Asymmetric hash function cryptographic operations provide the system with security and authenticity. Both the sender and receiver need to agree on parameters of the elliptical curve.

h. RobSAD [25]:

This technique provides an effective method for detecting Sybil attacks. When two or more nodes have identical trajectories of motion, Sybil node is established. Two different techniques on vehicles driven by different drivers are unable to maintain the same patterns of motion because each driver drives based on his own requirement and comfort.

i. Holistic protocol [25]:

In this protocol, each vehicle is authenticated by RSU. By sending a "Hai" text, vehicles are registered with RSU. In response, the RSU creates and sends to the vehicle, a registration ID which consists of vehicle registration and license number. More encryption is provided by RSU-supplied certificate. Only if the node is authenticated by RSU or the node is blocked will information be exchanged.

8.5   Conclusion

Lightweight cryptography is also a method of encryption with a low footprint and/or computational complexity. This seeks to extend cryptography applications to restricted devices and is currently underway the associated international standardization and compilation of guidelines.

Hardware and Software implementation challenges on lightweight cryptography are discussed.

Classification of hash function construction mode and hash function algorithms of lightweight cryptography are explained and applications on sustainable lightweight cryptography are discussed.

References

1. Young, G.O., Synthetic structure of industrial plastics (Book style with paper title and editor), in: *Plastics*, 2nd ed., vol. 3, J. Peters (Ed.), pp. 15–64, McGraw-Hill, New York, 1964.
2. Lo, O., Buchanan, W.J., Carson, D., Power analysisattacks on the AES-128 S-box using differential poweranalysis (DPA) and correlation power analysis (CPA). *J.Cyber Secur. Technol.*, 1, 2, 1–20, 2016.
3. Li, S., Da Xu, L., Zhao, S., The internet of things: a Survey. *Inf. Syst. Front.*, 17, 2, 243–259, 2015. Apr.
4. Bogdanov, A., Knežević, M., Leander, G., Toz, D., Varici, K., Verbauwhede, I., {SPONGENT}: The Design Space of Lightweight Cryptographic Hashing. *IEEE Transactions on Computers*, 62, 10, 2041–2053, 2013.
5. Mouha, N., The Design Space of Lightweight Cryptography. *NIST Light. Cryptogr. Work. 2015*, pp, 1–19, 2015.
6. Banik, S., Bogdanov, A., Isobe, T., Shibutani, K., Hiwatari, H., Akishita, T., Regazzoni, F., Midori: A Block Cipher forLow Energy, in: *Proceedings, Part II, of the 21st International Conference on Advances in Cryptology—ASIACRYPT 2015—Volume 9453*, Auckland, New Zealand, Springer-Verlag New York, Inc., pp. 411–436, 2015.
7. Biryukov, A. and Perrin, L., State of the Art in Lightweight Symmetric Cryptography. *IACR Cryptology ePrint Archive*, 511, pp. 1–55, 2017.
8. Avanzi, R., The QARMA Block Cipher Family. AlmostMDS Matrices Over Rings With Zero Divisors, NearlySymmetric Even-Mansour Constructions With Non-Involutory Central Rounds, and Search Heuristics for Low-Latency S-Boxes. *IACR Trans. Symmetric Cryptol.*, 1, 4–44, Jan. 2017.
9. Wu, W., Wu, S., Zhang, L., Zou, J., Dong, L., LHash: A Lightweight Hash Function. 8567, 291–308, 2014.
10. Guo, J., Peyrin, T., Poschmann, A., The PHOTON family of lightweight hash functions. *IACR Cryptology ePrint Archive*. 2011. 222–239, 2011.
11. Gupta, B., Tiwar, M., Improving Performance of Source Camera Identification by Suppressing Peaks and Eliminating Low-Frequency Defects of Reference SPN, IEEE Signal processing letters PP 99, 1–5, July 2018.
12. Chakraborti, A., Datta, N., Nandi, M., Yasuda, K., Beetle Family of Lightweight and Secure Authenticated Encryption Ciphers, *IACR Transactions on Cryptographic Hardware and Embedded System*, 2018, 2, 218–241, 2018.
13. Hirose, S., Ideguchi, K., Kuwakado, H., Owada, T., Preneel, B., Yoshida, H., *A Lightweight 256-Bit Hash Function forHardware and Low-End Devices: Lesamnta-LW*, pp. 151–168. Lecture Notes in Computer Science, vol 4727. Springer, Berlin, Heidelberg 2011.
14. Bogdanov, A., Knudsen, L.R., Leander, G., Paar, C., Poschmann, A., Robshaw, M.J.B., Seurin, Y., Vikkelsoe, C., PRESENT: An Ultra-Lightweight Block Cipher. *Cryptogr.Hardw. Embed. Syst.—CHES 2007*, 4727, 450–466, 2007.

15. Buchanan, W.J., "QUARK." [Online]. (2018). Available: http://asecuritysite. com/encryption/quark. [Accessed: 30-Jul-2018].
16. Buchanan, W.J., "Mickey V2 Light Weight StreamCipher." [Online]. (2017). Available: http://asecuritysite.com/encryption/mickey. [Accessed: 30 Jul-2017].
17. Engels, D., Fan, X., Gong, G., Hu, H., Smith, E., Ultra-lightweight cryptography for low-cost RFID tags: hummingbird algorithm and protocol. Centre for Applied Cryptographic Research (CACR) Technical Reports. 29, 1–16, 2009.
18. Gunathilake, N., Buchanan, W., Asif, R., Next Generation Lightweight Cryptography for Smart IoT Devices: Implementation, Challenges and Applications. 2019.
19. Lee, I. and Lee, K., The internet of things (IoT): Applications, invest-ments, and challenges for enterprises. *Bus. Horiz.*, 58, 4, 431–440, 2015.
20. Buchanan, W.J., Li, S., Asif, R., Lightweight cryptography methods. *J. Cyber Secur. Technol.*, 1, 3-4, 187–201, 2017.
21. Oren, Y. and Feldhofer, M., WIPR—public-key identification on two grains of sand. Tech. Rep., in: *Proceedings of RFIDSec'08*, Malaga, Spain, pp. 15–27, 2008.
22. Wu, J. and Stinson, D., How to Improve Security and Reduce Hardware Demands of the WIPR RFID Protocol, in: *Proceedings of IEEE International Conference on RFID*, Orlando, Florida, USA, 192–199, 2009.
23. Jahan, M., Zhao, Q., Seneviratne, A., Light Weight mechanisms for Cloud Data. *IEEE Trans. Parallel Distrib. Syst.*, 29, 5, 1131–1146, May 2018.
24. Hammad, B.T., Jamil, N., Rusli, M.E., Z`aba, M.R., A survey of Lightweight Cryptographic Hash Function. *Int. J. Sci. Eng. Res.*, 8, 7, 806–814, July, 2017.
25. Jadoon, A.K., Wang, L., Li, T., Zia, M.A., A Lightweight Cryptographic Techniques for Automotive Cybersecurity. *Wirel. Commun. Mob. Comput.* 1640167, pp. 1–15, 2018.

9

Pre-Learning-Based Semantic Segmentation for LiDAR Point Cloud Data Using Self-Organized Map

K. Rajathi* and P. Sarasu

Department of Computer Science & Engineering, Vel Tech Rangarajan Dr. Sagunathala R&D Institute of Science and Technology, Chennai, India

Abstract

This chapter presents a framework for reflexive understanding the issues surrounding challenges like smart cities, agricultural environment for autonomous vehicle, and mobile rover's navigation purpose. Reflexive environment perceiving system have many applications like reverse engineering, modelling, autonomous car, autonomous robots, Simultaneous Localization and Mapping (SLAM) vision of navigation. In reflexive perception of environment, sensors play a vital role. Light Detection and Ranging (LiDAR) is an active sensor used in many research applications. LiDAR is remote sensing method used to examine the surface of the earth. Nowadays stunning systematic investigation is going on with LiDAR sensor by dint of its accuracy. It is an active sensor used to detect the object with high accuracy. The main concern in LiDAR is first, visualizing the real time error-free reflexive environment perception and, secondly is construction of local map for perceived environment. The main issue in modeling the agricultural or smart environment using LiDAR is to make the system to understand and interpret the environment in the right way to the user. Initially, semantic segmentation was developed for the roadside habitat and industrial purposes not for smart cities agricultural environment. To achieve this we propose a new framework and a new pre-learning process is framed to train the system using SOM clustering algorithm regardless of illumination. Pre-learning process gives a small knowledge about the environment. This process is implemented and tested with the real time data, the result is analyzed for further rectification.

Corresponding author: k.rajathimtech@gmail.com

G. R. Kanagachidambaresan (ed.) Role of Edge Analytics in Sustainable Smart City Development: Challenges and Solutions, (171–188) © 2020 Scrivener Publishing LLC

Keywords: Semantic segmentation, Self-Organized Map, SOM, unsupervised learning, LiDAR point cloud, environment perception and modelling, smart environment

9.1   Introduction

Autonomous vehicle (AV) is the most trusted area of research. In AVs, the automotive functionality is deployed in four different modules. The first module is environment perception where the AV can be trying to understand the perception on their own. It can able to answer the following question, "where are objects located?" and "What are surrounding me?" The second module is localization and mapping where the AV can answer "where am I?" In this, the AV is automated to find its location with respect to object and its location. The third module is path planning and navigation system. In this, the AV is trained with the environment & localization. It can able to take decision about their next desired move from the trajectory planning. In the fourth module, motion and control, wheel speeds are automated.

Our main objective is perceiving real-time error-free reflexive environment using LiDAR sensor. LiDAR sensor generates data with different file format like LAS, point cloud. This research handles LiDAR point cloud data. A point cloud is a set of data points in space. Point clouds are generally produced by 3D scanners, which measure many points on the external surfaces of objects around them. A point cloud is a collection of points with x, y, and z coordinates that include properties such as intensity, color, timeframe, etc. A point cloud is not organized. Even though nowadays a camera sensor is used in day to day life in many places like surveillance camera, traffic signal, security purpose, etc. A Camera is not enough for accuracy, distance and illumination related application. Robotic 3D scanner is used in the medical filed. In case of scanning the surface of the human body, a high resolution is required, so precise laser scanner is used based on triangulation principle. These scanners are very accurate. Such a scanner should also use laser emitter compatible with Class 1 or Class 1M in order to avoid damage of a patient's eyes in case of scanning his face [1].

The next section describes the related work of semantic segmentation of LiDAR point cloud. In section 3 proposed work have been introduced. This section contains data acquisition, semantic segmentation, region of interest, registration of point cloud and Self Organized Map (SOM) clustering algorithm. Section 3 explores experimental result and Section 4 discusses about conclusion and future work of this proposed work.

9.2   Related Work

9.2.1   Semantic Segmentation for Images

Semantic segmentation is a process of mapping each pixel in an image to a class label. Semantic segmentation takes an image as input and creates an output as a region or structure. Semantic segmentations are applied in robot vision and understanding, autonomous driving, and medical purpose. In the field of object detection & classification [2], Tian and Liu proposed a framework to employ CNN architecture for object detection to fuse with Simultaneous Localization and Mapping (SLAM) which gave better performance in both object detection and semantic segmentation in a 3D environment. In 2018, Akai and Yoichi proposed novel approach [3] for localization & graphical model to calculate the robot's pose. They suggested to extent their work to create a model for localization failures. Aytayalan and Yuksed proposed a new semantic segmentation model [4] that combines with hyperspectral image with LiDAR data in 3D space using fully connected CRF algorithm. CNN predicted dense depth maps to reconstruct 3-dimention. In this research CNN semantic segmentation is used to generate global map and semantic label fusion. Further this may extend to improve depth estimation with respect to geometric maps [5]. Deep semantic classification for LiDAR data is proposed by Dewan and Burgaurd. This work received information with motion clues to estimate the point wise segmented classification using Fast-Net [6] and applying Bayes filter for labeling movable & non-movable points. A novel method is presented to convert 2D mono scopic images into 3D stereoscopic images using background subtraction algorithm and key frame extraction for environment perception [17].

9.3   Semantic Segmentation for LiDAR Point Cloud

In 2013, Cristiano Premebida proposed an approach for pedestrian detection [7] using Bayesian strategy is use to fuse data from LiDAR, Camera along with semantic information. Proposed segmentation and classification for 3D LiDAR turrestial data. This work uses hierarchical segment learning method, and takes semantic class object and test set of data from the LiDAR and then trains the LiDAR data augmented with segment. Finally, it generates the semantic segment class label for each point. This system first detects and removes the major structural elements from the environment, and it computes the feature vector to form the remaining point. By using feature vector, regions are identified. This work concludes that the classifier can learn for semantic segment for smaller data. Further this can be extended for comparison and combination with object recognition. Three dimensional localization tracking algorithm is also proposed for wireless sensor network in the year 2014 [15].

Wang, Shi, Yun, Tai, and Liu introduced a generation of spherical images and key features of the network structure to form the point cloud data. They proposed a network structure called pointSeg [8] which consists of three functional layers. The first layer is a fire layer which is able to construct lightweight layer, which is very similar to Alexnet. The next layer is Squeeze reweight layer to obtain feature representation vector. The third layer is an enlargement layer, to find the context information using pooling layer. All experiments are done in single 1080ti GPU under CUDA 9 and CUDNN V7. In pointSeg the RANSAC method is used and to give a better result. The proposed pointSeg is a method not giving the expected performance for the small level object.

Biasutti, Bugeau, Aujol, and Bredif proposed the Range–Image U Net for semantic segmentation [9] of 3D LiDAR point cloud data. This method builds the raw 3D point cloud data into a dense image which is called as the Range Image using quasi-uniform angular steps. The U Net architecture's first half 3×3 convolutional followed by 2×2 max pooling and down sampling the features. The second half of the U Net is 2×2 up convolutional and 1×1 convolutional. Cross entropy function is used for finding the loss function from the network. The researchers concluded that RIU Net is comparatively simple and fast with other state of art algorithms. This work planned to extend with focal loss function.

Ben-Shabat proposed representation builds on Fisher Victor which is based on a likelihood set of vectors associated with GMM (Gaussian Mixture Model). Modified fisher vector model [10] is used as uniform model, but is not as effective as maximum likelihood. However, the learning rate is improved comparatively. 3DmFV architecture is used to solve part segmentation using per point classification method. Misclassification was found for similar kind of objects for example table desk, dresser, night stand, etc. Wang, Yu, and Huang proposed pointNet [11]. The main aim of this work is to produce a class label for each instance and object instance label for each pixel from the LiDAR point cloud data using deep learning network. Similarity matrix is derived from the raw point cloud data and used in feed forward feature extraction network. PointNet/pointNet++ is used to extract the feature, from this feature similarity matrix and confidence matrix are combined to produce the group proposal and semantic prediction module helped to produce class proposal. Finally, all are merged together for instance segmentation. To reduce similarity matrix size, this work may extend with generating groups using seeds which were selected based on SGPN (Similarity Group Proposal Network). In medical field Matlab-based modeling the sensor helps to remotely monitor the environment using Monrovian model [16].

Table 9.1 [12] below shows a few existing methods and architecture proposed for semantic segment for point cloud data and also for image.

Existing research show that, the main data source for semantic segmentation is LiDAR sensor along with a camera or RGB-D. LiDAR point cloud is segmented with the alignment of RGB image. A camera is high informative data source but it is dependent with illumination and lighting. A few applications are not dependent with light or illumination. To overcome this, we proposed a mono model data source where only the LiDAR point cloud is taken for visualizing the real-time error-free reflexive environment perception for autonomous navigation. Existing work show that, an architecture or a framework is cast-off to carry out the semantic segmentation using supervised learning technique in a structured environment. We proposed a mono model pre-learning-based semantic segmentation for unstructured environment and also for small environment using SOM.

9.4 Proposed Work

9.4.1 Data Acquisition

In our research VLP16 PUCK sensor is used to collect the raw data. Table 9.2 shows the attributes and its details of LiDAR sensor. The main uses of LiDAR technology is for mapping. For experimental purpose a small portion of our university lane is captured and stored as packet capture (PCAP) file format. Wire shark is a popular Network Packet Analyzer tool, used to open Packet capture file. PCAP files contain a number of frames. Each frame contains X, Y, Z coordinate information, intensity, time stamp, start and end of the frame. This captured frames that are processed using MatlabR2019b. Velodyne LiDAR object is created and it contains model, IP address, port terminal timeout, calibration file, number point cloud available, streaming as property.

9.4.2 Our Approach

From existing study, we find that LiDAR sensor is aligned with camera. We tried to prove that LiDAR sensor is enough to reconstruct the

Table 9.1 LiDAR configuration.

S. no.	Method used	Architecture name	Work proposed
1	Cityscapes test	HRNetV2 + OCR	Object-Contextual Representations for Semantic Segmentation
2	PASCAL VOC	DeepLabv3+	Encoder-Decoder with Atrous Separable Convolution for Semantic Image Segmentation
3	PASCAL Context	OCR (HRNetV2-W48)	Object-Contextual Representations for Semantic Segmentation
4	ADE20K val	ACNet(ResNet-101)	Adaptive Context Network for Scene Parsing
5	ScanNet	MinkowskiNet	4D Spatio-Temporal ConvNets: Minkowski Convolutional Neural Networks
6	Semantic3D	RandLA-Net	RandLA-Net: Efficient Semantic Segmentation of Large-Scale Point Clouds
7	ADE20K	LaU-regression-loss	Location-aware Up sampling for Semantic Segmentation
8	LIP val	SCHP (ResNet-101)	Self-Correction for Human Parsing
9	Cityscapes val	HRNetV2 (HRNetV2-W48)	Deep High-Resolution Representation Learning for Visual Recognition
10	CamVid	DeepLabV3Plus + SDCNetAug	Improving Semantic Segmentation via Video Propagation and Label Relaxation

(*Continued*)

Table 9.1 LiDAR configuration. (*Continued*)

S. no.	Method used	Architecture name	Work proposed
11	COCO-Stuff test	OCR (HRNetV2-W48)	Object-Contextual Representations for Semantic Segmentation
12	PASCAL VOC 2012 val	ExFuse (ResNeXt-131)	ExFuse: Enhancing Feature Fusion for Semantic Segmentation
13	Freiburg Forest	SSMA	Self-Supervised Model Adaptation for Multimodal Semantic Segmentation
14	ScanNetV2	SSMA	Self-Supervised Model Adaptation for Multimodal Semantic Segmentation
15	SUN-RGBD	SSMA	Self-Supervised Model Adaptation for Multimodal Semantic Segmentation
16	SYNTHIA-CVPR'16	SSMA	Self-Supervised Model Adaptation for Multimodal Semantic Segmentation
17	ShapeNet	SGPN	SGPN: Similarity Group Proposal Network for 3D Point Cloud Instance Segmentation
18	KITTI Semantic Segmentation	DeepLabV3Plus + SDCNetAug	Improving Semantic Segmentation via Video Propagation and Label Relaxation
19	NYU Depth v2	Dilated FCN-2s RGB	Efficient Yet Deep Convolutional Neural Networks for Semantic Segmentation

Table 9.2 LiDAR configuration.

Attributes	Values
Make	Velodyne LiDAR
Model	Puck LITE
Weight	590 g
Output	Dual return & 16 Channels
Range	100 M
Capacity	Up to ~600,000 points per second
FOV	360° Horizontal, ±15° Vertical

environment without the help of any other sensor. In our work we are using the existing state of art algorithms for getting accurate result. These algorithms are adopted within the proposed framework. Existing research work uses the supervised data to process the image data. Unsupervised learning is not investigated for unstructured environment. Unsupervised algorithms designed for limited image data and still in under research. To overcome this, we introduce a pre-learning-based semantic segmentation, which make the system to get the prior knowledge of real world which called experience (e). Figure 9.1 shows the point cloud data capture from LiDAR sensor and the right side figure shows unorganized point cloud data.

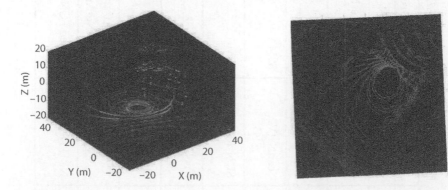

Figure 9.1 Point cloud data from LiDAR captured PCAP file (Left), Unorganized Point Cloud Data (Right).

9.4.3   Pre-Learning Processing

Pre-learning process is a very significant area of this research. Since the research is focused on mono model sensor we took the raw LiDAR data. It is a stream of data which is depicted in Figure 9.1. Point cloud data is not organized. The first step is to set the PCAP file reader using velodyne-FileReader function. This function takes a file name and the device name as a parameter. From the unorganized point cloud, the voledyne point cloud object is created. Point cloud object taken as an input and the ground region is segmented removed from the point cloud. Distance thresholds is set as 0.5. Labels are assigned for the ground plan. Cluster labels and number of cluster are the output. Cluster labels returned as M by N matrix of integer. All points in a cluster are assigned the same integer cluster label, ranging from 1 to number of cluster. Invalid points such as Not a Number (NaN) or inf are assigned the label 0. NaN and inf are defined by the IEEE754 2008 standard for handling floating point numbers. The number of cluster of valid points returned as a non-negative number. Now point cloud data are organized and segmented with color based.

Algorithm: preLearning(pointCloud)
Input: Raw LiDAR point cloud data;
Output: point wise segmented 2D with labels.

1. Start capture the environment
2. Convert PCAP file into point cloud object
3. Remove ground segment from the point cloud data
4. Remove the invalid points from point cloud
5. Split the image frames and Repeat for each frame 1 to n
    a. Each point's weights are initialized.
    b. A ground truth input vector is created for Building.
    c. Every point is examined to calculate which one's weights are most like the input vector.
    d. Then the neighborhood similarity is calculated. The amount of neighbors decrease over time.
    e. The winning weight is rewarded with becoming more like the sample vector. The neighbours also become more like the sample vector.
    f. Repeat step b for N iterations.
6. End for
7. Assign color index weight for each clustered point.
8. Do point cloud registration for consecutive frames.

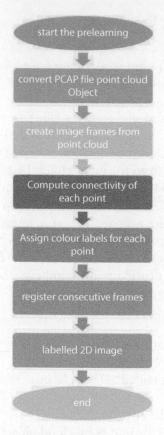

Figure 9.2 Work flow of pre-learning module.

    9. Generate labeled segmented 2D Image frames
   10. End

The above algorithm describes the logical flow of pre learning module. Performance of the algorithm is good. LiDAR data occupies more space, speed and space efficiency is average. Figure 9.2 shows the work flow of the pre learning module of our work. Since this frame work modelled for unstructured or smart environment, this pre learning module gives an experience in the form of vector representation.

9.5   Region of Interest (RoI)

Expose region of interest is the next important task in pre-learning process. Ground truth app provides an easy way to mark rectangular region of interest.

In our research ground truth values are selected manually. First unlabeled data are loaded in workspace. Next intended objects are defined with label definition. The same are exported into workspace. Here the regions are labeled based on the Color index (CI) by finding the similarity of the point. Color index is a vector representation of RGB from the range 0 to 255. These two arguments are considering as very crucial one. Labels are set of elements which is related with Color index which is assigned by the LiDAR sensor manufactures. By taken this two inputs we can manually assign a labels with bounding box which is consider as an object from unknown or unstructured or smart environment.

$$L = \{0, 1, 2, 3, ...N\}$$

$$CI = \{255, 255, 255\}$$

9.6   Registration of Point Cloud

Image fames from point cloud were read for registering the image sequence. Normal-distributions transform (NDT) algorithm is used for image registration. It will merge consecutive image frames from the point cloud. It generates the mono model 2D image with label. This labels and its coordinate points are added as feature for vector representation.

9.7   Semantic Segmentation

The segmentation is a task to sort out the point of the point clouds into the small, coherent and connected subset. After this task, the points are classified with label based on similarly. Each sub-set of these points has unique features. Point cloud process has three pipe lined process. Figure 9.3 shows the proposed framework of semantic segment.

Semantic understanding plays a vital role in reverse engineering, autonomous car, it is chunk of localization and vision based navigation system for autonomous robotic system. Different types of segmentations are there so for. The regional segmentation of point clouds is a classification process of data points with geometric parameters in clustering-based methods. Graph-based segmentation methods are stimulating the structure of the neighbor graph. Still these algorithms have some disadvantages. Detecting boundaries, interpolation problem in case of similarity closed objects, etc. To rectify these problems local descriptor is proposed to extract the

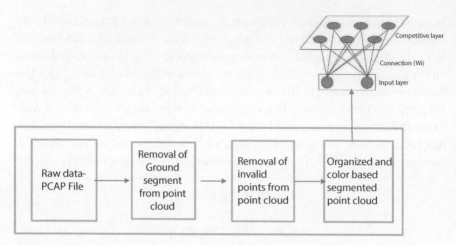

Figure 9.3 Proposed framework of semantic segmentation.

features and we create our own new dataset from the local descriptor. Fast Point Fast Histogram (FPFH) [13] method is used to for extract the local feature. Figure 9.4 shows the step-down process of point cloud.

9.8   Self-Organized Map (SOM)

Pre-learned point cloud data are taken and trained in SOM. Input data taken from the same work space. Initially building is taken as an input

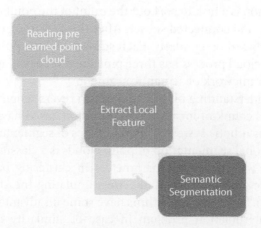

Figure 9.4 Step down process of 3D point cloud data.

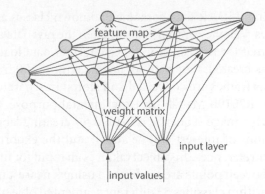

Figure 9.5 SOM architecture.

of region of interest. No of classes taken a 10. After that trained the given data. In building class, two different sub labels are named as "Block4" and "Block6". Figure 9.5 shows SOM classifies 9x9 feature map in unsupervised manner. Weight distance and number of hit for building alone. SOM differs from other artificial neural network as they apply competitive learning to error correction. SOM starts with initializing weight vectors. From that sample vector selected randomly and the weight vector is searched to find which weight best represents the sample. Each weight vector has neighboring weights that are close to it. The weight rewarded by being able to become more like the chosen sample vector. Figure 9.5 shows the architecture of SOM The weight updates and changes of the neighborhood is represented as below,

$$W_{ij}(t + 1) = W_{ij}(t) + \alpha_i(t)[x(t) - W_{ij}(t)] \tag{9.1}$$

Where,
   W—weight vector
   $W_{ij}(t)$—Weight of the connection
   t—current iteration
   $\alpha_i(t)$—learning rate
   x(t)—input vector

9.9 Experimental Result

For experimental purpose we captured a small portion of our institute building, road, ground, trees, open stage, stone benches, lane, pillar, our flag, rain water cannel, etc. in the evening as a PCAP (Packet Capture Data) file for processing. LiDAR data contains 25 known classes and around 28 unknown classes. Veloviewer tool helps to open the raw data and converted as a csv file format for further process. Csv format data loaded and point cloud object was created. Our data set having almost 100 frames in every point cloud. This frames are converted and stored in separate location.

We are using R2019b Matlab for experimental purpose. Ground truth is selected and the image sequence is loaded for creating labels. By adding new labels, regions of interest will be added and the export to the workspace for further reference. This object taken as an input for further process. Connectivity between points are established using k nearest neighbor algorithm. This algorithm classifies 53 different segmented objects. Among this 53 objects 9 objects are labeled with predefined names. One class is named with 'unknown' category. Clusters were identified from organized point cloud. Each clusters having unique color index value. Each color assigned for one label. Red color assigned as building label, green color assigned for trees, yellow color for concrete work, purple color for unknowns. Remaining all are not taken into consideration for pre learning. Figure 9.6 depicts color wise segmented frame. This frame clearly shows our block 4 and block 6 as building class, trees, lanes, cement benches, open terrace, etc. The right side figure shows the contour image of the point cloud.

Figure 9.7 shows the SOM topology for the sample building, weight distance, number of hit for buildings. Figure 9.8 shows the SOM topology for our point cloud data. Weight distance and neighbor connection of points. Figure 9.9 shows the 2D image frames of point cloud as left and contour generation of the point cloud in right side.

Figure 9.6 Segmented point cloud for 3D object.

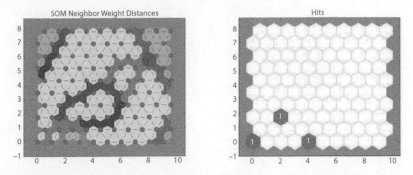

Figure 9.7 Weight distance for building (Left), No. of hits for building (Right).

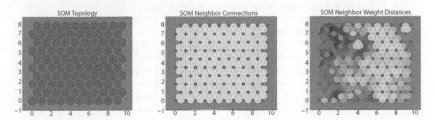

Figure 9.8 Point cloud—SOM topology (Left), Neighbor connection (Center), Neighbor wight distance (Right).

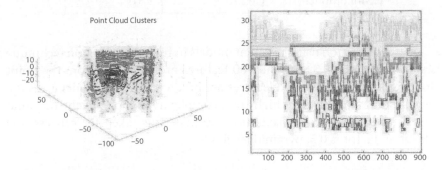

Figure 9.9 Segmented point cloud as image frames (Left), Contour Generation (Right).

Figure 9.10 shows regenerated 2D image of the point cloud data. Still this image is not having clear meaning full information but the unknown environment is reconstructed for further analyzed. This image frames used in the trained image net for testing purpose. Testing phase takes more than 3 days to validate the result. Few objects are misclassified. Error computed from the output subtracted from the target. Right side image shows the error rate of the samples.

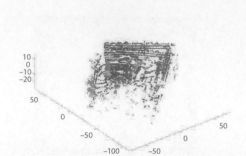 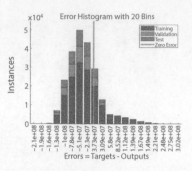

Figure 9.10 Regenerated 2D image (Left), misclassification rate (Right).

Table 9.3 Comparison of feature detection.

Feature detection model	Accuracy	Timing
MinEigan	0.855	0.06s
FAST	0.882	0.03s
BRISK	0.852	0.05s
SURF	0.907	0.05s
MonoModel	0.910	1.51s

Feature detection using different models in image registration technique is shown in Table 9.3. Around 700 features are identified from the point cloud, among that only 200 features are predicted. Mono model gives the high accuracy but it takes high time complexity comparatively. In mono model feature detection maximum 100 iterations taken for process, the relaxation factor is 0.5, pyramid level is 3.

9.10   Conclusion

We proposed a mono model pre-learning-based semantic segmentation for unstructured and for smart environment. Our proposed work gains the experience from the point cloud using pre-learned process. SOM is in-cooperated with pre-learning process. Point cloud is regenerated as 2D image frames using mono model image registration technique. Further this work may have extended for real-time data for smart environment.

Time complexity of mono model need to be improved further. Part of our work in MatLab for generating image frames from point cloud is published in R2018b platform.

References

1. Chromy, A. and Zalud, L., Robotic 3D scanner as an alternative to standard modalities of medical imaging. *SpringerPlus*, 3, 13, 2014.

2. Tian, G., Liu, L., Ri, J.H., ObjectFusion: An Object Detection and Segmentation framework with RGB-D SLAM and Convolutional Neural Networks. *Neurocomputing*, 345, 3–14, 2019.

3. Akai, N., Morales, Y., Murase, H., Simultaneous pose and reliability estimation using convolutional neural network and Rao–Blackwellized particle filter. *Adv. Rob.*, 32, 17, 930–944, 2018.

4. Yuksel, S. and Aytaylan, H., Fully-Connected Semantic Segmentation of Hyperspectral and LiDAR Data. *IET Comput. Vis.*, 13, 3, 285–293, 2018.

5. Tateno, K., Tombari, F., Laina, I., Navab, N., CNN-SLAM: Real-time dense monocular SLAM with learned depth prediction. *2017 IEEE Conference on Computer Vision and Pattern Recognition (CVPR)*, Honolulu, HI, pp. 6565–6574, 2017. open access, arXiv:1704.03489.

6. Dewan, A., Oliveira, G., Burgard, W., Deep semantic classification for 3D LiDAR data, in: *Conference: 2017 IEEE/RSJ International Conference on Intelligent Robots and Systems (IROS)*, September 2017.

7. Dohan, D., Matejek, B., Funkhouser, T., Learning Hierarchical Semantic Segmentations of LIDAR Data, in: *2015 International Conference on 3D Vision*, pp. 273–281, 2015.

8. Wang, Y., Shi, T., Yun, P., Tai, L., Liu, M., *PointSeg: Real-Time Semantic Segmentation Based on 3D LiDAR Point Cloud*, arXiv:1807.06288 [cs.CV].

9. Biasutti, P., Bugeau, A., Aujol, J.-F., Bredif, M., *RIU-Net: Embarrassingly simple semantic segmentation of 3D LiDAR point cloud*, 17 Jun 2019, arXiv:1905.08748v3 [cs.CV].

10. Ben-Shabat, Y., Lindenbaum, M., Fischer, A., *3D Point Cloud Classification and Segmentation using 3D Modified Fisher Vector Representation for Convolutional Neural Networks*, arXiv:1711.08241v1 [cs.CV] 22.

11. Wang, W., Yu, R., Huang, Q., Neumann, U., *SGPN: Similarity Group Proposal Network for 3D Point Cloud Instance Segmentation*, 30 May 2019, arXiv:1711.08588v2 [cs.CV].

12. https://paperswithcode.com/task/semantic-segmentation.

13. Zhao, T., Li, H., Cai, Q., Cao, Q., Point Cloud Segmentation Based on FPFH Features, in: *Proceedings of 2016 Chinese Intelligent Systems Conference. CISC 2016*, vol. 405, Y. Jia, J. Du, W. Zhang, H. Li (Eds.), Lecture Notes in Electrical Engineering, Springer, Singapore, 2016.

14. Akwensi, P.H., Kang, Z., Yang, J., Fisher Vector Encoding of Super voxel-Based Features for Airborne LiDAR Data Classification. *IEEE Geosci. Remote S.*, 1–5, 2019.
15. Vinothkumar, C., Prabakaran, S., Prabakaran, R., Kanagachidambaresan, G.R., WSN based Three Dimensional Location Tracking Algorithm, in: *International Conference on Computing and Control Engineering*, 2012.
16. Kanagachidambaresan, G.R., Dhulipala, V.R.S., Vanusha, D., Udhaya, M.S., Matlab Based Modelling of Sensor network using ZigBee Protocol, in: *International Conference on Computational Intelligence and Information Technology*, pp. 773–776, Springer Berlin, Heidelberg, 2011.
17. Kavitha, M. and Kannan, E., 2D to 3D Conversion using Key Frame Extraction. *Indian J. Sci. Technol.*, 9, 28, 2016.

10

Smart Load Balancing Algorithms in Cloud Computing—A Review

K.R. Jothi[1]*, S. Anto[1], M. Kohar[1], M. Chadha[1] and P. Madhavan[2]

[1]*Vellore Institute of Technology, Vellore, India*
[2]*SRM Institute of Science and Technology, Chennai, India*

Abstract

Smart Load Balancing is crucial for productive tasks in the cloud computing environment. As cloud computing is evolving rapidly and clients are demanding additional facilities and desirable outcomes, load balancing for the cloud has turned into an exceptionally fascinating and significant study area. Numerous algorithms and techniques were proposed to give proficient systems and procedures to assign the customer's requests to accessible cloud backend instances. Methodologies like these, expect to upgrade the general execution of the cloud and give the client all the more fulfilling and productive facilities. We explore and review various proposed methodologies and algorithms to solve various cloud computing problems like task scheduling and load balancing. We compare and contrast these paradigms to give an outline of the recent techniques in the domain.

Keywords: Cloud computing, fault tolerance, network overhead, load balancing, task scheduling

10.1 Introduction

Cloud load balancing is characterized as the strategy for breaking the remaining tasks at hand and computing properties in cloud computing. It enables a load balancer that can evenly distribute and divide the workload or demands between a large number of networks, end stations, and back-end servers. Cloud load balancing incorporates holding the course of the remaining tasks at hand, traffic, and requests that exist over the Internet.

Corresponding author: prof.krj@gmail.com

G. R. Kanagachidambaresan (ed.) Role of Edge Analytics in Sustainable Smart City Development: Challenges and Solutions, (189–218) © 2020 Scrivener Publishing LLC

With the extension of cloud-based administrations, the inquiry about how to handle the tasks at hand amongst an enormous VM group has turned out to be progressively significant. In this paper they tend to the issue with an approach for making a load balancer in the two physical machine's layer and virtual machine's layers, in addition, they also incorporated a forecasting algorithm to make sure the temporary stake does not activate unnecessary virtual machines migration, and in virtual machine's layers they also reason an advantage calculation model so as to determine if the relocation of employments in virtual machines under a similar PM is an advantage for the entire framework. The assessment outcomes they gave demonstrates that the dynamic migration of VMs brings about load balancing. The current proposed load balancing strategies in distributed computing are not competent enough and [2] the existing VM resource distribution for cloud computing condition mostly take into account the present condition of the structure however only sometimes thinks about structure's variety and past information, which consistently prompts load imbalance of the structure. This system handles the problems like load im-balancing and increased moving overheads by standard algorithms after scheduling. Investigational results reveal that this technique can carry out load balancing and practical resource utilization both when framework load is steady and varied.

There are many exceptional and exciting algorithms that can be implemented in a cloud for load balancing, such as Dhinesh Babu and Krishna [10] propose a methodology called HBB-LB, which means to realize a well-distributed load across VMs for increasing the efficiency. The suggested methodology likewise balances the task priorities on the machines so that the estimate of holding uptime of the tasks in the line is insignificant. They have compared and contrasted the proposed methodology with current load balancing and scheduling algorithms. The investigational outcomes demonstrate that the algorithm is successful when contrasted with existing techniques. This methodology outlines that there is a noteworthy improvement in standard execution time and a decrease in holding up time of tasks online.

Mondal et al. and Maguluri et al. [24, 26] propose a confined optimization method which is the SHC technique utilized for designation of coming tasks to the VMs. Execution of the algorithm is examined both according to quality and quantitatively utilizing CloudAnalyst which is a CloudSim-based Visual Modeler for investigating cloud computing sectors and real-time applications. FCFS and Round Robin techniques are compared. Chen et al. [25] tells us about an improved load balancing method presented on the ground of the Min–Min algorithm so as to diminish the makespan and increment the resource use (LBIMM). Simultaneously, Cloud suppliers offer PC assets to clients on payment for each utilization base. To suit the requests of various clients, they may offer varying degrees of quality for provisions. At that point, the expense per asset unit relies upon the services chosen by the client. Consequently, the client gets certifications concerning the given assets. To observe the promised guarantees, customer-priority was considered in this proposed PA-LBIMM so the interests of the customers could be fulfilled at their best.

The availability of cloud frameworks is one of the significant worries of cloud computing, and accessibility is a reoccurring and a developing worry in software-based frameworks [13]. In clouds, load balancing, as a technique, is provided over various data centers to promise the system accessibility by reducing use of PC apparatus, programming failures and reducing the severity of plan of action restrictions. This work talks about the load balancing in cloud computing and after that, shows a contextual examination of framework accessibility for a Hospital Database Management arrangement.

Proficient task scheduling algorithm can meet clients' prerequisites and improve asset usage, in this manner, upgrading the general execution of the cloud computing condition. In any case, the task scheduling for grid computing is regularly about the static task prerequisites, and the assets usage rate is additionally low. Fang et al. [21] shows us the two-level task scheduling mechanism dependents on load balancing in cloud computing. This task scheduling mechanism can meet the client's necessities yet besides gets increased resource use, which was outlined by the simulation outcomes in the CloudSim toolkit and is in accordance with the new properties of cloud computing, such as flexibility, virtualization and so forth. Ramezani et al. [27] proposes a Task-centered System Load Balancer utilizing PSO that accomplishes framework load balancing only by moving extra assignments from an over-utilized virtual machine instead of relocating the whole overloaded VM. They also structure an enhancement model to move these extra tasks to the new host VMs by applying Particle Swarm Optimization (PSO).

In today's world, there are numerous calculations for load balancing in a cloud and it's essential to investigate them. Al Nuaimi et al., Randles et al. and Geetha & Robin [20, 22, 33] depict the various methods that were recommended in the past to give proficient systems and algorithms to assign the customer's requests to accessible Cloud hubs. These techniques plan to improve the general execution of the Cloud and give the client all the more fulfilling and effective administrations. Legitimate examination of the various algorithms proposed to determine the issue of load balancing and resource planning for Cloud Computing are given. They examine and contrast these algorithms with a given outline of the most recent methodologies in the field.

Load Balancing is advantageous with practically any kind of administration, similar to HTTP, SMTP, DNS, FTP, and POP/IMAP. It also raises reliability through repetition. A devoted equipment gadget or program gives the balancing service. Cloud-based servers farms can achieve increasingly exact versatility and accessibility utilizing server load balancing.

10.2   Research Challenges

10.2.1   Security & Routing

It is vital to safely transfer the client's request to the backend instances through effective load balancing. The request should not be tampered or lost in any case and should be routed to the backend nodes using routing protocols. Different load balancing algorithms use different routing mechanisms to safely transfer client requests like minimum-cost routing or path-based routing mechanisms. The client can send their requests using various protocols and priorities which are taken care of by these mechanisms.

10.2.2   Storage/Replication

A 100% replication mechanism does not take productive capacity usage into the record. This is based on the fact that similar data will be put away in all of the replication nodes. Complete duplication techniques force increased costs since more stockpiling is essential. Be that as it may, fractional replication calculations could spare pieces of the informational collections in every node (with a specific degree of overlap) in light of each node's abilities, for example, power consumption and overall capacity.

10.2.3   Spatial Spread of the Cloud Nodes

A few calculations are intended to be proficient just for an intranet or proximity nodes where correspondence delays are unimportant. Nonetheless, it is very problematic to plot a load balancing algorithm that can work for spatially disseminated nodes. This is based on the fact that unalike elements must be considered, for instance, the velocity of the framework joins among the nodes, the separation between the client and the task handling nodes, and the separations between the nodes engaged with providing the services. Because of this, there is a necessity to formulate a technique to govern load adjusting systems among all the disseminated spatial nodes while having the option to endure high delays viably.

10.2.4 Fault Tolerance

Management of load balancing and collecting data about the various nodes should be planned in a manner that maintains a strategic distance from having a single purpose of error in the algorithm. A few mechanisms which are centralized ones can give productive and successful systems for unraveling the load balancing in a particular example. Be that as it may, they have the issue of one controller for the entire system. In such cases, if the controller comes up short, at that point, the whole framework would come up short. All load balancing techniques should be planned to overcome this challenge.

10.2.5 Algorithm Complexity

Load balancing algorithms are required to be less unpredictable regarding execution and tasks. The higher execution unpredictability would prompt a progressively mind-boggling procedure, which might have a few undesirable execution problems. Besides, when the mechanisms require more data, what's more, higher correspondence for checking and control, delays would cause more issues, and the effectiveness will drop. Subsequently, load balancing techniques must be structured in the least complex potential structures.

10.3 Literature Survey

1. Addresses the issue with an arrangement for making a load balancing strategy in the two PMs and VMs layers, additionally they also introduce prediction technique to guarantee the brief point doesn't cause unnecessary VMs migration, and in VMs layers they additionally propose a benefit estimating model so as to choose whether the migration of tasks in VMs under a similar PM is advantageous for the entire framework. The assessment results they give demonstrating that generously, the dynamic reallocation of VMs causes load-adjusting.

2. This procedure calculates the influence on the framework beforehand, after sending the required VM assets and then selecting the least-effective arrangement, because of which it achieves the finest load balancing and lessens or stays away from dynamic migration. This procedure takes care of the problem of load balancing and high migration cost by customary calculations after planning. Exploratory outcomes show us that this technique can understand load balancing and sensible resource use both when the framework burden is steady and variant.

3. In this research, the authors studied diffusion plans for live load balancing on the topic of message passing multiprocessor systems. Primary outcomes consider circumstances in which these effective plans meet and their paces of union for discrete and random topologies.

4. A conventional detailing of the feeder reconfiguration issue for loss decrease and load balancing is provided, and a novel arrangement technique is introduced. The arrangement utilizes a pursuit over various radial setups made by considering switching of the branch exchange type. To control the pursuit, two diverse power flow estimation strategies with shifting degrees of precision have been created and tested.

5. Mainstream Web locales cannot depend on a sole potent server nor on autonomous mirrored-servers to help the regularly expanding client load. Dispersed Web server structures that straightforwardly plan customer requests offer an approach to meet unique adaptability and accessibility necessities. The creators audit the cutting edge in load balancing methods on dispersed Web-server frameworks and examine the effectiveness and constraints of the different methodologies.

6. In this paper, the author examines the issue of load balancing in P2P frameworks. They investigate the space of planning load-balancing calculations that utilize the thought of "virtual servers". They portray three plans that vary substantially in the measure of data used to choose how to re-organize load. Their re-enactment results demonstrate that even the least complicated plan can adjust the load inside 80% of the ideal worth, while the most unpredictable plan can adjust the load inside 95% of the ideal worth.

7. This paper depicts a novel strategy for accomplishing load balancing in broadcast communications systems. A simulated system models an ordinary dispersion of calls amongst nodes; nodes conveying an abundance of traffic can wind up clogged, making calls to be lost. Notwithstanding calls, the system additionally supports a population of straightforward mobile agents with practices demonstrated on the trail-laying capacities of ants.

8. This paper fights barriers between the load balancing methodologies through a few physical relaxations of the system-wide association issue, whose arrangement is NP-hard. They give a low-intricacy circulated algorithm that meets to a close ideal arrangement with a hypothetical exhibition assurance, and they see that straightforward per-level biasing loses by a less factor, if the bias estimates A j are picked cautiously. Numerical outcomes demonstrate a huge (3.5×) throughput gain for cell-edge clients and a 2× rate addition for middle clients with respect to a boosting received power association.

9. Five Dynamic Load Balancing methodologies are displayed, which show the trade-off between 1) information—the precision of each balancing choice, and 2) overhead—the measure of included preparing and correspondence acquired by the adjusting procedure. Every one of the five techniques has been executed on an Inter iPSC/2 hypercube.

10. In this paper, the authors put forward a honey-bee inspired technique which is called HBB-LB, which is formulated to attain proportionally balanced VMs to increase efficiency and throughput. Moreover, the suggested algorithm handles the requirements of errands on the VMs so that the waiting time of the tasks in the line is reduced to an insignificant amount. We contrasted the projected calculation and prevailing task scheduling and load balancing techniques. The trial results demonstrate that the scheme is viable when contrasted with current algorithms. Their methodology represents that there is a noteworthy enhancement in standard execution time and a decrease in the waiting time of errands on line.

11. This paper investigates whether the assorted geological variety of Internet-scale frameworks can moreover be utilized

to give ecological increases. In particular, we investigate whether topographical burden adjusting can energize utilization of "green" sustainable power source and diminish the utilization of "dark-colored" petroleum product vitality. We make two commitments. To start with, we determine two conveyed calculations for accomplishing ideal topographical load balancing. Second, we demonstrate that if power is progressively estimated in the extent to the momentary part of the all-out vitality that is dark-colored, at that point, geological load balancing gives critical decreases in darker vitality use. In any case, the advantages depend unequivocally on how much frameworks acknowledge dynamic vitality valuing and the type of evaluating utilized.

12. A unique load balancing technique is proposed for a class of huge distance across multiprocessor frameworks. The technique depends on the "gradient model," which involves moving multiplied assignments to close by inert processors as indicated by a weight slope in a roundabout way settled by requests from inactive processors. The calculation is completely distributed and asynchronous. Worldwide equalization is accomplished by progressive refinements of many confined adjusts. The gradient model is detailed to be autonomous of framework topology.

13. This investigates and achieves load balancing in cloud computing and also shows a contextual analysis of framework accessibility in view of a regular Hospital Database Management. It guarantees the accessibility of the system through minimum PC equipment utilization, errors in programming and mitigating asset limits.

14. The authors argue in this paper that the load balancing objectives can be accomplished all the more basically and more cost-successfully. Initially, they propose the immediate utilization of the "power of two choices" worldview, whereby a thing is put away at the less stacked of (at least two) arbitrary choices. They then think about how associating a little consistent number of hash esteems with a key can normally be reached out to help other load balancing systems, including load-taking or burden shedding, just as giving common adaptation to non-critical failure components.

15. This research argues and demonstrates why the controller should over-use switch provision for wild card rules for a

progressively versatile arrangement that guides huge totals of customer traffic to server imitations. We present calculations that register succinct special case decisions that accomplish an objective dispersion of the traffic, and naturally conform to changes in load-balancing arrangements without disturbing existing associations. We execute these calculations over the NOX OpenFlow controller, assess their adequacy, and the authors also show a few other ways for future investigations.

16. This research demonstrates a technique to increase the effectiveness of the exhibition of web servers overhauling static HTTP demands. The thought is to offer inclination to demands for little documents or demands with short outstanding record size, as per the SRPT booking policy. The usage comes out to be at the kernel stage and includes handling the request in which attachment cushions are depleted into the system.

17. In this research paper, the load might be treated at the host where it arrives or can be routed to other host for processing. In the last scenario, a moving activity acquires a correspondence delay, notwithstanding the lining delay at the host on which the activity is handled. It is expected that the choice of moving a vocation does not rely upon the framework state, and henceforth has static nature. Execution is advanced by deciding the workload on each host that limits the average employment reaction time. A nonlinear improvement issue is detailed, and the properties of the ideal arrangement in the uncommon situation where the correspondence postponement does not rely upon the source-goal pair is appeared. Two proficient calculations that decide the ideal load on each host PC are displayed.

18. The authors propose a calculation of load balancing in heterogeneous, dynamic P2P frameworks. Our recreation results demonstrate that despite fast landings and flights of objects of generally fluctuating load, their calculation accomplishes load balancing for framework uses as great as 90% while migrating just about 8% of the load that touches base into the framework. Also, in a powerful framework where nodes arrive and withdraw, their calculation migrates under 60% of the workload the fundamental DHT moves because of load landings and take-offs. At last, they

demonstrate that their appropriated calculation performs just a little poorly than a comparable unified calculation, and that node heterogeneity benefits, not harms, the adaptability of our calculation.

19. They present calculations that accomplish a consistent factor in exact max-min reasonable data transfer capacity distribution. To start with, they compute a partial load balancing arrangement, where clients can be related with various APs at the same time. This arrangement ensures the most attractive data transmission allotment as far as max-min decency. At that point, by using an balancing strategy they acquire a proficient necessary affiliation. Specifically, they give a 2-estimation calculation to unweighted voracious clients and a 3-guess calculation for weighted and limited interest clients. Notwithstanding data transfer capacity reasonableness, they additionally consider time decency and show it tends to be unraveled ideally. They further expand their plans for the on-line situation where clients are capable of leaving or joining. Their reproductions exhibit that the proposed calculations accomplish near-ideal load balancing and max-min decency and they beat ordinarily utilized heuristic approaches.

20. In this paper, they research the various calculations out forward to solve the matter of load balancing and assignment booking in Cloud Computing. They discussed and contrasted these calculations to provide a diagram of the latest methods and paradigms in the domain.

21. The customary task planning for computing on a network or grid computing is to plan the errand straightforwardly to the host assets for execution, and it is not beneficial to meet the wide variety of necessities of clients. A two-level booking system dependent on load balancing is discussed in this research. The planning instrument considers the dynamic necessities of clients and the load balancing in cloud computing; consequently, to meet the various prerequisites of clients and expands the asset use. Using the CloudSim toolbox, they also simulate the mechanism.

22. This paper displayed a relative investigation of three circulated load-balancing calculations for Cloud computing situations. It was noticed that present business contributions dependent on a unified portion would stop to be adaptable

as interest overwhelms endeavors at distributing the load over all nodes in a framework. Hence a decentralized methodology is needed because of which load balancing rises as a global result from neighborhood node connections.

23. In this investigation, the OLB scheduling calculation is utilized to endeavor the fact that every single node is occupied, and the objective of load balance can be accomplished. In any case, the set-forth LBMM scheduling calculation that changed from Min–Min planning calculation can achieve the minimum run-time of every assignment on cloud computing conditions. Besides, in a summed-up case, the cloud computing system is not just static; it is dynamic. Then again, their proposed strategy will reach out to keep up and oversee when the node is underlying a three-level progressive cloud computing system in forthcoming work.

24. This research tells us about a stochastic slope climbing approach that has been used for load balancing in Cloud computing. The subtle registering-based methodology has been contrasted with two famous techniques which are RoundRobin and First Come First Serve. The outcomes are very reassuring, but the utilization of other famous processing systems is required for further improvement.

25. In this paper, two new structures of task scheduling calculation are proposed to diminish employment's run time, improve the load balance and fulfil clients' need requests in the cloud. As indicated by the outcome, the calculations proposed in this paper outflank the Min–Min calculation as far as makespan, load balancing and client need are concerned. The rest of the paper shows a review of past works about assignment planning with a solid accentuation on conventional Min–Min calculation.

26. In this research the authors have come up with a stochastic model for load balancing and planning for cloud computing groups. An essential commitment is the advancement of edge based non-preemptive VM configuration strategies. These arrangements can be made about throughput-ideal by picking sufficiently long outline terms, while the generally utilized best fit approach was demonstrated to be inefficient. Recreations demonstrate that long outline terms are great from a throughput viewpoint as well as appear to give great defer execution.

27. In this paper, writers structure an enhancement model to relocate these additional undertakings to the new host VMs by applying Particle Swarm Optimization (PSO). To study the PSO technique, the authors perform the cloud test system (CloudSim) bundle and use PSO as its assignment planning model. The recreation results demonstrate that the TBSLB-PSO strategy altogether decreases the time taken for the load balancing procedure contrasted with customary load balancing approaches. Moreover, in this proposed methodology the over-loaded VMs won't be stopped during the movement procedure, and there is no compelling reason to utilize the VM pre-duplicate procedure. Along these lines, the TBSLB-PSO technique will wipe out VM vacation and the danger of losing the last movement performed by a client and will expand the Quality of Service experienced by cloud clients.

28. The work proposed here examines how a hereditary calculation can be utilized to tackle the dynamic load balancing issue. A powerful load-balancing calculation is created whereby ideal or close ideal errand distributions can "develop" during the activity of the parallel registering framework. The calculation considers other load balancing issues, for example, limit approaches, data trade criteria, and inter-processor correspondence. The impacts of these and different issues on the accomplishment of the hereditary based load balancing calculation as contrasted and the principal fit heuristic are plot.

29. They have contemplated the issue of intracloud load balancing by versatile, dynamic relocation of VMs. Creators plan and actualize a load balancing paradigm and suggest a conveyed calculation BALANCE AND COMPARE dependent on testing to arrive at a balance arrangement. The trial results demonstrate that the calculation unites quick, however the creators additionally observe that the relocation for OpenVZ virtual machine is still moderate, creators will attempt the Xen virtual innovation for live movement later on work.

30. In this paper, an effective calculation is structured which deals with the load at the server by taking into account the present status of all accessible virtual machines for allocating the approaching requests shrewdly. The virtual

machine-appointa a load balancer, for the most part, centers around the effective usage of the assets. Creators demonstrated that their proposed calculation ideally disperses the load, and subsequent under/overuse (VMs) circumstances will not emerge.

31. In this paper, the creators researched the presentation ramifications of SSL convention for giving secure administration in a group-based server application, and put forward a back-end sending plan for optimizing server execution through better load balance. This ssl with bf plan misuses the basic client level correspondence for limiting the intra-group correspondence overhead. The proposed plan gives higher use and better load balance over all server nodes.

32. This study examines and compares the performance results of the SSL protocol, which provides reliable provisions for cluster-centered application servers. For enhancing the server performance, a backend forwarding method is suggested employing an enhanced load balancer. The proposed method over-utilizes the root user-level interaction to reduce the intra-cluster interaction costs. The system will be more robust in handling variable file sizes.

33. This research surveys the execution and Quality Metrics of load balancing techniques in Cloud Computing, Green and Mobile Cloud Computing Frameworks. They explain how in a given system, the load of Cloud Computing can be seen as a procedure of reallocating the total load to the distinct nodes of the specified system.

10.4   Survey Table

In order to develop our project, we need some inspiration and knowledge on the existing techniques on load balancing. To get to the bottom of the load balancing problem, we analyze a few papers implementing load balancing in p2p structures, distributed memory multiprocessors, telecommunication techniques, etc to know more about load balancing at a general level and not just in cloud computing. For the applications of load balancer in the cloud computing environment, there are many other types of research which have proposed algorithms like Honey bee behavior inspired load balancing of tasks and stochastic hill climbing—a soft computing approach which are unique in their way and we need to study them for the implementation of our project carefully. Many papers compare and contrast the current load balancing methods for cloud computing environment constructed on numerous simulations for different factors like utilization%, efficiency, loss reduction, cluster utilization.

The following survey table shown in Table 10.1 analyses the approaches for each paper and also tells us about the different parameters like tools used, methods used, configuration and result parameters, results, and conclusion. We also give our own remarks about each paper.

10.5   Discussion & Comparison

In this segment, we talk about numerous techniques that we surveyed in Section 3 of this paper. Centered on the difficulties examined in Section 2 of this paper, we compare and contrast these techniques. As reviewed, the various methodologies suggest definite answers for the load balancing that are suitable for a few circumstances, yet not others. The static algorithms are generally exceptionally effective as far as overhead is concerned because these algorithms do not have to screen the assets while executing. Hence, these algorithms perform very effectively in a steady domain. As in such operational properties do not vary with time, and they have consistent and commonly uniform loads.

The dynamic algorithms then again offer a vastly improved arrangement that can change the load powerfully dependent on the assets of the resources during execution. In any case, this property prompts increased operating costs on the framework as consistent checking and governing will include high traffic and m cause more deferrals. Few recently proposed dynamic load balancing algorithms attempt to keep away from this operational cost by using novel task distribution frameworks. Table 10.2 demonstrates an examination of comparison among the investigated algorithms. The correlation outlines the advantages and disadvantages of every calculation. It contours a correlation between the investigated calculations as far as the difficulties talked about in Section 2 are concerned.

10.6   Conclusion

In this paper, we reviewed numerous papers on the topic: Load Balancing for Cloud Computing. A Load Balancer is hugely successful and valuable in cloud computing as it is utilized to efficiently distribute the load among all nodes and offer similarity over all nodes, so no node is exhausted or

Table 10.1 Literature review of load balancing algorithms.

Ref. no.	Methods used	Tools used	Configuration parameters	Result parameters	Result	Conclusion	Your remarks
[1]	• Forward probability method • Benefit estimate method	• Virtual machine cluster environment	• CPU configuration • Memory configuration	• VM load • PM load • Prediction function	The workload is balanced effectively among VMs by the forward probability method.	The authors proposed an ALB policy built on VM in the cloud.	For the future work, diverse applications in the cloud should be considered by the authors.
[2]	• The method of spanning tree • Coding method	• VMware distributed resource scheduler	• Virtual machine • CPU utility	• Load of the physical machine • Migration cost	Rotating and least scheduling method performs poorly.	By considering past elements, the proposed method ensures better load balancing.	The real-world dynamic variations in the cloud are not taken into consideration.
[3]	• Diffusion approach	• Hypercube multiprocessor	• Communication models • Processors used	• Diffusion • Dimension exchange	The Dimension exchange method on a hypercube multiprocessor is superior to the diffusion approach.	In message-passing multiprocessor networks, authors studied numerous diffusion methods for dynamic ALB.	The eigenstructure of the duplication matrices that occur in dynamic load balancing has been used for the results.
[4]	• Simplified DistFlow method	• Fortran-7 • Sectionalizing switches	• Network configuration • Base-radial configuration • Base configuration	• Search level • Branch in-out • Loss reduction on kW	Estimation methods are computationally very efficient and in general, give conservative results.	The authors proposed a typical design of the feeder reconfiguration problem and gave a new scheme for improvement.	The algorithm searches over diverse radial arrangements formed by taking branch exchange type switching into consideration.

(Continued)

Table 10.1 Literature review of load balancing algorithms. (*Continued*)

Ref. no.	Methods used	Tools used	Configuration parameters	Result parameters	Result	Conclusion	Your remarks
[5]	• Distributed Web-server system	• HTTP • LINUX • Webserver	• Intermediate name servers • Number of machines on the web server system	• Maximum cluster utilization • Number of servers overloaded	A limited solution to added client requests could be LAN-dispersed Web Server clusters.	While allocating requests, network load and client proximity must be taken into account by the dispatching algorithm.	Dynamically assessing such information could be a problem because it frequently fluctuates in the Internet environment.
[6]	• Three algorithms varying in the extent of data used in rearranging load	• Binary modeling of the state • Binary modeling of a node • Heavy and light nodes	• Node configuration database • Storage configuration	• Number of probes to achieve balance • Portion of the load shifted to attain balance	With marginal load transfer, it is achievable to balance the load in ninety-five percent of the optimum value.	Three basic methods to attain load-balancing in systematized peer-to-peer systems are presented.	The authors address the problem of load balancing in P2P systems.
[7]	• Ant-based control	• Multiple mobile software agents • Visual works	• The age of the ant • Delay to the degree of congestion • The velocity of each ant is one node per simulation time step • The delay in time steps	• Least-cost route from source to destination • Call failures, mean • Standard deviation of call failures	Due to the extensive usage of arbitrary numeral makers, ants probably need added computation on the nodes of the network.	The authors implemented a completely decentralized adaptive control system for telecommunications networks.	Exclusive packets on the network to characterize the ants can be used such that these are treated in a different way by routers from packets.

(*Continued*)

Table 10.1 Literature review of load balancing algorithms. (*Continued*)

Ref. no.	Methods used	Tools used	Configuration parameters	Result parameters	Result	Conclusion	Your remarks
[8]	• Cell range expansion • Cell association method • Distributed algorithm for downlink HetNets	• SINRs and BS loads • Cellular networks • Three-tier HetNets	• Network configuration • User configuration • Security configuration	• Biasing Factor • Probability of tier • Density of tier	The BS densities for the many tiers do not affect the optimum biasing factors, but it is profoundly affected by per-tier transmit powers.	A group of new user association methods is proposed that realize load balancing in HetNets via a network-wide utilization maximization problem.	A logarithmic utilization maximization problem is formulated by the authors with optimum uniform resource allocation.
[9]	• Dimension exchange method • Hierarchical balancing method • Gradient model	• Intel iPSC/2 hypercube	• Receiver and sender configuration • Task dimension • Task size	• Granularity • Speedup	The DEM strategy is inclined to perform better than all other granularities.	The authors discussed two massive problems, that of the degree of information used in balancing decisions and of load balancing operating cost.	The system interconnection topology profoundly affects the effectiveness of the HBM and DEM.
[10]	• A nature-inspired algorithm • Self-organization • Arbitrary sampling of the system domain	• CloudSim simulator	• Number of tasks migrated • Number of virtual machines	• Makespan comparison • Response time • Degree of imbalance of VMs	Without increasing operating costs, the proposed algorithm gives excellent results.	Based on the behaviour of the honey bee foraging approach, the authors have suggested an algorithm for cloud computing environments.	The proposed HBB-LB is well suited for heterogeneous cloud systems also.

(*Continued*)

Table 10.1 Literature review of load balancing algorithms. (*Continued*)

Ref. no.	Methods used	Tools used	Configuration parameters	Result parameters	Result	Conclusion	Your remarks
[11]	• Gauss-Seidel iteration algorithm • Distributed gradient projection	• Trace-driven numerical simulation	• Availability of renewable energy • Demand response • Dynamic pricing	• Cost incurred by geographical load balancing • Delay cost • Energy cost	The simulation indicates that geographical load balancing can create a proficient scheme for demand-response.	The authors have proposed two distributed algorithms that calculate the provisioning decisions and optimum routing for Internet-scale systems.	The social influence of geographical load balancing has been studied in Internet-Scale systems.
[12]	• Based on the gradient model	• Rediflow	• Quantity of Xputers • Memory • Arrangement of the Xputers • Switch capacities	• Utilization %, Simulation time • Speedup	The gradient model has satisfactory results under logical technological suppositions.	In this paper, a cloud load balancing algorithm, called the gradient model, is proposed and compared with existing algorithms.	When the system scales up, any load balancing method that needs a centralized action looks unreasonable.
[13]	• Proactive scaling • Compression	• GroundSim • GreenCloud	• Transaction metrics • Activity based costing	• Response time • Utilization % • Data rate in Mbps • Health	To increase efficiency, the most available resources can be forwarded onto users by using the load balancer functionality.	The authors demonstrated the use of real-world load balancing techniques to increase the availability of cloud-computing environment and asset employment.	For providing the availability of cloud resources and resource monitoring, the authors used XMPP.

(*Continued*)

Table 10.1 Literature review of load balancing algorithms. (*Continued*)

Ref. no.	Methods used	Tools used	Configuration parameters	Result parameters	Result	Conclusion	Your remarks
[14]	• "Power of two choices" paradigm • Low-overhead searching	• A one-dimensional ring • Keys • Servers • Finger table	• Item configuration • Item hash value • Item storage	• Items per bin • Number of items	Load balancing is improved considerably, and a portion of idle peers is reduced by the use of virtual peers when assessed to a method without load balancing.	The authors argue to DHT's to permit a key to map to a set of d potential peers, rather than to an individual peer.	Using the "power of two choices" model, the authors demonstrate better load-balancing performance than the virtual peer's method initially suggested in Chord.
[15]	• Transitioning algorithm • Partitioning algorithm	• The NOX OpenFlow controller	• Cluster configuration • Session configuration • Web server configuration	• Throughput • Latency • Utilization • Standard deviation	The system easily adapts to fluctuations in target traffic allocation. A few packets guided to the controller have a negligible effect on throughput.	Load-balancing framework intensely maps sections of source IP addresses to duplicate servers, so that the client requests are promptly despatched.	Online applications make use of load balancing to utilize the backend servers fully.

(*Continued*)

Table 10.1 Literature review of load balancing algorithms. (*Continued*)

Ref. no.	Methods used	Tools used	Configuration parameters	Result parameters	Result	Conclusion	Your remarks
[16]	• Trace-driven simulation • Pre-emptive migration strategy	• UNIX • MOSIX • Research machines • Machines used for system administration.	• Client • Server • CPU • Storage.	• Migration cost • Mean slowdown • The standard deviation of the slowdown	It would be advantageous for applications to incorporate a preemptive load-balancing policy.	The advantages of load balancing are devalued by sole usage of the mean slowdown as a metric of system execution.	Various factors are ignored in the simulation that would influence the functioning of migration in real systems. Also, the authors have presumed that all activities are CPU-bound.
[17]	• Parametric-study algorithm • Single-point algorithm	• LINUX	• Number of resources • Speed configuration	• Communication time • Mean response time	The authors demonstrated that the group of nodes divisions into groups of source nodes, sink nodes, and neutral nodes.	The authors created a typical archetype for this distributed computer system.	Product-form queuing networks may represent communication networks and nodes.
[18]	• Simple greedy algorithm	• Extensive simulations • DHTs • Virtual servers • Consistent hashing	• User configuration • Web-server configuration	• System utilization • Load movement factor	The algorithm efficiently attains load balancing for system utilization up to 90% by shifting a mere 8% of the load.	The algorithm handles heterogeneousness in form of • Fluctuating object loads • Fluctuating node capacity.	The proposed algorithm can balance various kinds of resources, comprising bandwidth, processor cycles, and storage.

(*Continued*)

Table 10.1 Literature review of load balancing algorithms. (*Continued*)

Ref. no.	Methods used	Tools used	Configuration parameters	Result parameters	Result	Conclusion	Your remarks
[19]	• Rounding method of Shmoys & Tardos • Adjusted load balancing algorithm • SSF • LLF	• A mobile device equipped with client software	• Client configuration • Web-server configuration • Database configuration	• Utilization % • Bandwidth allocation	The simulations show that the proposed schemes, attain almost optimum load balancing and radically outperform popular heuristics.	The authors presented an approximation algorithm that promises the optimal solution.	As wireless LANs deployment is increasing to cover more areas gradually more trusted to transfer crucial info, they must be controlled in order to attain required system performance objectives.
[20]	• Static algorithms dynamic algorithms	• LINUX	• Spatial dispersal of the cloud nodes replication/storage • Complexity of algorithm • Point of failure	• Replication • Speed • Heterogeneity • SPOF • Network • Overhead • Spatially • Distributed • Implementation • Complexity • Fault • Tolerance	Some approaches are well suited for some situations, but not for all.	The authors reviewed the obstacles that should be passed to deliver the best and effective load balancing algorithm.	This paper is a comparison for all the existing algorithms for load balancing of VMs.

(*Continued*)

Table 10.1 Literature review of load balancing algorithms. (*Continued*)

Ref. no.	Methods used	Tools used	Configuration parameters	Result parameters	Result	Conclusion	Your remarks
[21]	• Task model • Host resource • Model	• CloudSim toolkit	• The task of computing resources • Network resources • Storage resources	• Resource utilization comparison • Make span comparison	When the difference between the number of hosts and tasks is small, the makespan in the cloud environment is higher than in the grid environment.	This paper discusses a two-stage scheduling technique for load balancing.	The resource utilization rate is low in the task scheduling in grid computing.
[22]	• Nature-inspired algorithm • Self-organization • Random sampling	• CloudSim	• Available resources • Allocated jobs	• Diversity vs. Throughput in an unchanging size • Size vs. Throughput for an unchanging diversity	The Honey-bee based load balancing performs better when a distinct population of service types is needed.	The authors compared three distributed load-balancing methods for Cloud computing set-ups.	Three potential distributed solutions suggested for load balancing motivated by Biased Random Sampling, Active Clustering, and Honeybee Foraging Behaviour were investigated.
[23]	• Cloud computing techniques based on ZEUS	• GreenSim	• Remaining CPU (MB/s) • Remaining memory in Mbps • The transmission rate in Mbps	• Threshold(Avg) • Efficiency	The authors used LBMM scheduling method to achieve minimal execution time on the node of each task.	In an attempt to keep each node busy OLB scheduling algorithm is used.	The authors merged the OLB algorithm and the LBMM algorithm that can deploy more resources for improved effectiveness.

(*Continued*)

Table 10.1 Literature review of load balancing algorithms. (*Continued*)

Ref. no.	Methods used	Tools used	Configuration parameters	Result parameters	Result	Conclusion	Your remarks
[24]	• Stochastic hill climbing algorithm	• CloudAnalyst simulation tool	• User base • Region • Simultaneous online users during peak hrs • Simultaneous online users During offpeak hrs	• Cloud configuration • DC specification • Response time in (ms) using SHC, • Response time in (ms) using RR • Response time in (ms) using FCFS	SHC performs better than almost all existing CPU scheduling algorithms.	The authors used the SHC algorithm in order to achieve load balancing in Cloud computing.	The usage of other soft computing methods should be investigated for more enhancement.
[25]	• LBIMM algorithm • Min-Min algorithm	• LINUX • Matlab	• Resource specification • Task specification.	• Make span • Mean resource deployment ratio • Mean VIP task completion time • Mean ordinary task completion time	LBIMM and PALBIMM give better makespan than Min-Min.	The authors proposed LBIMM and PA-LBIMM.	Proposed frameworks reduce the job's completion time.
[26]	• JSQ routing algorithms • Myopic max-weight scheduling algorithm	• Sonata-NFV emulator	• Number of backlogged VMs • Memory • CPU • Storage	• Mean delay • Traffic intensity	Good throughput is not produced by the best fit algorithm.	Stochastic simulation for application load balancing is considered by the authors for scheduling in cloud computing clusters.	In the results, they use simulations to compare to the performance.

(*Continued*)

Table 10.1 Literature review of load balancing algorithms. (*Continued*)

Ref. no.	Methods used	Tools used	Configuration parameters	Result parameters	Result	Conclusion	Your remarks
[27]	• PSO algorithm Cloudsim's task scheduling algorithm • MOPSO-based algorithm	• Cloud simulator (Cloudsim) package • Jswarm package	• VM properties • Task properties • Task mapping	• Total task scheduling time • Search time for suitable VMs	The time consumption of load balancing is profoundly reduced by TBSLB-PSO.	The TBSLB-PSO method is proposed.	The proposed algorithm minimizes task execution, and transfer time is reduced by the proposed algorithm.
[28]	• A dynamic load-balancing algorithm	• LINUX	• Client and web-server configuration • Database configuration • Speed configuration	• Average utilization • Run time • The flexibility of the load balancing mechanism	By escalating the flexibility of the method, processor utilization is considerably increased initially before reaching its peak value.	Central scheduler's use was efficient as it handled all load-balancing evaluations with minimum interprocessor interaction.	When compared to the first-fit algorithm, the threshold method used gave a better outcome.
[29]	• Sampling-based algorithm • Centralized algorithm	• OpenVZ	• Node Name • Machine Bit • Shared storage • IP Address • OpenVZ	• Live Migration • The time between two hosts in distinct conditions • System and software configuration • Distribution of VMs on hosts	The results show how the standard deviation decreases over time.	The issue of intracloud load balancing was investigated by the authors using the flexible live migration of VMs.	A basic model that reduces the migration time of VMs has been implemented.

(Continued)

Table 10.1 Literature review of load balancing algorithms. (*Continued*)

Ref. no.	Methods used	Tools used	Configuration parameters	Result parameters	Result	Conclusion	Your remarks
[30]	• Active-VM load balance algorithm	• CloudAnalyst • CloudSim Toolkit • CloudSim extensions	• User base • Region • Simultanecus online users during off-peak hours • Simultaneous online users during peak hours	• Number of virtual machines • Number of incoming requests	The proposed method does not have any resources under-deployment issues in the cloud.	The authors designed an effective algorithm to manage the load at the servers by taking the current status of all available VMs into consideration for designating the received requests wisely.	Load distribution on VMs is not proper as compared to other present Active-VM load balancing algorithm.
[31]	• Round Robin • Secure Sockets Layer with session • Secure Sockets Layer with bf	• Secure Sockets Layer • Simulator written in CSIM	• Cluster configuration • Session configuration • Web server configuration	• Throughput • Latency • Utilization • Standard deviation	Methods with reusable sessions, employed in proposed SSL models are crucial for reducing the fixed cost.	The core user-level communication is utilized by the proposed SSL with bf method, which minimizes the intra-cluster communication cost.	This paper investigates the working inferences of the SSL protocol.

(*Continued*)

Table 10.1 Literature review of load balancing algorithms. (*Continued*)

Ref. no.	Methods used	Tools used	Configuration parameters	Result parameters	Result	Conclusion	Your remarks
[32]	• Parametric-study algorithm • Single-point algorithm	• LINUX • MOSIX	• VM configuration • Usage configuration • Profile configuration	• Throughput, utilization % • Migration time	The SSL backend forward method minimizes the mean latency by roughly forty percentage.	This paper investigates the working of the Secure Sockets Layer protocol for a reliable cluster-oriented application server service.	The projected back-end forwarding method can be used to enhance the performance of application servers further.
[33]	• Static algorithms • Dynamic algorithms	• Software framework (Java/.Net) • AWS • Microsoft azure	• Client • Storage • Security	• Performance • Response • Time scalability resource • Utilization throughput fault • Tolerance • Process • Migration	It shows the different qualitative measure for a large number of scheduling techniques and algorithms.	This paper summarizes the performance analyses of Load Balancing Algorithms in the various frameworks like green and mobile cloud computing.	Compares and summarizes numerous load balancing algorithms with their quality metrics.

Table 10.2 Load balancing algorithms.

	Advantages	Disadvantages
Ant-based control	Ants can collect the information faster	Little extra computation required on the nodes.
Active-VM	In the new proposed active algorithm, there is no underutilization of the resources	In existing Active-VM algorithms initially, Virtual machines are overexploited, and later virtual machines are not utilized as much as earlier.
LBMM	Tasks are assigned to the nodes reliably.	Work passes through 3 layers before processing, thus making it slower than other algorithms.
Honey-Bee	Sorts the tasks according to priority	The task migration is very less compared to popular balancing algorithms.
Stochastic Hill Climbing	In most of the cases, SHC outperforms RR & FCFS.	Do not perform well in some cases.
TBSLB PSO	Considerably reduces the energy and time utilization of the load balancer.	It is expensive and utilizes a considerable amount of energy in the migration process.
CLDBM	The need for human administrators is reduced.	Its failure leads to wholes process failure.

under-loaded. Even though each load balancing strategy has its benefits and negative marks, the choice of an excellent load balancing method is built simply on the type of application, which helps for the smooth and easy handling of the work loads.

For instance, for web applications, a simple round-robin strategy would be adequate to take care of the download demands of the static websites. Some advanced load balancing methods like honey-bee or dynamic load balancing can be used for dynamic applications like real-time interactive applications. We discussed the numerous strategies and calculations utilized by various analysts for load balancing and parameters utilized.

We discussed the troubles that must be directed to give the most proper and viable load balancing methods. We similarly analyzed the ideal conditions and blocks of these methods.

Whatever may be the load balancing strategy, we decide for an application; the picked procedure ought to be a productive method to deal with the remaining load of the application efficiently. So, to creäte a load balancing framework proficient, the main load balancer module should be included with the capability of giving intelligent monitoring supervision to screen the current outstanding tasks at hand on the gathering of servers and furthermore the load balancer module must be competent enough to convey the remaining loads to the best accessible servers that are fit for taking care of the remaining tasks at hand superior to the others in the gathering of servers.

References

1. Wang, R., Le, W., Zhang, X., Design and implementation of an efficient load-balancing method for virtual machine cluster based on cloud service. *4th IET International Conference on Wireless, Mobile & Multimedia Networks (ICWMMN 2011)*, Beijing, pp. 321–324, 2011.
2. Hu, J. Gu, J., Sun, G., Zhao, T., A scheduling strategy on load balancing of virtual machine resources in cloud computing environment. *2010 3rd International symposium on parallel architectures, algorithms and programming*, IEEE, Dalian, pp. 89–96, 2010.
3. Cybenko, G., Dynamic load balancing for distributed memory multiprocessors. *J. Parallel Distr. Com.*, 7, 2, 279–301, 1989.
4. Baran, M.E. and Wu, F.F., Network reconfiguration in distribution systems for loss reduction and load balancing. *IEEE T. Power Deliver.*, 4, 2, 1401–1407, 1989.
5. Cardellini, V., Colajanni, M., Yu, P.S., Dynamic load balancing on web-server systems. *IEEE Internet Comput.*, 3, 3, 28–39, 1999.
6. Rao, A., Lakshminarayanan, K., Surana, S., Karp, R., Stoica, I., Load balancing in structured p2p systems, in: *International Workshop on Peer-to-Peer Systems*, Springer, Berlin, Heidelberg, pp. 68–79, 2003, February.
7. Schoonderwoerd, R., Holland, O.E., Bruten, J.L., Rothkrantz, L.J., Ant-based load balancing in telecommunications networks. *Adapt. Behav.*, 5, 2, 169–207, 1997.
8. Ye, Q., Rong, B., Chen, Y., Al-Shalash, M., Caramanis, C., Andrews, J.G., User association for load balancing in heterogeneous cellular networks. *IEEE T. Wirel. Commun.*, 12, 6, 2706–2716, 2013.
9. Willebeek-LeMair, M.H. and Reeves, A.P., Strategies for dynamic load balancing on highly parallel computers. *IEEE T. Parall. Distr.*, 4, 9, 979–993, 1993.

10. LD, D.B. and Krishna, P.V., Honey bee behavior inspired load balancing of tasks in cloud computing environments. *Appl. Soft Comput.*, 13, 5, 2292–2303, 2013.

11. Liu, Z., Lin, M., Wierman, A., Low, S.H., Andrew, L.L., Greening geographical load balancing, in: *Proceedings of the ACM SIGMETRICS Joint International Conference on Measurement and Modeling of Computer Systems*, ACM, vol. 39, issue 1, pp. 193–204, 2011, June.

12. Lin, F.C.H. and Keller, R.M., The gradient model load balancing method. *in: IEEE Transactions on Software Engineering*, vol. SE-13, no. 1, pp. 32–38, 1987.

13. Chaczko, Z., Mahadevan, V., Aslanzadeh, S., Mcdermid, C., Availability and load balancing in cloud computing, in: *International Conference on Computer and Software Modeling, Singapore*, IACSIT Press, vol. 14, pp. 134–140, 2011, September.

14. Byers, J., Considine, J., Mitzenmacher, M., Simple load balancing for distributed hash tables, in: *International Workshop on Peer-to-Peer Systems*, Springer, Berlin, Heidelberg, pp. 80–87, 2003, February.

15. Wang, R., Butnariu, D., Rexford, J., OpenFlow-Based Server Load Balancing Gone Wild. *Hot-ICE, 11*, pp. 12–12, 2011.

16. Harchol-Balter, M. and Downey, A.B., Exploiting process lifetime distributions for dynamic load balancing. *ACM T. Comput. Syst. (TOCS)*, 15, 3, 253–285, 1997.

17. Tantawi, A.N. and Towsley, D., Optimal static load balancing in distributed computer systems. *J. ACM (JACM)*, 32, 2, 445–465, 1985.

18. Godfrey, B., Lakshminarayanan, K., Surana, S., Karp, R., Stoica, I., Load balancing in dynamic structured P2P systems, in: *IEEE INFOCOM*, Hong Kong, vol. 4, IEEE, pp. 2253–2262, 2004.

19. Bejerano, Y., Han, S.J., Li, L.E., Fairness and load balancing in wireless LANs using association control, in: *Proceedings of the 10th Annual International Conference on Mobile Computing and Networking*, ACM, pp. 315–329, 2004, September.

20. Al Nuaimi, K., Mohamed, N., Al Nuaimi, M., Al-Jaroodi, J., A survey of load balancing in cloud computing: Challenges and algorithms, in: *2012 Second Symposium on Network Cloud Computing and Applications*, IEEE, London, pp. 137–142, 2012, December.

21. Fang, Y., Wang, F., Ge, J., A task scheduling algorithm based on load balancing in cloud computing, in: *International Conference on Web Information Systems and Mining*, Springer, Berlin, Heidelberg, pp. 271–277, 2010, October.

22. Randles, M., Lamb, D., Taleb-Bendiab, A., A comparative study into distributed load balancing algorithms for cloud computing, in: *2010 IEEE 24th International Conference on Advanced Information Networking and Applications Workshops*, IEEE, Perth, WA, pp. 551–556, 2010.

23. Wang, S.C., Yan, K.Q., Liao, W.P., Wang, S.S., Towards a load balancing in a three-level cloud computing network, in: *2010 3rd International Conference on Computer Science and Information Technology*, vol. 1, IEEE, Chengdu, pp. 108–113, 2013.

24. Mondal, B., Dasgupta, K., Dutta, P., Load balancing in cloud computing using stochastic hill climbing-a soft computing approach. *Procedia Technol.*, 4, 783–789, 2012.

25. Chen, H., Wang, F., Helian, N., Akanmu, G., User-priority guided Min-Min scheduling algorithm for load balancing in cloud computing, in: *2013 National Conference on Parallel computing technologies (PARCOMPTECH)*, IEEE, Bangalore, pp. 1–8, 2013.

26. Maguluri, S.T., Srikant, R., Ying, L., Stochastic models of load balancing and scheduling in cloud computing clusters, in: *2012 Proceedings IEEE Infocom*, IEEE, Orlando, FL, pp. 702–710, 2012.

27. Ramezani, F., Lu, J., Hussain, F.K., Task-based system load balancing in cloud computing using particle swarm optimization. *Int. J. Parallel Program.*, 42, 5, 739–754, 2014.

28. Zomaya, A.Y. and Yee-Hwei, T., Observations on using genetic algorithms for dynamic load-balancing. *IEEE Trans. Parallel Distrib. Syst.*, 12, 9, 899–911, 2001.

29. Zhao, Y. and Huang, W., Adaptive distributed load balancing algorithm based on live migration of virtual machines in cloud, in: *2009 Fifth International Joint Conference on INC, IMS and IDC*, IEEE, Seoul, pp. 170–175, 2009, August.

30. Domanal, S.G. and Reddy, G.R.M., Optimal load balancing in cloud computing by efficient utilization of virtual machines, in: *2014 Sixth International Conference on Communication Systems and Networks (COMSNETS)*, IEEE, Bangalore, pp. 1–4, 2014.

31. Kim, J.H., Choi, G.S., Das, C.R., A load balancing scheme for cluster-based secure network servers, in: *2005 IEEE International Conference on Cluster Computing*, IEEE, Burlington, MA, pp. 1–10, 2005.

32. Suresh, V.M., Karthikeswaran, D., Sudha, V.M., Chandraseker, D.M., Web server load balancing using SSL back-end forwarding method, in: *IEEE-International Conference On Advances In Engineering, Science And Management (ICAESM)*, IEEE, Nagapattinam, Tamil Nadu, pp. 822–827, 2012.

33. Geetha, P. and Robin, C.R., A comparative-study of load-cloud balancing algorithms in cloud environments, in: *2017 International Conference on Energy, Communication, Data Analytics and Soft Computing (ICECDS)*, IEEE, Chennai, pp. 806–810, 2017.

11

A Low-Cost Wearable Remote Healthcare Monitoring System

Konguvel Elango* and Kannan Muniandi

Department of Electronics Engineering, Madras Institute of Technology Campus, Anna University, Chennai, India

Abstract

One main area of research that has seen adoption of the technology is the healthcare sector. With the advancements in technology and miniaturization of sensor nodes, there have been many attempts to utilize the new technology in various areas to improve the quality of human life. This chapter is an attempt to solve a healthcare problem that the society faces. The main objective is to design and develop a wearable healthcare monitoring system. This system includes detection of a fall of a human subject under consideration, detection of heart rate and detection of body temperature. Remote viewing of the sensed data enables a health care specialist to monitor a patient's health condition. This wearable health monitoring system can be made with easily available sensors with an interpretation of making the system inexpensive.

Keywords: Healthcare monitoring, fall detection, remote monitoring, wearable sensors

11.1 Introduction

A remote health monitoring system is an extension of a hospital medical system where a patient's vital body state can be monitored remotely. Traditionally the detection systems were only found in hospitals and were characterized by huge and complex circuitry which requires high power consumption. Incessant advancements in the semiconductor technology

---

Corresponding author: konguart08@gmail.com

G. R. Kanagachidambaresan (ed.) Role of Edge Analytics in Sustainable Smart City Development: Challenges and Solutions, (219–242) © 2020 Scrivener Publishing LLC

led to manufacture of sensors and microcontrollers that are smaller in size, faster in operation, low in power consumption and affordable in cost. This has further seen development in the remote monitoring of vital life signs of patients especially the elderly. The remote health monitoring system can be applied in the following scenarios:

- A patient is known to have an unstable medical condition.
- A patient is prone to heart attacks or may have suffered one before.
- Situation leading to development of a risky life threatening condition.
- Athletes during training.

In recent times, several advancements have come up to address the various issues of a remote health monitoring. These systems have wireless detection system that sends the sensor information wirelessly to a remote server. Some have even adopted a service model that requires one to pay a subscription fee. In developing countries this is a hindrance as some people cannot use them due to cost issue involved. There is also the issue of internet connectivity where some systems to operate good quality internet for a real-time remote connection is required. Internet penetration is still a problem in developing countries. To address some of these problems there is a need to approach the remote detection from a ground-up approach to suit the minimal conditions currently available.

A simple patient monitoring system design can be approached by the number of parameters it can detect at a time. It can be categorized as single parameter monitoring system and multi parameter monitoring system. Using a single parameter monitoring system an approach to a remote health monitoring system was designed that extends healthcare from the traditional clinic or hospital setting to the patient's home.

11.1.1   Problem Statement

Remote health monitoring can provide biological information of elderly or chronically ill-patients, who avoid a long hospitalization. The implanted wireless sensors collect and transmit the signals of interest and a processor is programmed to receive and analyse the data. In this study, sensor data such as detection of fall, cardiac rate, brain signal data and body temperature are considered as the signals of interest. During the design, the following characteristics of the future medical applications were adhered to [1, 2]:

- Integration with current trends in medical practices and technology.
- Real-time, long-term, remote monitoring, miniature, wearable sensors.
- Long battery life of designed device.
- Assistance to the elderly and chronic patients.

11.1.2   Objective of the Study

This study aims at designing a healthcare module with detection of heart rate, fall of a patient, body temperature and analysis of the detected data. A health specialist can use the system to monitor remotely the status of the patient. An attempt has been made at designing a remote health care system with easily available components to make the system inexpensive.

- The fall detection module includes an accelerometer and microcontroller. The data collected was transmitted wirelessly to a receiver module.
- The heart rate detection involves a non-invasive infrared fingertip detector and a microcontroller.
- The body temperature sensor is connected to a microcontroller.
- All the sensor data are transmitted to a remote sever, from which it can be analysed and monitored.

The entire design process from signal detection to data analysis is presented. For the devices that require instant intervention by a specialist doctor, it is foremost important that they should be autonomous, non-invasive to the patient in everyday life activities. The designed module is easy to wear, smaller in size, shock-proof and consumes less power. To collect and manage the information signal from patient, integrated circuits and microprocessors are implemented. The main advantages of the system are fall detector allows free movement of the patient and method of acquiring the heart rate is completely non-invasive.

The significance of the study includes solving the healthcare problem with engineering approach by developing a remote health care system and bridging the gap between the consultant and patient with modern non-expensive sensors. This also helps the senior citizens who are unaccompanied in home for various reasons, whose fall detection is a concern. Falls result in serious injuries such as fractures, trauma or even fatalities. A handy fall detector circuit and heart rate sensor could be configured to detect the occurrence of fall and monitor the pulse.

11.2 Related Works

11.2.1 Remote Healthcare Monitoring Systems

The study on "Remote Healthcare Monitoring Systems" covers areas of interest in both electrical engineering and medical sciences, which leads to the emerging field of Biomedical Engineering. Remote health monitoring systems are based on wearable sensors attached to the patient's body that collects data and transfer to a remote database or a server. The data is then accessed remotely by a healthcare specialist who can monitor and may make a vital decision based on the data, if necessary. The literature refers a remote healthcare monitoring system as "Mobile Health" or "mHealth" during "feature phone only" era [3]. At that time, a mHealth alliance that identifies barriers, gaps in scaling and usage of mobile communication technology in healthcare sector.

According to the Journal of Neuro-Engineering and Rehabilitation [4], most of non-invasive techniques used in acquiring critical signals from the human body are of micro-Volt (μV) in nature. The information from the acquired signals is extracted by using microcontrollers. The instrumental and biological noises are then removed using Digital Signal Processing (DSP) modelling techniques. Advancements in wireless sensors networks have led to numerous developments that are continuously being adopted by healthcare sectors. In near future, the healthcare sector will be an integrated one with pervasive wireless wearable sensor networks, infrastructures in clinical trials, augmentation of data collection and real time response.

In smart phone era, medical techniques and several sensors are incorporated in many mobile phones, wearable smart watches and bands, which collect biological data in a non-invasive way and the data is uploaded instantly to an online storage, generally known as cloud storage. These devices adopt the concept of Internet of Things (IOT). A data log of a patient under study can then be generated any time if needed. This reduces the number of patient's visits to the hospital as health-care specialist can intervene with the patient's data chart before they turn critical instantly. Patients with chronic health conditions such as Congestive Heart Failure (CHF), Chronic Obstructive Pulmonary Disease (COPD), diabetes, asthma and hypertension get benefit from the remote health care management taking advantage of remote patient monitoring. Once the patient is referred to the remote healthcare management by a healthcare specialist in the hospital, it offers,

- Access to a mobile application/web page that can be used from their home.
- Use of an intuitive, step-by-step application based on pre-scheduled questions that they need to answer, may be several times a day based on the need.
- Seamless integration with electronic-medical devices that can continuously capture the data and shares with remote healthcare management servers.

The remote healthcare management offers healthcare specialists,

- Access to a centralized view of all registered patients, to tailor workflows, protocols and interventions, creating customized care plans.
- Easy analysis of results, empowering them to adjust treatment based on best-practice guidelines and protocols.
- Alerts and reminders based on the continuously being monitored data.
- Sophisticated care coordination through better organization of multidisciplinary teams, assignment of interventions and tasks, and the ability to view past, present and future interventions.
- Asset management, making it easy to manage device's location and user.

The remote healthcare management systems also includes,

- Collection of physiological information such as cardiac activity, body temperature and day-to-day activity to monitor the occurrence of fall.
- Tracking the patients' results on a regular basis, the healthcare team can provide the treatments as required.
- In a longer term, remote health care management system provides guidance to patients about their present health conditions.

- Increased patient satisfaction and quality of care, because of closer interaction with health professionals, reduced anxiety as well as fewer emergency-room visits and hospital stays.
- The remote health care solution leads to increased healthcare team productivity, enabling more evidence-based care and more efficient patient case management for more patients.
- Enhanced collaboration by the remote health care programs to help enhance collaboration between healthcare providers. Acute care discharge planning is enhanced using the remote health care management solution.

11.2.2 Pulse Rate Detection

Instead of conventional manual method of detecting pulse rate, a light signal from a Light Emitting Diode (LED) from one side of the finger and measure the intensity of light received on the other side using Light Dependent Resistor (LDR). Whenever the heart pumps the blood, more light is absorbed by increased blood cells and decrease in the intensity of light received on the LDR is observed [5] through reflection mode or transmission mode, as shown in Figure 11.1. As a result, the resistance value of LDR increases which can be converted into voltage variation using a signal conditioning circuit like an Operational Amplifier. A programmed microcontroller can be used to receive an interrupt for every pulse detected and count the number of interrupts or pulses in a minute or for any time interval.

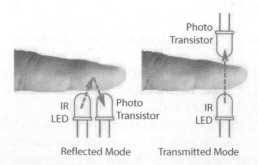

Figure 11.1 Pulse rate detection.

11.2.3 Temperate Measurement

The LM35 is one of the conventionally used low cost centigrade precision temperature sensor with an electrical output relative to temperature (in °C) when compared to a thermistor. This has an advantage over linear temperature sensors calibrated in °Kelvin (K), as the handler is not required to do the conversions. The LM35 does not necessitate any external calibration to provide typical accuracies of ±0.25 °C at room temperature and ±0.75 °C at a temperature range of −55 to +150 °C. Low cost is guaranteed by trimming and calibration at the wafer level. The advantages such as low output impedance, linear output, and accurate intrinsic calibration make interfacing to readout circuitry exclusively easy. It can be used with single power supplies, or with plus and minus supplies. As it operates with only 60 μA, it has very low self-heating, less than 0.1 °C in still air. The LM35 sensor series is available packaged in hermetic TO-46 transistor packages, while LM35C/CA and D are available in the plastic TO-92/220 transistor package [6].

11.2.4 Fall Detection

Unintentional fall of elderly or chronically ill patient is a major problem in public health as it causes many disabling fractures and psychological consequences which reduce the non-dependability of an individual. If a pattern of activities of a person can be detected falls can be prevented [7]. With recent developments in Integrated Circuit (IC) industry and telecommunication, systems that encompass accelerometers and gyro meters find its necessity in medical profession and it can be repurposed. The accelerometer in the smart phones can also be configured to detect the occurrence of a fall for chronically ill or elderly people [8]. For the chronically ill or people prone to falls, it is important to monitor their behaviours. Athletes can also be benefited by this monitoring and logging their training regimes. The human physiological data is collected for their normal situations of activity. A commercial device available in the market that addresses the fall detection issue is the home fall detection sensor by AlertOne services [9]. A smartphone with an accelerometer in it can also be used for fall detection by use of an app which provides interface between accelerometer data and remote health management servers. Recent advancements in development of Micro Electro Mechanical Systems (MEMs) made the sensors miniaturized to small wearable ICs. Several implementation strategies for health care monitoring and communication are discussed in [10–16].

11.3   Methodology

11.3.1   NodeMCU

The proposed system block diagram is shown in Figure 11.2. NodeMCU ESP8266 is used as a microcontroller unit. The NodeMCU is an open-source firmware and development kit that helps you to prototype your Internet of Things (IOT) product with a few Lua high-level programming language. It is open-source, interactive, programmable, low cost, simple, and Wi-Fi enabled. It has advanced Application Programming Interface (API) for hardware Input-Output, which can dramatically reduce the redundant work for configuring and manipulating hardware. Programming is similar to Arduino, but interactively in Lua script. Event driven API for network applications, which facilitates developers writing code running on MCU in *Node.js* style which greatly speed up your IOT application developing process. The development kit based on ESP8266, integrates General Purpose Input Output (GPIO), Pulse Width Modulation (PWM), Inter Integrated Circuitry (IIC), 1-Wire and Analog to Digital Converter (ADC) all in one board. The Pin configuration of NodeMCU ESP8266 is shown in Figure 11.3 and Table 11.1.

Electrical Characteristics:

> Working Voltage: 3.3 V
> Maximum IO Driving Power IMAX: 12 mA
> Maximum IO Voltage Level VMAX: 3.6 V
> Current Consumption: 100 mAmp

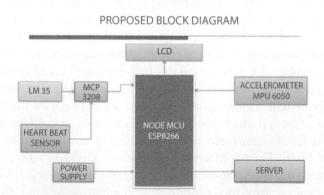

Figure 11.2 Proposed block diagram.

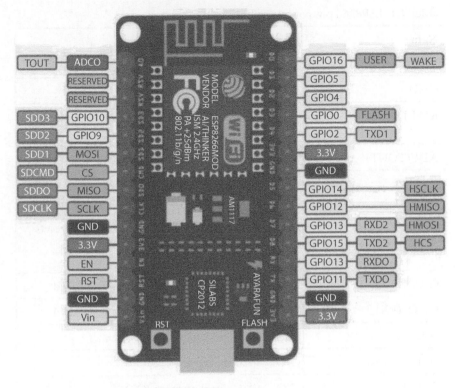

Figure 11.3 NodeMCU ESP8266 pin configuration.

11.3.2   Pulse Rate Detection System

Pulse rate detection sensor is a well designed plug-and-play heart-rate sensor for Arduino which can be used easily to acquire the heart rate data. The sensor clips onto a fingertip or earlobe and plugs right into Arduino with some jumper cables. It also includes an open-source monitoring mobile application that graphs your pulse in real time. The front of the sensor is the pretty side with the heart logo that makes contact with the skin which is shown in Figure 11.4. On the front side, a small round hole is provided, where the LED shines through from the back, and there is also a little square for ambient light sensor. The LED shines light into the fingertip or earlobe, or other capillary tissue, and sensor reads the light that bounces back. The back of the sensor is where the rest of the parts are mounted so that they would not get in the way of the sensor on the front [17].

The cable is 24" flat colour coded ribbon cable with 3 male header connectors. Red wire is input voltage of ranges from +3 V to +5 V. Black

Table 11.1 ESP8266 pin configuration.

Name	Type	Function
VCC	P	Power 3.0~3.6 V
GND	P	Ground
RESET	I	External reset signal (Low voltage level: Active)
ADC(TOUT)	I	ADC Pin Analog Input 0~1 V
CH_PD	I	Chip Enable. High: On, chip works properly; Low: Off, small current
GPIO0(FLASH)	I/O	General purpose IO, If low while reset/ power on takes chip into serial programming mode
GPIO1(TX)	I/O	General purpose IO and Serial TXd
GPIO3(RX)	I/O	General purpose IO and Serial RXd
GPIO4	I/O	General purpose IO
GPIO5	I/O	General purpose IO
GPIO12	I/O	General purpose IO
GPIO13	I/O	General purpose IO
GPIO14	I/O	General purpose IO
GPIO15(HSPI_CS)	I/O	General purpose IO, Connect this pin to ground through 1,000 Ω resistor to boot from internal flash

wire is for ground. Purple wire gives the output Analog heart rate signal. Insulation from sweat or any other fluids are necessary for better operation of the sensor. The pulse rate sensor is an exposed circuit board which should be carefully maintained and introduction of unwanted noises may be avoided. So, a thin film of vinyl sticker is used for insulation and protection. The back of the sensor has even more exposed contacts than the front, so utmost care should be taken while implanting the sensor. The easiest and quickest way to protect the back side from undesirable sorting or noise is to simply stick a Velcro bag.

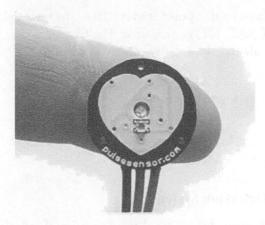

Figure 11.4 Pulse rate sensor.

Heart rate sensor was designed to read the patient's beats per minute (bpm). The technique used to measure the heart rate is based on Near Infra-Red (NIR) spectroscopy. NIR involves uses light with wavelength of 700–900 nm to measure blood volume. At these wavelengths most tissues do not absorb light—other than hemoglobin. A silicon phototransistor, moulded into a flat side-facing package, and a Gallium Arsenide (GaAs) Infra-Red Light Emitting Diode (LED) were used in the sensor. The amount of light that was detected by the phototransistor varied with the patient's heart pulse, as the amount of absorbed IR light changed with the flow of blood, which is directly linked to the heart rate.

This signal was then amplified, filtered, and sent to the microcontroller to be analyzed. The heart rate signal at the collector of the photo-transistor and at the output sensor was mounted in the finger ring as this position proved to give the best response. The signal (analog) originally was too small to detect, and without amplification proved to be too noisy to extract the heart rate. Because of this, operational amplifiers were used to extract the heart rate signal. After amplifying, the signal was fed to comparator, resulting output in the form of pulses. The standard heart rates for babies, children and adults are 70~190 bpm, 80~130 bpm and 60~100 bpm respectively.

The heart rate measurement is interfaced with microcontroller through its digital port for further processing. The heart rate is measured by using the hardware interrupt facility of the microcontroller. The heart rate as is a square wave pulse of varying duty ration. The time period of the wave is measured using the Timer and in combination with hardware interrupt.

The Timer generates a tick pulse at every 10 s. The total tick count in one period (BPM_T_COUNT) is measured. The frequency and heart rate per minute is then calculated using the equation,

$$Frequency = \frac{1,000,000}{BPM\_T\_COUNT} \tag{1}$$

$$BPM = Frequency * 60 \tag{2}$$

11.3.3   Fall Detection System

The MPU-6050 sensor [18] is used for detection of fall of human body. It has 3-axis accelerometer that uses separate proof masses for each axis. Acceleration along a particular axis induces displacement on the corresponding proof mass, and capacitive sensors detect the displacement differentially. The MPU-6050's architecture reduces the accelerometer's susceptibility to fabrication variations as well as to thermal drift. When the device is placed on a flat surface, it will measure 0 g on the X- and Y-axes and +1 g on the Z-axis. The accelerometers' scale factor is calibrated at the factory and is nominally independent of supply voltage.

Each sensor has a dedicated sigma-delta ADC for providing digital outputs. The full scale range of the digital output can be adjusted to ±2 g, ±4 g, ±8 g, or ±16 g. The Digital Motion Processor (DMP) is embedded within the MPU-6050 which offloads computation of motion processing algorithms from the host processor. The DMP acquires data from accelerometers, gyroscopes, and third party sensors such as magnetometers, and processes the data. The resulting data can be read from the DMP's registers, or can be buffered in a FIFO.

The DMP has access to one of the MPU's external pins, which can be used for generating interrupts. The purpose of the DMP is to offload both timing requirements and processing power from the host processor. Motion processing algorithms should run at a high rate, often around 200Hz, in order to provide accurate results with low latency. The DMP can be used as a tool in order to minimize power, simplify timing, simplify the software architecture, and save valuable MIPS on the host processor for use in the application.

The MPU-6050 contains a 1,024-byte FIFO register that is accessible via the Serial Interface. The FIFO configuration register determines which data is written into the FIFO. Possible choices include gyro data, accelerometer data, temperature readings, auxiliary sensor readings, and FSYNC input. A FIFO counter keeps track of how many bytes of valid data are contained in the FIFO. The FIFO register supports burst reads. The interrupt function may be used to determine when new data is available. The bias and LDO section generates the internal supply and the reference voltages and currents required by the MPU-6050. Its two inputs are an unregulated VDD of 2.375 to 3.46 V and a VLOGIC logic reference supply voltage of 1.71 V to VDD. The LDO output is bypassed by a capacitor at REGOUT. The MPU-6050 has an auxiliary I 2C bus for communicating to an off-chip 3-axis digital sensors. This bus has two operating modes namely I2C Master Mode and Pass-Through mode. In I2C Master Mode the MPU-6050 acts as a master to any external sensors connected to the auxiliary I2C bus whereas in Pass-Through Mode the MPU-6050 directly connects the primary and auxiliary I 2C buses together, allowing the system processor to directly communicate with any external sensors.

In I2C Master Mode the I2C Master can be configured to read up to 24 bytes from up to 4 auxiliary sensors and a fifth sensor can be configured to work single byte read/write mode. In Pass-Through mode the auxiliary I2C bus control logic of the MPU-6050 is disabled, and the auxiliary I2C pins AUX_DA and AUX_CL (Pins 6 and 7) are connected to the main I2C bus (Pins 23 and 24) through analog switches which is useful for configuring the external sensors, or for keeping the MPU-6050 in a low-power mode when only the external sensors are used.

Accelerometer can be used to detect fall of human body. Accelerometer has three axis namely x-axis, y-axis, z-axis. Any 2 axis is sufficient to detect fall of human body. When the accelerometer is placed straight coinciding with standing position of human body, the person is having no issues and no fall is detected. When the accelerometer is deviated from the rest position to front or rear maximum then the human is said to have fallen down. There also exist chances at times human tend to fall sideways right or left. All the possible chances of fall are considered and rough readings of any two axis of accelerometer are taken at all corresponding positions of fall. With the help of program we incorporate the readings into the code burnt in nodeMCU ESP8266 using which we detect the fall of human body.

11.3.4   Temperature Detection System

The LM35 (Figure 11.5) series are precision integrated-circuit temperature sensors, whose output voltage is linearly proportional to the Celsius

Figure 11.5 LM35.

(Centigrade) temperature. The LM35 thus has an advantage over linear temperature sensors calibrated in °Kelvin, as the user is not required to subtract a large constant voltage from its output to obtain convenient Centigrade scaling. The LM35 does not require any external calibration or trimming to provide typical accuracies of ±1/4 °C at room temperature and ±3/4 °C over a full −55 to +150 °C temperature range. Low cost is assured by trimming and calibration at the wafer level. The LM35's low output impedance, linear output, and precise inherent calibration make interfacing to readout or control circuitry especially easy. It can be used with single power supplies, or with plus and minus supplies. As it draws only 60 μA from its supply, it has very low self-heating, less than 0.1 °C in still air.

The LM35 is rated to operate over a −55° to +150 °C temperature range, while the LM35C is rated for a −40° to +110 °C range (−10° with improved accuracy). Features are calibrated directly in °Celsius (Centigrade), Linear + 10.0 mV/°C, scale factor 0.5 °C, accuracy guarantee able (at +25 °C), Rated for full −55° to +150 °C range n Suitable for remote applications n Low cost due to wafer-level trimming operates from 4 to 30 volts, less than 60 μA current drain, low self-heating 0.08 °C in still air n Nonlinearity only ±1/4 °C typical low impedance output, 0.1 Ω for 1 mA load. The sensor circuitry is sealed and therefore it is not subjected to oxidation and other processes. With LM35, temperature can be measured more accurately than with a thermistor.

The skin temperature measurement is done using an integrated circuit, the LM35temperature sensor. The Sensor gives an analog output depending on the measured temperature. This voltage has to be measured by the microcontroller using an Analog-to-Digital converter

Figure 11.6 Accelerometer sensor MPU6050.

(ADC). This sensor is mounted within the wrist strap, positioned in such a way that it is in contact with the skin, allowing it to measure the external temperature of the skin. From the skin temperature, the body temperature is estimated. There can be different methods to estimate the exact body temperature from skin temperature, but with a rough estimation usually the body temperature is 5.1 °C higher than skin temperature when the body temperature is measured at the ear by the National DM-T2-A thermometer used by a general practitioner compared to the skin temperature. Because an exact measurement of body temperature is not required, this method is suitable. Rather, relative changes are monitored within set threshold, which sets off the alarm. This allows the device to detect changes in body temperature that could indicate the patient is undergoing any of the following conditions: trauma, injury, heart attack, stroke, heat exhaustion, and burns. The Output of the ADC has to be converted into the right value. The accuracy of the measurement is shown in Figure 11.6 and is seen that at steady state the error is within 0.5 °C.

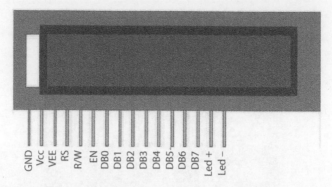

Figure 11.7 LCD pin configuration.

11.3.5   LCD Specification

Liquid Crystal Display screen is an electronic display module and find a wide range of applications. A 16×2 LCD display is very basic module and is very commonly used in various devices and circuits. These modules are preferred over seven segments and other multi segment LEDs. The reasons being: LCDs are economical; easily programmable; have no limitation of displaying special & even custom characters, animations and so on.

A 16×2 LCD means it can display 16 characters per line and there are 2 such lines. In this LCD each character is displayed in 5×7 pixel matrix. This LCD has two registers, namely, Command and Data. The command register stores the command instructions given to the LCD. A command is an instruction given to LCD to do a predefined task like initializing it, clearing its screen, setting the cursor position, controlling display, etc. The data register stores the data to be displayed on the LCD. The data is the ASCII value of the character to be displayed on the LCD. The pin configuration is shown in the Figure 11.7 and Table 11.2.

11.3.6   ADC Specification

MCP3208 (Figurer 11.8) ADC is used along with MCU ESP8266. MCP 3208 works at V_{DD} from +2.7 V to +5.5 V Power Supply, DGND stands for Digital Ground, AGND stands for Analog Ground, CH0–CH7 are Analog Inputs, CLK stands for Serial Clock, DIN is Serial Data Input pin, DOUT is Serial Data Output pin. CS/SHDN stands for Chip Select/Shutdown Input pin, VREF is Reference Voltage Input pin. The Pin configuration of MCP3208 is given in Table 11.3.

Table 11.2 LCD pin configuration.

Pin no.	Function	Name
1	Ground (0 V)	Ground
2	Supply voltage; 5 V (4.7 V–5.3 V)	V_{CC}
3	Contrast adjustment; through a variable resistor	V_{EE}
4	Selects command register when low; and data register when high	Register Select
5	Low to write to the register; High to read from the register	Read/write
6	Sends data to data pins when a high to low pulse is given	Enable
7	8-bit data pins	DB0
8		DB1
9		DB2
10		DB3
11		DB4
12		DB5
13		DB6
14		DB7
15	Backlight V_{CC} (5 V)	Led+
16	Backlight Ground (0 V)	Led-

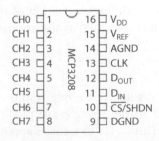

Figure 11.8 MCP3208 ADC pin configuration.

Table 11.3 MCP 3208 pin description.

PIN	Description
DGND	Digital ground connection to internal digital circuitry.
AGND	Analog ground connection to internal analog circuitry.
CH0–CH7	Analog inputs for channels 0–7 for the multiplexed inputs. Each pair of channels can be programmed to be used as two independent channels in single-ended mode or as a single pseudo-differential input, where one channel is IN+ and one channel is IN.
Serial Clock (CLK)	The SPI clock pin is used to initiate a conversion and clock out each bit of the conversion as it takes place.
Serial Data Input (DIN)	The SPI port serial data input pin is used to load channel configuration data into the device.
Serial Data Output (DOUT)	The SPI serial data output pin is used to shift out the results of the A/D conversion. Data will always change on the falling edge of each clock as the conversion takes place.

11.4 Results and Discussions

11.4.1 System Implementation

The proposed system is kept insulated in a box as shown in the Figure 11.9 and it is tied to patients arm as shown in the Figure 11.10.

11.4.2 Fall Detection Results

The fall detection values for different position of the sensor are recorded for a period of time and it is tabulated as shown in Table 11.4.

11.4.3 ThingSpeak

The temperature sensor results, pulse rate results and fall detection sensor results are evaluated using ThingSpeak platform. ThingSpeak is an open source Internet of Things (IoT) website application and Application Programming Interface (API) to store and retrieve data from sensors using

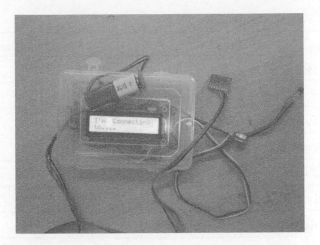

Figure 11.9 Proposed system.

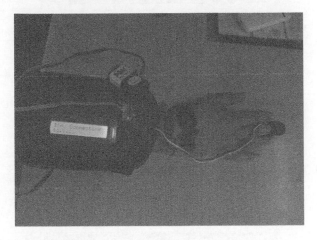

Figure 11.10 System fitted into arm.

the Hypertext Transfer Protocol (HTTP) and MQ Telemetry Transport (MQTT) protocol over the Internet or via a Local Area Network (LAN). ThingSpeak enables the creation of sensor logging applications, location tracking applications, and a social network of things with status updates. The recorded sensor values are shown in Figures 11.11, 11.12 and 11.13. The results can also be downloaded to a computer in different formats from ThingSpeak servers. A dashboard view of ThingSpeak server with Channel ID 466958 is shown in the Figure 11.14.

Table 11.4 Fall detection results.

		Axis			Recorded value		
S. no.	Position	X	Y	Z	X	Y	Z
1.	Face-Up	0	0	90	331	335	406
2.	Face-Down	0	180	180	329	327	271
3.	Face-Side	0	90	90	263	335	338
4.	Face-Side	0	−90	−90	266	329	341
5.	Left Tilt	90	0	−90	333	337	410
6.	Right Tilt	−90	0	90	263	335	338

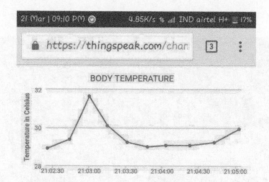

Figure 11.11 Temperature results in ThingSpeak web application.

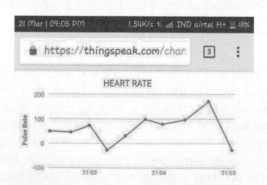

Figure 11.12 Heart rate results in ThingSpeak web application.

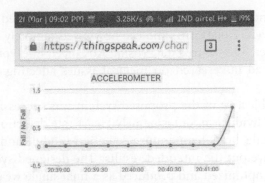

Figure 11.13 Accelerometer results in ThingSpeak web application.

Figure 11.14 Dashboard view for channel ID: 466958.

11.5 Conclusion

A low cost remote patient monitoring system was designed, implemented and presented around the concept of Internet of Things. Personal physiological data from the patient is collected that simulates fall detection, body temperature and the heart rate. The readings are collected in a database of ThingSpeak (IOT platform) and can be viewed remotely by a doctor or Healthcare giver. The secured data (using Advanced Encryption Standard) can also be used in research on medical issues affecting the elderly or chronically ill.

The main objective of the proposed system was successfully achieved. All the four individual modules namely Heart rate detection module, fall detection module, body temperature detection module and remote viewing module gave out the intended results. The designed system modules can further be optimized and produced as a final single wearable module. More important fact that came up during design is that all the circuit components used in the remote health detection system are available locally and are of affordable cost. With development in the integrated circuit industry, Micro Electro Mechanical Systems (MEMs) and microcontrollers have become affordable; have increased processing speeds, miniaturized and power efficient. This has led to increased development of embedded systems that the healthcare specialists are adopting. These embedded systems have also been adopted in the Smartphone technology too.

With increased internet penetration in most developing countries through mobile phones, its uses such as Internet of things (IoT) will become adopted at a faster rate. The Remote Health Care system utilizes these concepts to come up with a system for better quality of life for people in society. From an engineering perspective, the work has several concepts acquired from the electronics engineering study and is being practically applied.

11.6 Future Scope

The following are the list of potential recommendations for future exploration.

- In fall detection, a gyro-meter and Global Positioning System (GPS) sensor can be added to pinpoint accurately the location.
- Designing a smartphone application to read on-board sensors and remotely detect physiological data.
- Further investigations can be made by incorporating many sensors to acquire physiological data such as diabetes, locomotion issues, fitness tracking and internal organ related issues.

- Buying a channel in ThingSpeak is highly recommended for getting instant data updates every second, sending 90,000 messages a day, more number of users, creating alert system, control and talkback features.

References

1. Asthana, S., Megahed, A., Strong, R., A recommendation system for proactive health monitoring using IoT and wearable technologies, in: *2017 IEEE International Conference on AI & Mobile Services (AIMS)*, IEEE, pp. 14–21, 2017, June.
2. Arai, K., Wearable physical and psychological health monitoring system, in: *2013 Science and Information Conference*, IEEE, pp. 133–138, 2013, October.
3. http://www.devicelink.com/mddi/archive/04/09/018.html, Oct. 15, 2004
4. Milenković, A., Otto, C., Jovanov, E., Wireless sensor networks for personal health monitoring: Issues and an implementation. *Comput. Commun.*, 29, 13–14, 2521–2533, 2006.
5. https://wiki.analog.com/university/courses/alm1k/alm-lab-heart-rate-mon
6. http://www.ti.com/lit/ds/symlink/lm35.pdf
7. Noury, N., Fleury, A., Rumeau, P., Bourke, A.K., Laighin, G.O., Rialle, V., Lundy, J.E., Fall detection-principles and methods, in: *2007 29th Annual International Conference of the IEEE Engineering in Medicine and Biology Society*, IEEE, pp. 1663–1666, 2007, August.
8. Arai, K., Wearable physical and psychological health monitoring system, in: *2013 Science and Information Conference*, IEEE, pp. 133–138, 2013, October.
9. https://www.alert-1.com/content/fall-detection-technology/1390.
10. Saranya, V., Shankar, S., Kanagachidambaresan, G.R., Energy efficient clustering scheme (EECS) for wireless sensor network with mobile sink. *Wireless Pers. Commun.*, 100, 4, 1553–1567, 2018.
11. Kanagachidambaresan, G.R. and Chitra, A., Fail safe fault tolerant mechanism for wireless body sensor network (WBSN). *Wireless Pers. Commun.*, 80, 1, 247–260, 2015.
12. Kanagachidambaresan, G.R. and Chitra, A., TA-FSFT thermal aware fail safe fault tolerant algorithm for wireless body sensor network. *Wireless Pers. Commun.*, 90, 4, 1935–1950, 2016.
13. Dhulipala, V.S. and Kanagachidambaresan, G.R., Cardiac care assistance using self configured sensor network—A remote patient monitoring system. *J. Inst. Eng. India Ser. B*, 95, 2, 101–106, 2014.
14. Esakki, B., Ganesan, S., Mathiyazhagan, S., Ramasubramanian, K., Gnanasekaran, B., Son, B., Choi, J.S., Design of Amphibious Vehicle for Unmanned Mission in Water Quality Monitoring Using Internet of Things. *Sensors*, 18, 10, 3318, 2018.

15. Elango, K. and Muniandi, K., VLSI Implementation of Area and Energy Efficient FFT/IFFT core for MIMO OFDM applications, in: *Annals of Telecommunications*, Springer, pp. 1958–9395, December 2019.
16. Elango, K. and Muniandi, K., Hardware Implementation of FFT/IFFT algorithms incorporating efficient computational elements, *J. Electr. Eng. Technol.*, Springer, 2093-7423, 14, 4, 1717–1721, April 2019.
17. https://pulsesensor.com/
18. https://playground.arduino.cc/Main/MPU-6050/

12

IoT-Based Secure Smart Infrastructure Data Management

R. Poorvadevi[1], M. Kowsigan[2*], P. Balasubramanie[3]
and J. Rajeshkumar[4]

*[1]Department of Computer Science and Engineering,
Sri Chandrasekharendra Saraswathi Viswa Mahavidyalaya, Kanchipuram
[2]Department of Computer Science and Engineering,
SRM Institute of Science and Technology
[3]Department of Computer Technology, Kongu Engineering College
[4]Department of Information Technology,
SNS College of Technology*

Abstract

Internet of Things (IoT) connects millions of objects to connect, share and communicate the data across the wireless network. The application of IoT on the smart city management to improve the quality of the lifestyle through connected devices. The network of sensors connected on the wireless space collaboratively collect the data of the object intended for tracking and monitoring. The smart city infrastructure developments making use of this advanced connected devices to increase the performance of smart communication ecosystem model. The smart sensors are deployed on the space where the real-time analysis initiated to trigger the events appropriately. The minimization of resource consumption and maximize the utilization of smart device becomes the major objective of any smart city development model. The data collected through IoT sensors are pushed to cloud storage system where the real-time analysis will take place by using the strength of the cloud infrastructure. The artificial intelligence-based machine learning algorithms applied over the data collected through IoT sensors for decision making process.

Keywords: Smart city management, smart communication, wireless network

Corresponding author: mkowsigan@gmail.com

G. R. Kanagachidambaresan (ed.) Role of Edge Analytics in Sustainable Smart City Development: Challenges and Solutions, (243–256) © 2020 Scrivener Publishing LLC

12.1   Introduction

The smart city-based infrastructure management system improves the quality of the service provided by the government and individual through smart IoT based applications. The IoT applications are applied in the various level of infrastructure development which includes smart home automation, smart energy consumption, smart transportation and smart water resource management etc., the application involves reduced management cost, resource consumption and wastage management.

The open network with wireless communication introduces number of security issues related to the sensor communication. The collaborative multiple sensor interaction must be coordinated effectively to avoid the conflicts on the data transmitted to the server. The sensor with minimal security enforcement leads to the loss of control over the confidential data.

The private data captured by the public sensors must be protected from the number of security breaches. The compromised sensor may leak the data to the malicious intruders. The sensor on the collaborative environment is very much essential for the smart city infrastructure.

12.1.1   List of Security Threats Related to the Smart IoT Network

- Compromised IoT sensor node
- Compromised Wireless Sensor Network
- Intruder penetration
- Traffic analysis
- Data access control mechanism.

The proposed research article focuses on the data security and privacy on the IoT infrastructure while establishing the smart city applications. The secure sensor and communication devices ensure the confidentiality of the smart city data management process.

12.1.2   Major Application Areas of IoT

- Consumer applications (E.g.: smart phones, smart watches and smart homes)
- Business applications (E.g.: smart Intelligent cameras, vehicles location identity, Logistics management, smart sensors)
- Governmental applications (E.g.: Smart Infrastructure development, traffic monitoring and disaster recovery alerts).

12.1.3   IoT Threats and Security Issues

Centralized instruction and control along with APIs are efficiently controls the real time process of IoT operations. The applications centralized nature will create a number of opportunities for attacks in the IoT service access platform [1].

- Unpatched vulnerabilities
- Weak authentication
- Vulnerable APIs.

12.1.4   Unpatched Vulnerabilities

It focusing on the connection and sharing based issues or the demand from the users to manually perform the software updates operations and allow the device to newly discover the various security vulnerabilities.

12.1.5   Weak Authentication

Easily predictable passwords are the major problem for occurring weak authentication. When the devices are left in the remote access location, automatically attackers are trying to the steal the information.

12.1.6   Vulnerable API's

A common gateway to command and control center (C&C center) based API's are targeted in man-in-the middle attacks and DDoS attacks [2].

12.2   Types of Threats to Users

- Data Theft
  Due to vast amounts of data generation and process in IoT device, an individual user's information like e-browsing history, purchase information and transaction details and other personal health information are easily hacked by the intruder.
- Physical Harm
  When sensitive data are extracted from the IoT devices may find physical threats to IoT platform [9].

12.3   Internet of Things Security Management

An IoT device makes the application with more specific security and higher level priority with the support of internet ecosystem.

For various device specific users, they will specify basic security level best practices and provide the option for changing default security passwords and blocking unwanted remotes access.

Vendors and device manufacturers, on the other hand, should take a broader approach and invest heavily in securing IoT management tools. Steps that should be taken include:

- Automatically monitoring and identifying devices running with outdated software and Operating Systems.
- Creation of smart and challenging password.
- Removal of unused ports and device access through remote device.
- Implementing safe and secure access control policy for APIs.
- Protecting end to end communication from compromise attempts and Distributed Denial of attacks.

All the applications are process specific contents and the C&C center will process the segment into the higher level of security and privacy implication parameters. It can be accessed via a connected peer group system.

12.3.1   Managing IoT Devices

To Manage IoT operations the function should maintain the internal inbuilt software and external communication with interfacing devices.

The deployment of IoT system must address the number of challenges which includes an IoT system and its connected devices security, interoperability, power and processing capabilities, scalability and availability. These issues are addressed through either by adopting standard protocols or using services offered by a vendor.

Figure 12.1 shows the functional interaction among the various IoT sensors with IoT-based smart objects. The IoT edge devices are connected with the IoT cloud server and also provide the additional view of managing data under the multi cloud strategy. The process of software maintenance, configurations, firmware updates to patch bugs

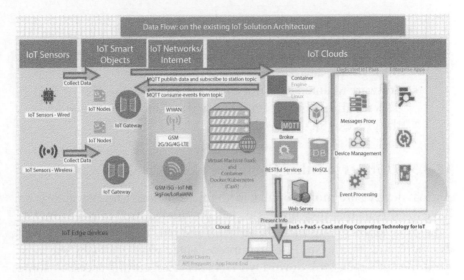

Figure 12.1 IoT based secure solution architecture for data management.

and vulnerabilities are highlighted in the architecture. The provision of resources and authentication of device identity performed through secure technology.

12.3.2   Role of External Devices in IoT Platform

- Communication Devices
  Communication devices interfaced with application program interface to collect and transfer the data across the sensor and application server. Once the device manufacturer announces its API, the other devices or applications can make use of this for data communication. The remote devices are controlled through this API.
- Provisioning and Authentication
  Provisioning: It is a process of registering a device into the IoT infrastructure.
  Authentication: It is a process of verifying the device credentials which is registered under the IoT infrastructure.
- Configuration and Control
  Configuration control ensures the various configurable parameters are performed with the knowledge and consent of management.

- Monitoring and Diagnostics
  The abnormal and normal behaviour of the device interaction and communication can be monitored and identified through this device.
- Software Maintenance and Updates
  This identifies the system security flaws and bugs related to the process [8].

12.3.3   Threats to Other Computer Networks

As IoT devices are more popular in the field of smart infrastructure, so have the threats that they pose. This has manifested itself in all manner of cyber-attacks, including widespread spam and phishing campaigns, as well as Dodo's attacks. This leads to an unprecedented wave of attacks, the most notorious of which took down Dyn DNS services, cutting access to some of the most popular domains in the world including Etsy, GitHub, Netflix, Spotify and Twitter.

Botnets:
Cybercriminals can utilize botnets to attack IoT devices that are connected to several other devices such as laptops, and smart phones.

Denial of service:
Denial of service can be used to slow down or disable a service to hurt the reputation of an organization.

Man-in-the-middle:
With MITM an attacker can intercept communication between Multiple IoT devices which leads to critical devices malfunctions.

Identity and data theft:
Hacker can attack Iot devices such as smart watches, smart meters, and smart home devices to gain sensitive information about several users and organizations.

Social engineering:
Personally identifiable information can be illegally accessed by attackers to gain confidential information such as bank details. Purchase history, and home address for social engineering attacks.

Advanced persistent threats:
A cybercriminal can target Iot devices to gain access to personal or corporate networks.

Ransomware:
Hacker can lock out users from their Iot-enabled devices and refuse to grant access until they receive a ransom.

Remote recording:
Attackers can use zero-day exploits in lot devices to secretly record audio and video footage [10].

12.4   Significance of IoT Security

The lack of security among the IoT device is the major issue on the development of smart city infrastructure. The unstable market of smart electronic devices makes the process more complicate. The security can be given low priority as the focus is on time-to-market and return-on-investment metrics.

A lack of awareness among consumers and businesses is also a major obstacle to security, with the convenience and cost-saving benefits of IoT tech appearing to outweigh the potential risks of data breaches or device hacking. Figure 12.2 shows the schematic representation of IoT Security.

12.4.1   Aspects of Workplace Security

1. Physical access control
2. Physical surveillance
3. Badges

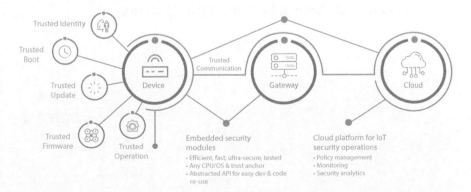

Figure 12.2 Schematic representation of IoT security.

4. Tokens
5. Security lighting
6. Alarm system.

12.4.2   Important IoT Security Breaches and IoT Attacks

Security experts have long warned of the potential risk of large numbers of unsecured devices connected to the internet since the IoT concept first originated in the late 1990s. A number of attacks subsequently have made headlines, from refrigerators and TVs being used to send spam to hackers infiltrating baby monitors and talking to children. It is important to note that many of the IoT hacks don't target the devices themselves, but rather use IoT devices as an entry point into the larger network. Attacks on industrial networks have only continued, with malware such as Crash Override/Industry over, Triton and VPN Filter targeting vulnerable IoT and industrial IoT systems [3].

12.5   IoT Security Tools and Legislation

There are many IoT security frameworks, but no single enterprise-accepted standard is currently available. The easy implementation of an IoT device security system can help, however; tools and checklists are available to help businesses develop and implement IoT device security. The GSM Association, the IoT Device Security Foundation, the Industrial Internet Consortium, and others have published such frameworks. A public service announcement FBI Alert Number I-091015-PSA was released on September 2015 by the Federal Bureau of Investigation to warn about the possible vulnerabilities of IoT devices, to offer consumers' safety and advocacy recommendations. Figure 12.3 shows the block diagram for designing IoT Security.

Figure 12.3 Block diagram for designing IoT security.

The IoT Cyber security Implementation Act was passed by Congress in August 2017, which would restrict the use of default passwords, unknown vulnerabilities and a system for fixing apps for IoT Device Security sold in the US government. It set out a foundation for security measures that all manufacturers should take when they created devices sold to the government [7].

12.6 Protection of IoT Systems and Devices

12.6.1 IoT Issues and Security Challenges

The major issue faced by any IoT based application is security. The data security and privacy ensures the retention of end user in the field of IoT. The following are the most common security issues related to IoT:

- Data Privacy

The IoT represents collection of data storage in cloud, and analysis mechanisms in enhanced manner. Any device connected to the Internet, with more elements requiring protection, including the network, device, infrastructure or the application.

- Authentication and Authorization

The Internet of Things Authenticate the data received from the sensor through some security algorithms. The authentication process ensures the data privacy. The further level of analysis work take into picture from the data verified through authentication process.

- Encryption

It is the process of converting data from one form to another by applying number of rotations and translation over the data to make it unreadable format. The standard encryption algorithms are user to perform this type of conversion. This type of operation protects the data from the attackers while in motion and rest. The decryption algorithm is used to recover the encrypted data at the other side to get it original data [4].

- Traffic Analysis

Monitor and understand the data format while it is in process by the attackers. The stream of data formats are analyzed through breached network entity. The lack of security enforcement leads to this type of traffic analysis attack.

- Distributed Denial of Service (DDoS)

Overload the particular network communication channel to restrict the data exchange between the peer ends fall under the Distributed Denial of Service (DDoS). This type of services makes the network unavailable for the authenticated user for the routine communication between the target ends. The inclusion of secure Tunneling and Virtual Private Network (VPN) etc., avoid this type of security breaches.

- Security and Privacy Attack on the Data

The sensitive data leakage is a major issue in any open interface device. The government and confidential data leakage lead into number of challenges. The data leakage by the authorized user becomes the more challenging part as compared to the attacker.

12.6.2   Providing Secured Connections

Secure connections are achieved through deployment of private VPN networks. The IoT devices connected to the internet lose its control over the data. The minimization of sharing public network will restrict the number of security breaches over the communication channels. However, the trick isn't to connect the internet to them and that is the reason why you would want to use a VPN or virtual private network. However, it is not enough. For more safety, you will require a VPN that is ideal for your device. For example, if you are accessing internet using MacBook, you will need to look for the best VPN suited for Mac. It's one of the most effective ways to connect your device to the internet securely.

Securing the Passwords

Easy guessing password open the number of security challenges to the data privacy. Very often password changes also lead into the complex password maintenance. It is hard to remember lengthy password and dynamic changes. The user must try to use the phrase for password or user can also use password manager. The best passwords are the ones that contain uppercase letters, special characters, numbers, lowercase letters, and so on. If user password is longer, then it's better.

Resource Access

Accessing the limited resources on the secure smart infrastructure need to identity the device uniquely. The identity of the device limits the access of resources at various levels.

Updates
The customer expectations over the regular device security updates are increases a lot. The manufacturers also need to work hard to improve their products by releasing the new updates regularly. This updates will ensure the quality of the secure end devices in the IoT infrastructure.

Cloud Services
The cloud computing technology allows the end user to create, deploy and provision the computing resources like server, storage and network etc., from the remote location at any time. The cloud security is the one of the major challenge need to be addressed in an effective way to ensure the hassle free environment for the cloud user.

UPnP
Standard Universal Plug and Play, which make devices including routers, cameras or printers vulnerable to attack from the cyber-attacks. It helps in setting up devices, yet from a security perspective, it's best for you to consider turning off UPnP [5].

12.7   Five Ways to Secure IoT Devices

- Start with Your Router

A secure smart home, therefore, starts with your router. It is the hub that connects all your devices to the IoT and enables them to operate. Most

Figure 12.4 Smart router device.

people use the router that their ISP provided them with, however, it's always best to invest in a router that is better and offers a higher degree of security as standard. There is nothing wrong with using the router your ISP provided, but it's not going to be massively secure [11]. Figure 12.4 shows the smart router device.

- Create a Secondary or 'Guest' Network

All your Wi-Fi router's networks should be secured with a strong encryption method and robust password. For routers, the standard and most secure encryption method is called WPA2. This should always be used, even for guest networks.

For passwords, avoid things that are common and easy to guess. A strong password is composed of letters, numbers, and symbols, and each network should have a unique one. You can use a password manager to help you remember them all. Never use your router's default username and password.

- Check Your IoT Device Settings and Keep Them Updated

Avoid putting off software updates as these are often patches for security vulnerabilities. Many IoT devices will prompt you when an update is available, but it's good due diligence to check manufacturer websites often.

- Enable Two-Factor Authentication

Two-factor authentication is an additional security layer on top of a device's password that requires secondary authentication—a one-time code sent via email or SMS—before access is granted. When used properly, two-factor authentication can stop the bad guys gaining access to your accounts and taking control of your IoT devices [6]. Figure 12.5 shows the two factor authentication.

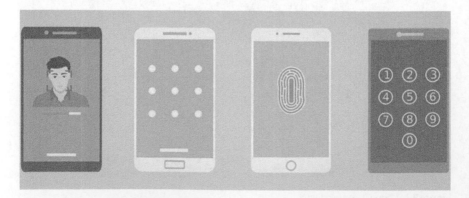

Figure 12.5 Two factor authentication.

- Disable UPnP Features

IoT devices tend to have Universal Plug in and Play (UPnP) features, enabling different devices to find and connect to one another. Whilst this is convenient and eliminates the need to configure each device individually, the protocols rely on local networks to connect to each other and these are vulnerable to third-party attackers. When an attack occurs, UPnP lets multiple devices be accessed at the same time.

12.8   Conclusion

The above chapter listed out various security threats in the aspect of smart city management. Protections of various IoT device identity and security techniques are suggested at various levels.

References

1. Sha, K., Wei, W., Yang, T.A., Wang, Z., Shi, W., On security challenges and open issues in Internet of Things. *Future Gener. Comp. Sy.*, 83, 326–337, 2018.
2. Yuchen Yang, H.Z., Wu, L., Yin, G., Li, L., A survey on security and privacy issues in internet-of-things. *2015 10th Int. Conf. Internet Technol. Secur. Trans.*, IEEE, vol. 4, pp. 202–207, 2015.
3. Tewari, A., Gupta, B.B., Security, privacy and trust of different layers in Internet-of-Things (IoTs) framework. *Future Gener. Comp. Sy.*, 1–13, 2018, 10.1016/j.future.2018.04.027.
4. Ferrag, M.A., Maglaras, L.A., Janicke, H., Jiang, J., Authentication Protocols for Internet of Things: A Comprehensive Survey. *Secur. Commun. Netw.*, 2017, 1–41, 2017.
5. Glissa, G., Meddeb, A., 6LowPSec: An End-to-End Security Protocol for 6LoWPAN. *Ad Hoc Netw.*, 82, 100–112, 2018.
6. Riahi Sfar, A., Natalizio, E., Challal, Y., Chtourou, Z., A roadmap for security challenges in the Internet of Things Digit. *Commun. Netw.*, 4, 2, 118–137, 2018.
7. Gao, H., Study of the application for the security state assessment about the internet of things based on grey correlation algorithm. *J. Manuf. Autom.*, 34, 11, 2012.
8. Lin, J., Yu, W., Zhang, N., Yang, X., Zhang, H., Zhao, W., A survey on internet of things: Architecture, enabling technologies, security and privacy, and applications. *IEEE Internet Things*, 4, 5, 1125–1142, 2017.
9. Yang, Y., Wu, L., Yin, G., Li, L., Zhao, H., A survey on security and privacy issues in Internet-of-Things. *IEEE Internet Things*, 4, 5, 1250–1258, 2017.

10. Deogirikar, J. and Vidhate, A., Security attacks in IoT: A survey, in: *2017 International Conference on I-SMAC (IoT in Social, Mobile, Analytics and Cloud)(I-SMAC)*, IEEE, pp. 32–37, 2017.
11. Alam, M.M., Malik, H., Khan, M.I., Pardy, T., Kuusik, A., Le Moullec, Y., A survey on the roles of communication technologies in IoT-based personalized healthcare applications. *IEEE Access*, 6, 36611–36631, 2018.
12. Kowsigan, M. and Balasubramanie, P., A novel resource clustering model to develop an efficient wireless personal cloud environment. *Turk. J. Electr. Eng. Co.*, 27, 2156–2169, 2018.

A Study of Addiction Behavior for Smart Psychological Health Care System

V. Sabapathi* and K.P. Vijayakumar

SRM Institute of Science and Technology, Kattankulathur, Chennai, India

Abstract

There are diverse relating to addiction vmakers in this digital world. Addiction means regularly things in terms of physically and psychologically. It may be physical object addiction like cigarettes, mobile phones and drugs. It is psychological or virtual addiction such as playing virtual reality games. Addiction may be a passionate thing if it is returns positive results; it may be disease if it returns negative results. Addiction behavior such as virtual games which hides the real world and makes mentally restricted thinking from other things, such as real world issues. Video games and virtual reality games make very controllable and restricted thinking. In other words, these kinds of games reduce thinking power and memory loss to those players. These addictive games motivate the minds to do the things continuously and consistently. This survey chapter mainly focuses on the basic criteria of addiction and addiction points, the factors that influences the addiction behavior, and various types of addiction and their effects.

Keywords: Addiction behaviors, virtual reality games, drug addiction

Corresponding author: sabapathi2000@gmail.com

G. R. Kanagachidambaresan (ed.) Role of Edge Analytics in Sustainable Smart City Development: Challenges and Solutions, (257–272) © 2020 Scrivener Publishing LLC

13.1 Introduction

Factors of addiction content analyzing which was the major role for smart health care system towards psychological addiction are the mentality for making compulsive and addictive process. The addictive mentality has been generated via the exploring the new experience. The new things were induced by peers, family, media and society as well as the environment. Once the feeling of happiness was created the neural system generate the reward system as mesolibmic neural via activation of dopamine. Then, that experience becomes habitual behind the reward of neuro-biological systems. This experience becomes habitual which leads to compulsiveness. Once that experience is different from the previous one, the reward degrades. These things become addictive concerns which may be substance-based addiction disorder (SBA) and when the behavior becomes effects and consequences then we can refer it as behavior-based addiction (BBA).

The organization of this chapter is given as follows. Section 13.2 describes the basic criteria of the addiction and addiction point. In Section 13.3, influencing factors of addiction behavior is explained. Types of addiction and their effects are explained in Section 13.4. Finally Section 13.5 concludes this chapter.

13.2 Basic Criteria of Addiction

Addiction is categorized in terms of psychological and behavior concerns. The addiction factors become consistently made to use them. Addiction may occur

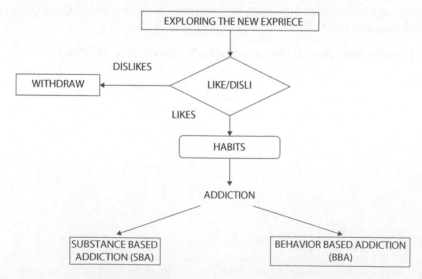

Figure 13.1 Basic addiction criteria.

Figure 13.2 Addiction point.

as a habitual function on substance or non-substance as shown in Figure 13.1. Substance as physical addiction include cigarette, mobile game, alcohol, etc. Non-substance addiction include behaviors like smoking sensation, playing mentality, eating or consuming too much among behavioral level of habits. The addiction happens by the way of stimulating by the age group of peers activity, environment, media, family groups and society, etc.

Exploring new experience is caused by many direct and indirect media. Direct media include the peers, family and the society where the people are part of. These media have higher impact than indirect media. Direct media directly communicate, sharing points as shown in Figure 13.2. These media activities, exploring experience, relationship, behavior have more impact towards the addiction content.

Indirect media refers to communication through various communication technologies or there is no direct communication with each peer. Despite the technology-evolved world, there are numerous ways how marketing media motivates addiction content. For example e-commerce enhances the online shopping addiction which leads to compulsive buying. The media and advertisement broadcasting to the adults and society lead to an indirect addiction content promotion.

13.3   Influencing Factors of Addiction Behavior

There are many direct and indirect factors that influence and stimulate addictive behavior. Some of these major factors are shown in Figure 13.3 and are described as the basic and fundamental of addictive behaviors and their influences.

13.3.1   Peers Influence

Based on age group and gender, there are different types of factors that influence people with addiction in the way of physical and behavior

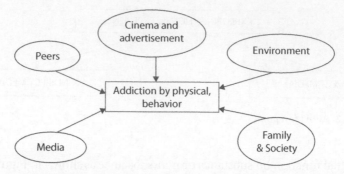

Figure 13.3 Key factors to influence the addiction behavior.

concerns. During childhood or in the 3–10 age groups, there will be physical gaming addiction like video game addiction. The playing will be considered behavior addiction.

Regardless of age group, the peers are considered as a major influence towards the physical or non-substance addiction. The addiction actually starts from physical and become behaviors as habits. For example, kids are eager to eat dark chocolate because of physical attraction, and then it becomes an eating habit. Later on it becomes an addiction. In this context, the addiction is known as passionate. Based on age group, peers behaviors, and their addiction, this can be categorized as following peers who introduce their experiences to their friends, which will be physical or behavior stimuli to others.

Table 13.1 shows that based on age group, there are numerous kinds of addiction factors which are explored or introduced to the child either by peers or society. In childhood playing environment or where they doesn't understand their addiction behaviors and influences. Grown-up day's peers and society even more add to new kind of stimuli factors to make addictive content over the people. The basic addiction and their consequences have to be evaluated for further knowledge.

13.3.2   Environment Influence

There is major influence from the environment, that is, the geographic locality. If a child is born in an urban place or city, their entire activity would comprise playing, eating or consuming things are different. Living in urban or rural areas in India there are playing of outdoor games and eating more natural food. In the city there will be more likely indoor games like video games in the gadgets. Food consumption would likely include processed or preserved food. Based on locality, climate, friends, playing games becomes and plays a vital role as addiction factors.

Table 13.1 Based on age group and their addiction behaviors.

S. no.	Age group	Element of addiction	Stage of addiction	Physical or behavior addiction concern
1	3–13	Video game or indoor game	Physical or psychological attraction over the addiction element	Explore based on availability Ex: videogames, cricket, chocolates
		Outdoor or real games		
		Food cravings		
2	14–21	Peers influence	Taking guidelines from peers and make as habitual	Due to peers, media they can influence and due to physical concerns changes in psychological behavior
		Media influences		
		Cinema casting influences		
3	22 and above	Consuming alcohol	Habitual becomes real time, compulsive activity	Habits become compulsive which habitual becomes reality consequences
		Illegal activities		
		Reality realization		

13.3.3   Media Influence

There is a major influence by the media in this digitized decade like film, advertisement, social media, and internet. The internet has many addicting content such as web games, social media, pornography, online shopping and communication, etc. These become a high-level starting origin for physical and virtual addiction habits. For example, one can learn about the world through the media and inform them of current happenings. But unfortunately, rather than positive news, they are immersed with the negative news. Advertisement gets easily popular or as a major talk. Due to media influence, an adult can easily be addicted. Web games can psychologically make them into group of players virtually connected through an online game series. This results to adults with very narrow minds as controlled by virtual games. In cinemas, there were castings doing something like drug-taking which attract adults into doing the same and influence them as habits. Pornography videos as pools are readily available in web servers. Majority of adults have smart phones with their hand. These smart phones provide all the information regardless of their age group, which tempt adults to watch pornographic videos. It causes illegal or unusual sex activity at a very early stage in their adult life. Figure 13.3 shows the basic and fundamental of addictive behaviors and their influences. It generates positive results like if the habit becomes playing the game well. Based on the consequences of the results of the addiction, the addiction is known as passionate.

13.3.4   Family Group and Society

There is definite relevance between habit of parent and childhood. Occasional drinking, consuming cigarette of parents, family members and society have a major play on an adult's habitual functions. Once a parent consumes a cigarette, there is possibility that their child will have the same smoking habit. The family and friends and most of the people in the society consume alcohol or cigarette means, there is more possibility to have that child have that habit. In this connection there is overall cycle relevance to addiction behavior habits of individual.

13.4   Types of Addiction and Their Effects

Any kind of addiction that is starting is an attempt for exploring a new kind of experience. Once that behavior provides happiness or makes familiarization to the society then it will be the triggering towards the addiction

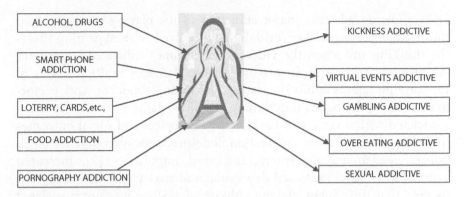

Figure 13.4 Addiction and consequences.

point. Substance-based addiction (SBA) as shown in Figure 13.4 uses substance and has a new experience such as drugs, new kind of foods or other goods. Using substance use disorder, this evolves as habits then the user gets a behavior-based addiction (BBA). Alcohol and other drugs often give a new kind of kick to the user.

Smartphone addiction composites many content to addictive portions such as online gaming, offline gaming, social media addiction, online shopping, pornography watching. Each of these addiction provides a different experience for every smart phone user. Gambling addiction is a kind of addictive event which tends to make money as lucky anxiety, desires. In majority of instances of gambling, a player loses their productive time and their money. Initially an entertainment event becomes a compulsive addictive disorder. Some people who are playing and gambling use numerous kinds of gambling such lottery buying and scratching. Food becomes addictive because of habitual food consumption and genetic disorder. This kind of food addiction cause many health diseases such as obesity, diabetes, blood pressure, etc. Food addicts are heavy food consumers regardless of age or gender. High-triggering foods also become the initial habit for food addiction. Online shopping which influences to buy what the trend is in the market without any necessity. Compulsive and addictive buying is a kind of psychological addiction. Pornography addiction is the tendency of sexual experience viewing and which can cause heterosexual and abnormal sexual behavior. Age group, peers behaviors, and their addiction can be categorized into the following.

13.4.1 Gaming Addiction

During childhood, a child connects through games which may indoor games or outdoor games based on peers and environment influences.

Over a few decades the major addiction in the playing games evolved into virtual gaming as the world digitally evolved. Virtual gaming affects the thinking and when the video game becomes enhanced it becomes pathological when this strong attachment damages multiple levels of functioning such as family life, social functioning, school or work performance, or psychological functioning [1]. Video game addiction has been associated with a variety of negative psychological and social outcomes including decreased life satisfaction, loneliness, social competence [2], poorer academic achievement, increased impulsivity [3], increased aggression [4], and increased depression and anxiety [5]. It is important to note that time spent playing video games alone was not associated with these negative social, emotional, and psychological outcomes and that these negative outcomes are specifically related to video game addiction [6]. Aspects of tolerance and withdrawal are seen with concomitant physical discomfort [7].

13.4.2 Pornography Addiction

Due to the advent of the smartphone and internet many things are easily accessible by adults like information through video, images, news, etc. In recent days, majority of adults having smart phones especially younger ones, are curios and knew about the existence of sexual affairs. Unfortunately, with some of the adults, watching pornography becomes a compulsive disorder. There were many indirect stimuli factors for watching pornography by their peers, media, and society. The unknown things especially while the people are in their adolescent period watch pornography as an entertainment then it will become habitual, This habit provides low self-esteem, anxiety, depression regardless of gender and there were many psychological and emotional things that happens and has an impact with negative consequences. In developed countries, the majority of adults with internet access have seen internet pornography [8–11]. Moreover, in nationally representative studies of adults in the U.S., up to 46% of men and 16% of women are reportedly intentionally consuming internet pornography with in the past week [12]. Together, these findings suggest that internet pornography use is a frequent behavior. However, this use is also controversial, with wide ranging debates about its effects and potentials for harm [13–16]. The abnormal sexual cravings lead to a sexual addiction disorder. It causes multi-partner relationship and sexual addiction. It's an addiction if the abnormal behavior towards the sexual acti1vity regardless gender and age and health condition.

13.4.3   Smart Phone Addiction

Smart phones have a major role for the current digitalized globalization formation. After the advent of internet that often use personal computers, the smart phone arrives. Internet usage was booming. A Smart phone is a handheld device which possesses all information about the users and their interpersonal relevant information like text messages, video, audio, images. The smart phone uses in many aspects such as communication, transactions and financial applications, entertainment applications and information as shown in Figure 13.5 and knowledge gathering. When the people were use mobile phones, when they were used for certain amount of time, when it required and conscious and controllable thing. But addiction in the sense, mobile phone addiction is defined as the disordered capabilities to control impulsive emotions without the impact of intoxicants [17] and was categorized as a behavioral addiction [18, 19]. Smart phone becomes a very active media, virtual market has a pool which has a lot of useful and also unnecessary content. Especially in the adolescents period the smart phone provides as facilitate and which is the major physical device for providing many virtual addictive content to the users.

For the communication purpose there were many applications which connect known and unknowns' friends/peers relationship. These communication applications were good when they interact and exchange useful information regarding business, knowledge and emergency needy. At the same time especially in girls, the social media and other communications

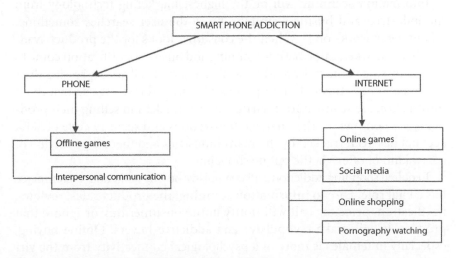

Figure 13.5 Smart phone content for triggers addiction.

applications becomes more dangerous if they were connected unknown persons, it will very pathetic due to malactivity of known or unknown. There is many security issues are arriving due to miscommunication between wrong contacts.

Entertainment purpose applications, there were many applications are make virtual adductors. Watching videos, dating with strangers like entertainment applications in the smart phone provide major gateway. Pornography watching, sexual behaviors, introvert behavior, gaming addiction like that has been increasing which leads to the greatest negative behavior and poor academic performances and low society relevancy. Often during notification checking, a number of entertainment applications have led many to security issues. In social media, sharing photographs has been used for malactivity and information scanning has been a vital role via the entertainment applications.

Business and financial tracking are possible due to the smart phone and arrives to people have via online applications. People can track their financial level and can transform or manipulate their financial accounts via mobile smart banking systems. There were many malware, hijacking money from the account by illegal access as theft happens. Addiction concerns happen when people keep looking at their financial trading via notification and keep on using and connecting to the financial websites. Due to this, the habit becomes an addiction, which will affect those people making them less concentrated to their personal relationship. The stress, depression, anxiety, mood modification become physiological and cognitive issues.

Information scanning will be the highest marketing technology from the industrial and business strategy. Once the user searches something, e-commerce works on it. When the consumer looks for the product available in the market, information scanning and business notification come to their browsing contact. Recently, social media users all are expressing their interest and likes through their photos, videos, and text, etc., so that those information are scanned from virtual market tracks and selling their products via e-commerce. The financial transactions and security code of bank account has been tracked by the many industries and there is possibility of a new kind of offer via the online shopping.

In online shopping addiction and compulsive buying addiction, e-commerce has a vital role. Due to information scanning, the product sales, reviews, notification, price tags all will notify until consumer buy or ignore that product. It will make compulsive and addictive buyers. Online buying, especially in females is more of a psychological connectivity from the virtual attraction of those things in the market of e-commerce. The product seller using tactics and keep on introducing their products in an attractive way to the consumer. Once the buyer likes the product that may be the cosmetics, dress or anything, the seller always advertise and promote which will be the online consume addiction. More than buying the products, due to the mobile applications which create the compulsive buying addiction. Financnial status has been tracked by the many e-commerce industry and they concentrate for planning of their marketing strategy.

13.4.4   Gambling Addiction

Gambling addiction starts as a fun or entertainment activity then it becomes an addiction called compulsive activity. Activity like lottery ticket scratch cards, cards playing for money such as activity become an addictive and compulsive activity. This addictive playing event is a kind of gambling addiction. The gambling addiction makes many adults spend their time and money at most for gambling.

Gambling is a kind of entertainment addiction which leads to addictive play. The gambling are evolved in many sports, which tends make more money. So that many adults were addicted via that addiction which stimulate to playing continuously as gambling.

13.4.5   Food Addiction

Eating habit addiction is a food addiction that refers to having a heavy food craving and over-eating which leads obesity and many health issues. Food-addicted people are not satisfied in terms of amount of food especially and very often the food addict having as frequent meals. They ate abnormal amount of food as addictive mentality. Its leads many healthy and psychological issues. If the food addicted people do not have sufficient amount of food, they becomes very depressed and experience physiological dysfunction. The food craving becomes compulsive in taking and they become very fatty which cause much health issue like blood pressure and diabetes too. It's a kind of substance addiction. The substance of food may be natural or processed or hybrid. Compare to natural food, the processed food i a high potential craving substance. Neuroimaging research has demonstrated that highly processed foods, defined as foods with added amounts of fat, refined carbohydrates, and/or salt, (e.g., pizza, chocolate, potato chips), and cues signaling their availability, engage reward-related neural circuitry in a similar manner as drugs of abuse [20], whereas minimally-processed foods (e.g., fruits, vegetables) have less reward potential [20, 21]. So, the neural reward system keep on motivating to take food craving leads as food addiction.

13.4.6   Sexual Addiction

Sex is a natural dimension and a behavior of the human species whereas drug addiction involves the consummation of substances that is external to the individual's body [25]. It's a kind of relationship path way for relationship in the society [23] and defined 'sexual addiction' in terms of the individual having a pathological relationship with sex. Adding to this, Goodman [24] states that the concept of 'sexual addiction' is based on the proposition that out of control sexual activity shares the same traits associated with traditional forms of addiction. Impulsive–compulsive spectrum appears as the syndromic base condition of addiction in general, and of sexual addiction in particular, which is characterized by a pleasure-seeking appetite and an uncontainable urge to put something into practice; it is a visceral overwhelming "hunger" that disregards both the risk and its negative effects. Such a craving stands on obsessive, impulsive and compulsive factors [22] that induce the individual to experience his/her sexuality not as a symbolic function of the desiring fusion of bodies, but as a realization of the urge to put something into practice in order to contain those intense, no modulated emotions that were not mentalized in early relationships with primary caregivers.

13.4.7   Cigarette and Alcohol Addiction

Over the few decades, the substance use addiction disorder like cigarette and alcohol addiction has been increasing. Cigarettes and alcohol have major role in the substance-use disorder rather than other opioids. These addictions have major primitive for many healthy distractions which cause sickness to the users as well as strangers and environment pollution. Cigarettes have polluted the air to the environment and strangers. Tobacco use has a vital role in addiction behavior of users making it a compulsive and addictive consumption. This kind of substance has a good number of potential addictive constituents like nicotine, which causes a kick or a more psychological craving mindset. Burgeoning alcohol use is relevant to more numbers of cancers and health issues. Alcohol use addiction (AUA), and alcohol use disorders (AUD) are a major and primitive role which affect lifetime prevalence rates as high as 29.1% among adolescents aged 18 and older [26]. Many research articles reviewed state 1 in 10 deaths among working age adults are from alcohol-related causes each year in the United States [27].

13.4.8   Status Expressive Addiction

In social media websites, like the application Whatsapp, the user becomes more expressive and is a kind of addiction. Addictive in the status expressive means currently many users taking selfies, photographs, videos, etc., upload in virtual network applications. Adults especially become more expressive and tend to explore through their status updating through the applications. Many applications like TikTok and Whatsapp, Facebook, Twitter, etc. These applications used stimulate via their reward points as likes and views. Social media users are triggered by rewarding point as number of likes and views. In this connection, many users were taking selfies or videos expressing in the media applications. This status updating becomes a psychiatry disorder when it becomes regularly and keep on updating the status. It's a kind of addictive and compulsive status expressive disorders. Immediate expressive people have become more addictive towards the application.

13.4.9   Workaholic Addiction

Some of the people become workaholic in terms of heavy and compulsive hard work. Even during holidays, the workaholic persons work and think about the working. It's a kind of compulsive and addictive issue. It is also a psychiatry issue and those workaholic people were working heavily spend their time more towards their professional careers.

Addiction happens in workaholic people. If they don't have work they felt very anxious, depressed and have other psychological issues. Those that have, they are dedicated and are fully and heavily concentrated.

13.5   Conclusion

Overall addiction and origin of addiction factors and their consequences were discussed. Addiction relief is supported with a smart health care system towards the psychiatry issue. The smart health care includes both physical and psychological. Addiction is more relevant to a physical and psychologically system. Identifying and analyzing origin factors towards the addictive system and it will be a significant development in the way of smart health care system as physical and psychological addictive treatment for relief. Addiction monitoring and providing treatment will have important aspects in the smart health care system.

In the future, the addiction of each which described in above content has to be taking as immersive research required. Relevance between psychological and physical addictive effective issues have to be analyzed and effect over the addiction research has to be explored for relief from addictive agents.

References

1. Gentile, D.A., Choo, H., Liau, A., Sim, T., Li, D., Fung, D., Khoo, A., Pathological video game use among youths: a two-year longitudinal study. *Pediatrics*, 127, 319–329, 2011. http://dx.doi.org/10.1542/peds.2010-1353.

2. Lemmens, J.S., Valkenburg, P.M., Peter, J., Development and validation of a game addiction scale for adolescents. *Media Psychol.*, 12, 77–95, 2009. http://dx.doi.org/10.1080/15213260802669458.

3. Gentile, D., Pathological video-game use among youth ages 8 to 18: A national study. *Psychol. Sci.*, 594, 594–602, 2009. http://dx.doi.org/10.1111/j.1467-9280.2009. 02340.x.

4. Griffiths, M.D., Kuss, D.J., King, D.L., Video game addiction: Past, present, and future. *Curr. Psychiatry Rev.*, 8, 308–318, 2012. http://dx.doi.org/10.2174/157340012803520414.

5. Mentzoni, R.A., Brunborg, G.S., Molde, H., Myrseth, H., Mår Skouverøe, K.J., Hetland, J., Pallesen, S., Problematic video game use: estimated prevalence and associations with mental and physical health. *Cyber. Behav. Soc. Netw.*, 14, 591–596, 2011. http://dx.doi.org/10.1089/cyber.2010.0260.

6. Brunborg, G.S., Mentzoni, R.A., Frøyland, L.R., Is video gaming, or video game addiction, associated with depression, academic achievement, heavy episodic drinking, or conduct problems? *J. Behav. Addict.*, 3, 27–32, 2014. http://dx.doi.org/10. 1556/JBA.3.2014.002.

7. Greenfield, D., The addictive properties of internet usage, in: *Internet addiction: A handbook and guide to evaluation and treatment*, K.S. Young and C.N. de Abreu (Eds.), John Wiley & Sons, Hoboken, N.J, 2011.

8. Price, J., Patterson, R., Regnerus, M., Walley, J., How much more xxx is generation x consuming? Evidence of changing attitudes and behaviors related to pornography since 1973. *J. Sex Res.*, 53, 12–20, 2016. http://dx.doi.org/10.1080/00224499.2014.1003773.

9. Rissel, C., Richters, J., de Visser, R.O., McKee, A., Yeung, A., Caruana, T., A profile of pornography users in Australia: Findings from the second Australian study of health and relationships. *J. Sex Res.*, 54, 227–240, 2017. http://dx.doi.org/10.1080/00224499.2016.1191597.

10. Wright, P.J., A longitudinal analysis of U.S. adults' pornography exposure. *J. Media Psychol.*, 24, 67–76, 2012. http://dx.doi.org/10.1027/1864-1105/a000063.

11. Wright, P.J., U.S. males and pornography, 1973–2010: Consumption, predictors, correlates. *J. Sex Res.*, 50, 60–71, 2013. http://dx.doi.org/10.1080/00224 499.2011.628132.

12. Regnerus, M., Gordon, D., Price, J., Documenting pornography use in America: A comparative analysis of methodological approaches. *J. Sex Res.*, 53, 873–881, 2016.

13. Duffy, A., Dawson, D.L., das Nair, R., Pornography addiction in adults: A systematic review of definitions and reported impact. *J. Sex. Med.*, 13, 760–777, 2016. http://dx.doi.org/10.1016/j.jsxm.2016.03.002.

14. Rasmussen, K.R., A historical and empirical review of pornography and romantic relationships: Implications for family researchers: Pornography and romantic relationships. *J. Fam. Theory Rev.*, 8, 173–191, 2016. http://dx. doi.org/10.1111/jftr.12141.

15. Short, M.B., Black, L., Smith, A.H., Wetterneck, C.T., Wells, D.E., A review of internet pornography use research: Methodology and content from the past 10 years. *Cyberpsych. Beh. Soc. N.*, 15, 13–23, 2011. http://dx.doi.org/10.1089/cyber.2010.0477.

16. Short, M.B., Wetterneck, C.T., Bistricky, S.L., Shutter, T., Chase, T.E., Clinicians' beliefs, observations, and treatment effectiveness regarding clients' sexual addiction and internet pornography use. *Community Ment. Health J.*, 52, 1070–1081, 2016. http://dx.doi.org/10.1007/s10597-016-0034-2.

17. Leung, L., Linking psychological attributes to addiction and improper use of the mobile phone among adolescents in Hong Kong. *J. Child. Media*, 2, 2, 93–113, 2008. https://doi.org/10.1080/17482790802078565.

18. Takao, M., Takahashi, S., Kitamura, M., Addictive personality and problematic mobile phone use. *CyberPsychol. Behav.*, 12, 5, 501–507, 2009. https://doi.org/10.1089/cpb.2009.0022.

19. Yen, C.-F., Tang, T.-C., Yen, J.-Y., Lin, H.-C., Huang, C.-F., Liu, S.-C. *et al.*, Symptoms of problematic cellular phone use, functional impairment and its association with depression among adolescents in Southern Taiwan. *J. Adolesc.*, 32, 4, 863–873, 2009. https://doi.org/10.1016/j.adolescence.2008.10.006.

20. Tang, D.W., Fellows, L.K., Small, D.M., Dagher, A., Food and drug cues activate similar brain regions: a meta-analysis of functional MRI studies. *Physiol. Behav.*, 106, 3, 317–324, 2012 Jun 6. (PubMed PMID: 22450260).

21. Killgore, W.D., Young, A.D., Femia, L.A., Bogorodzki, P., Rogowska, J., YurgelunTodd, D.A., Cortical and limbic activation during viewing of high- versus low-calorie foods. *Neuroimage*, 19, 4, 1381–1394, 2003 Aug. (PubMed PMID: 12948696. Epub 2003/09/02.

22. Caretti, V. and Craparo, G., Psychopatolgical Issues Of Technological Addiction. New diagnostic criteria for addiction, in: *Annual Review of Cybertherapy and Telemedicine 2009. Advanced Technologies in the Behavioral, Social and Neurosciences*, B.K. Wiederhold and G. Riva (Eds.), IOS Press, Amsterdam, 2009.

23. Carnes, P., *Out of the Shadows: Understanding Sexual Addiction*, Hazelden, Minnesota, 2001.
24. Goodman, A., *Sexual Addiction: An Integrated Approach*, International Universities Press, Madison, CT, 1998.
25. Hughes, B., Understanding 'sexual addiction' in clinical practice, *Procedia Soc. Behav. Sci.*, 5, 915–919, 2010.
26. Grant, B.F., Goldstein, R.B., Saha, T.D., Chou, S.P., Jung, J., Zhang, H., Pickering, R.P., Ruan, W.J., Smith, S.M., Huang, B., Hasin, D.S., Epidemiology of DSM-5 alcohol use disorder: Results from the National Epidemiologic Survey on Alcohol and Related Conditions III. *JAMA Psychiatry*, 72, 757–766, 2015. https://doi.org/10.1001/.jamapsychiatry.2015.0584.
27. Stahre, M., Roeber, J., Kanny, D., Brewer, R.D., Zhang, X., Contribution of excessive alcohol consumption to deaths and years of potential life lost in the United States. *Prev. Chronic Dis.*, 11, E109, 2014. https://doi.org/10.5888/pcd11.130293.

14

A Custom Cluster Design With Raspberry Pi for Parallel Programming and Deployment of Private Cloud

Sukesh, B.[1], Venkatesh, K.[2*] and Srinivas, L.N.B.[2]

[1]Department of Information Technology, SRM Institute of Science and Technology, Kattankulathur, India
[2]Department of Information Technology, SRM Institute of Science and Technology, Kattankulathur, India

Abstract

Super Computers build on the principle of combining group of computers to provide more processing power than one computer can alone. The domain of parallel computing and supercomputing present challenges both for today and future technologies, but building a cluster requires expensive and bulk hardware such as pc's or the implementation of virtual machines. Power consumption is one of the major constraints used in building supercomputing clusters. Low power embedded processors are used in large clusters in reducing power usage rather than use of high-end server CPUs. Single Board computer such as Raspberry pi has conquered several areas such as IOT, parallel and distributed computing within a short span. The design of cluster computing with RPi and its operations are important to the future enhancements of computer science. In this chapter, design and implementation of a cluster with 1 master node and 3 slave nodes is reported. MPICH and MPI4PY are used for parallel programming analysed speed of computation on each node. This chapter also shows an approach where we deploy one of the private clouds called as Nextcloud on RPi. A user who is using Nextcloud on his private server has full control over his data. One other approach for performance and workload distribution is that we can implement RPi Cluster where any number of Rip's can be interconnected to form a cluster. As this works with low cost and gives high performance these are termed as HPC Clusters. These RPi clusters can also replicate data centre features. We can use these clusters for hosting web services, media centre etc.

Keywords: RPi Cluster, Nextcloud, master node, slave node, MPI, MPICH, MPI4PY

*Corresponding author: venkatesh.k@ktr.srmuniv.ac.in

G. R. Kanagachidambaresan (ed.) Role of Edge Analytics in Sustainable Smart City Development: Challenges and Solutions, (273–288) © 2020 Scrivener Publishing LLC

14.1   Introduction

There is an ever-increasing demand for low-cost, compact and computationally-efficient computers around the globe. Parallel computing is one way to meet the need for more computational power. This has also contributed to the fact that in computer technology research parallel computers play an important role. Intensive semi-conductor engineering design helps a base for parallel computing [1, 2]. Computer clusters within the TCP/IP [3, 4] network create parallel computing. The parallel process of estimation takes place when the exchange of messages [5] takes place. MPI [5] and PVM [6] are best known examples of parallel computing within TCP/IP network.

Local personal computer networks are the foremost computers to develop clusters. The emergence of microcomputers, laid path to single-board computer, helps to extend the use of parallel computer clusters. Normally these SBCs have standard communication interfaces (USB, Ethernet, and HDMI) that allow them to communicate with the peripheral devices and different networks required. Microcomputers from RPi [7] and Beagle Bone [8] serve SBC. Raspberry Pi supports TCP/IP parallel computing. Figure 14.1 shows the network configuration enabling internet access to the cluster in which the cluster will be a part of the server environment. It will meet the user requests based on the parallel processing for the software support.

RPi has good characteristics in formation of computer cluster with processor and memory features and also connectivity to Ethernet. This paper

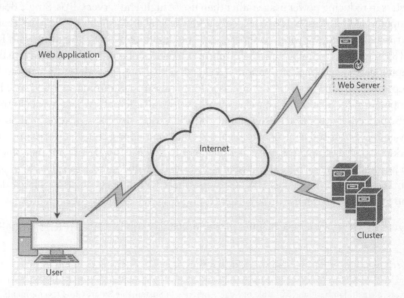

Figure 14.1 The structure of cluster supported via internet.

is intended to view cluster implementation on the linked Raspberry Pi 4 module in the TCP/IP network [9, 10]. Working with personal computer-based clusters has shown their important ability to support parallel computing. The acceptability of such systems should be given more attention, as they were significantly cheaper than costly supercomputers.

The RPi has a built-in Ethernet port that allows you to communicate it to a switch or router. A cluster can be formed by interconnecting several RPi devices to a switch. As for PC we have one CPU here the RPi contains a single ARM processor [11], however several RPi's are combined to give us more computing power. This ultimately leads to the creation and programming of clusters based on the concept of the MPI.

An additional goal was to learn the possibility of using the Python programming language for parallel programming based on MPI theory [12]. Eventually, the cluster was intended to be a forum where computer science students would become acquainted with parallel computing and parallel programming's foremost concepts [13].

The majority of the journal will be structured as follows. The second section explains the creation and use of Raspberry Pi cluster. The third section helps to understand the importance of parallel computing on Raspberry pi using MPI, which describes RPi cluster architecture and MPI implementation. The fourth section makes u understand the deployment of Next Cloud on RPi cluster. The fifth chapter explains the practical implementation, the final results and discussion. In the below Figure 14.2 consists of a group of computers which are linked equally or closely and work together to allow them to be viewed as a single unit. The cluster components are normally connected to each other by fast local networks and each node runs its own event.

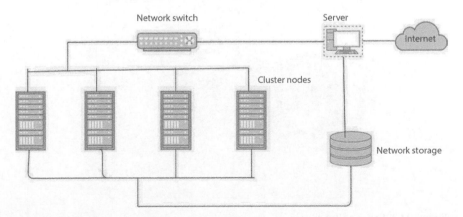

Figure 14.2 A cluster computing configuration.

14.2 Cluster Design with Raspberry Pi

Cluster is a set of SBCs that are interconnected which helps to gain performance in both parallel and distributed environment [14]. In cluster design multiple RPi's are connected using switch in network using MPI and PVM. Here we used four RPi 4 modules in implementing cluster.

14.2.1 Assembling Materials for Implementing Cluster

In order to assemble Cluster, Network hardware and cables are required to set up and necessary devices are required to communicate with the RPi's boot loading software. Following Figure 14.3 represent the entire setup of raspberry pi cluster in which one rpi is considered as a master node and remaining as a slaves node.

The list of recommended and optional items needs for Raspberry pi Cluster:

1. One Raspberry Pi 4, with 4 GB RAM
2. Three Raspberry Pi 4, with 2 GB RAM
3. Micro HDMI-capable
4. USB keyboard
5. USB mouse
6. 6-port powered USB hub
7. 4 Ethernet/RJ45 network cables
8. 5-port network switch

Figure 14.3 Setup of Rpi cluster.

9. An existing Internet connection
10. 4 Micro SD cards
11. Cluster stack
12. USB Portable hard drives (optional)

14.2.1.1 Raspberry Pi4

The RPi which is one of the SBCs is mostly used in educational institutions and research purpose. Most of the IOT projects use this RPi. Pi is used in research as desktop pc or server without any limits. It is based on Linux OS. The latest RPi 4 unlocks more computing power and increase in on-board connectivity. Figure 14.4 is the appearance of Raspberry pi 4 model with following specification.

14.2.1.2 RPi 4 Model B Specifications

- A 1.5Ghz quad-core 64bit ARM Cortex-A72 CPU
- 4 GB RAM
- Gigabit Ethernet Port
- Supports Dual-band 802.11ac
- Bluetooth 5.0
- USB 3.0 ports and 2 USB 2.0 ports

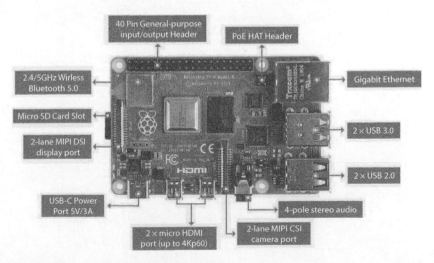

Figure 14.4 Raspberry Pi 4 model [15].

- Dual Monitor support resolutions up to 4K
- Micro HDMI Video Output.
- SD Card Slot
- 40-pin GPIO

14.2.2   Setting Up Cluster

SBCs should be named as nodes in a cluster that are linked in various ways [16, 17] depending on the method of communication. They are linked through an Ethernet router in a local network. As shown in Figure 14.5, the main aspect of this cluster is the scalability. For fewer directory changes, new nodes can be introduced without limitations [18]. This scenario involves incorporating network switches or routers as well as the system for cooling. The cluster cooling is done using heat sinks as well as cooling fans based on the literature review. In addition, this would require a separate storage space, depending on the number of units involved.

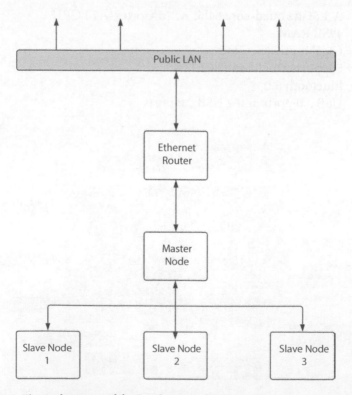

Figure 14.5 The Architecture of the Raspberry pi cluster.

14.2.2.1   Installing Raspbian and Configuring Master Node

Raspberry Pi's loaded Debian Linux as the operating system. With Raspberry Pi's it is easy to get an operating system (OS) installed since the OS is installed on a micro-SD card. When the OS is pre-installed, it can be used and configured accordingly based on our need.

The Raspberry pi Cluster uses the following configurations and software packages which are installed on Raspberry Pi

14.2.2.2   Installing MPICH and MPI4PY

Along with the installation of OS, we need to install MPI software on each RPi module. Even if MPICH3 version is installed, MPI4PY should be installed which helps in programming cluster nodes in Python Language. Then the RPis can communicate together using Message Passing Interface (MPI). This allows the write and run of programs created for a cluster and helps the programs to run in parallel.

14.2.2.3   Cloning the Slave Nodes

In a cluster every node has its Unique host name and all nodes are cloned using SD card to have same system software. The SSH protocol allows all nodes to work with. Each node's IP addresses are stored in the system directory. Every node contains the location of this file and uses MPICH3 in node communication.

14.3   Parallel Computing and MPI on Raspberry Pi Cluster

It is particularly important to use networked computers to run loosely coupled processes in parallel. That local network of computers can therefore be used as a basis for parallel computing. Parallel computation is focused on exchanging of messages in loosely coupled systems [19]. Appropriate code support was introduced to provide requirements for parallel computing. MPI and PVM are the common systems.

For programming the parallel computer clusters [20], we use a protocol known as MPI. Typically, using MPI helps model distributed storage architectures, but it can now run on almost any hardware platform, distributed memory [21], shared memory, hybrid, etc. MPI helps in having good communication, flexibility and portability.

For the better formation of clusters, we have small, powerful, efficient SBC such as Rpi [22]. To form a cluster, we should have few RPi nodes and if this does not meet your requirement you can add few more nodes to extend your cluster [14]. Each program which runs on RPi uses the underlying OS (Raspbian).

Once installation of Raspbian is done on every node, we have to generate Secure Shell keys for every IO address. This helps in the encryption of login and makes easy communication with each and every node. SSH can be enabled via Wi-Fi, and after configuration of SCP (Secure Copy) and SFTP, files and directories can be transferred from one node to another [23]. For the specific node we can run commands, and we can switch node names, or even shut down a node. Extra memory can be made available for each node or head node only for the cluster we are building [24].

For programming nodes in python language, the MPICH3 and MPI4PY library is installed here [25]. Eventually, we need secure shell keys that can control the Raspberry Pi module without using the username and password [26]. Figure 14.6 shows a clear picture of the MPI cluster's used hostname, IP addresses and SSH keys.

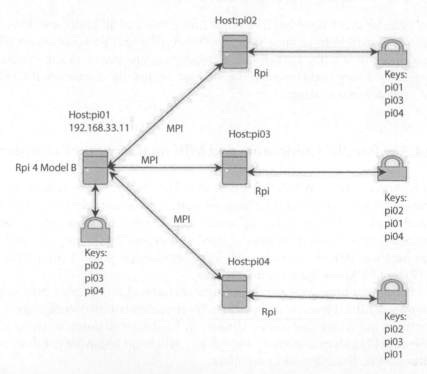

Figure 14.6 Hostname and SSH keys on Raspberry Pi cluster.

14.4 Deployment of Private Cloud on Raspberry Pi Cluster

The cloud resources are taken and used by third-party cloud service provider and these services are rendered on the Internet. AWS is one of the public clouds. We use a public cloud for all resources. These resources are managed by a cloud provider. Using this public cloud resources, you can share them with your known organisations also. The resources can be easily managed using particular accounts on internet. Private cloud here differs with public cloud where this is used by only particular organization or a company. This organization will have its data secured in nearby its data centres or it takes help from third party resource providers. Here in private cloud as it is only for a particular organization all the data of it is connected to a secure private network where only that organization has access. As such this kind of cloud deployment helps organization in need for their requirements. Private clouds are mostly used in large enterprises, government purposes, etc.

14.4.1 Nextcloud Software

There are few parameters where protection is required for data where these are tough situations for third party providers. This is the purpose in which we use Nextcloud where there is no need of any third-party and anyone can install and use the resources. Nextcloud is a client-server software suite designed to create and use file management services. Operations with Nextcloud are similar to Dropbox. Nextcloud is one of the free software that anyone on their own computers can use.

14.5 Implementation

14.5.1 NextCloud on RPi Cluster

NextCloud is one of the private clouds where anyone can use to run on their own servers. Here for the implementation of the NextCloud on RPi cluster, we need to follow the below steps:

Step 1: Do install few known packages such as Apache Web Server and PHP.
- sudo apt install apache2
- sudo apt-get install php7.3 php7.3-gd sqlite php7.3-sqlite3 php7.3-curl php7.3-zip php7.3-xml php7.3-mbstring

Step 2: As for the further procedure install MariaDB server for database.

- sudo apt install mariadb-server

Step 3: In the installation process of MariaDB follow accordingly with the user requirements, which is mostly yes.

Step 4: Download the NextCloud packages from the NextCloud site.

Step 5: Once the package is downloaded, unzip it and finally we need to give specific IP address of the RPi in which this got installed. In Figure 14.7 user can see the login page of Nextcloud on Rpi after successful installation.

14.5.2   Parallel Computing on RPi Cluster

For the implementation of parallel computing on RPi cluster, we here follow below described steps. Following Figure 14.8 shows the installation of MPICH3 packages and in Figure 14.9 you can see the generation of SSH keys.

Step 1: Foremost installation starts with MPICH3. Create a directory for MPICH3

- sudo mkdir mpich3
- cd ~/mpich3

Step 2: Then download the latest version of mpich form the site and extract in the mpich3 folder.

- sudo wget http://www.mpich.org/static/downloads/3.3.2/ mpich-3.3.2.tar.gz

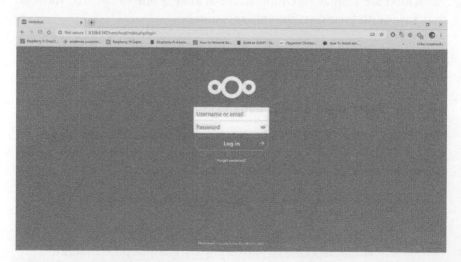

Figure 14.7 Nextcloud page on Rpi.

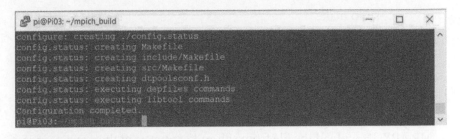

Figure 14.8 MPICH Package installation.

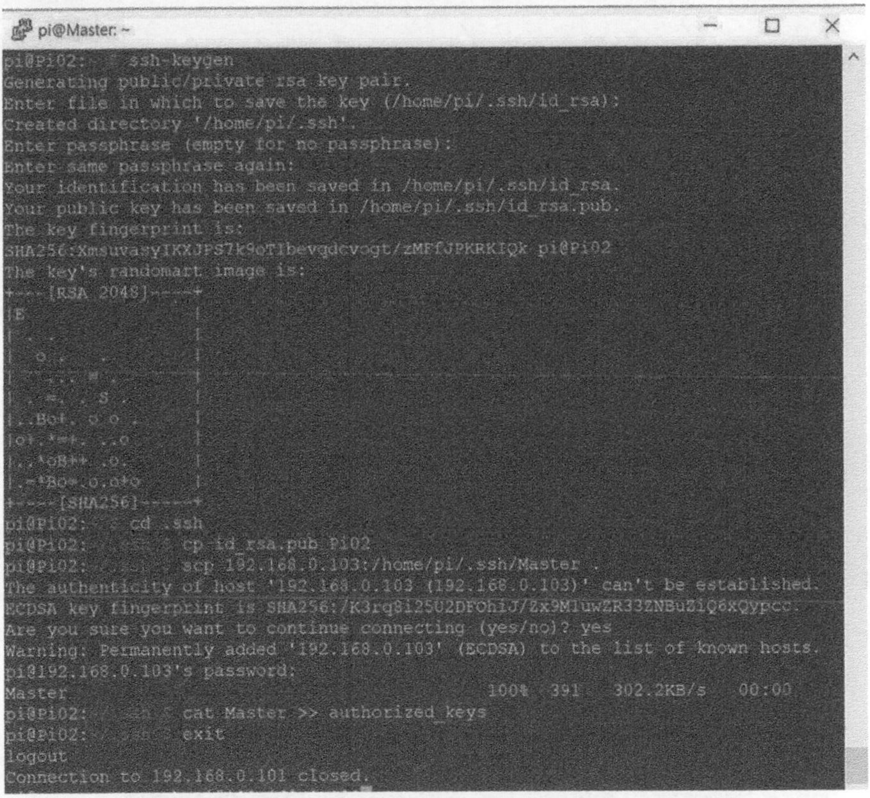

Figure 14.9 Generation of SSH keys.

Step 3: Fortran or C language are the prerequisites for the mpich installation
- sudo apt -get install gfortran

Step 4: Now configure and also install mpich such as,
- sudo/home/pi/mpich3/mpich-3.3.2/configure-prefix=/home/rpimpi/mpi-install

- sudo make
- sudo make install

Step 5: Test the MPI with the below command

- mpiexec -n 1 hostname

Further along the implementation we need to install MPI4py and also SSH keys need to be generated.

MPI4PY: Download the file from site and extract as in the previous process like below. This procedure needs to be done on all RPi's.

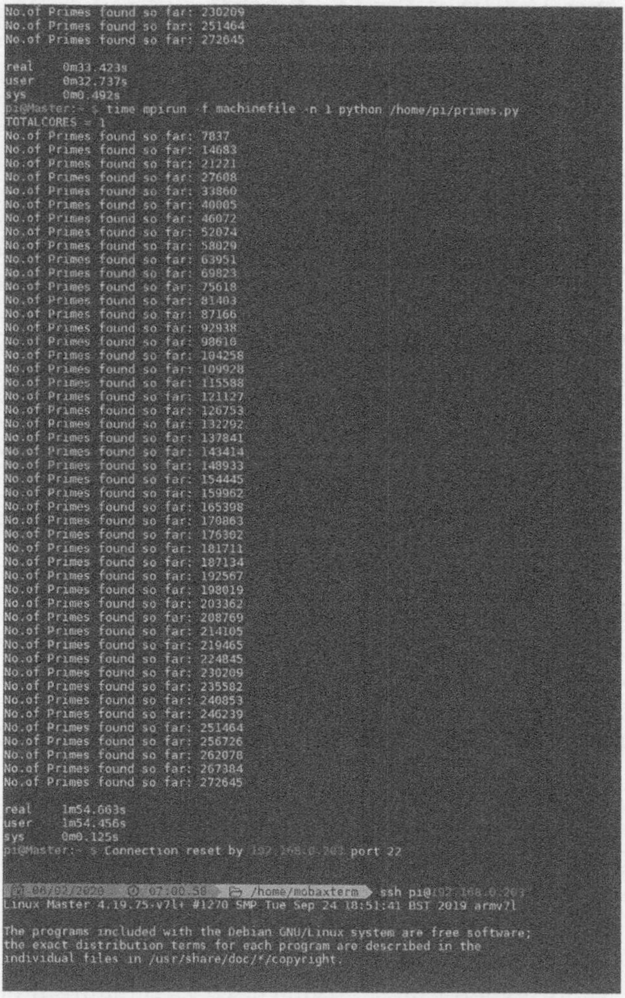

Figure 14.10 Time taken to execute the program on single core.

- wget https://bitbucket.org/mpi4py/downloads/mpi4py-3.0.3. tar.gz

SSH Keys Generation: To communicate with each RPi we need to specify credentials every time. So, if we generate SSH keys for each RPi and if this key is shared with every RPi in the network, communication will be easy among Pi's. Hence MPI will make it possible to communicate with any RPi without worrying about the credentials. In the above mentioned Figures 14.10 and 14.11 shows the variation of time taken to execute the program on single core as well as on different cores.

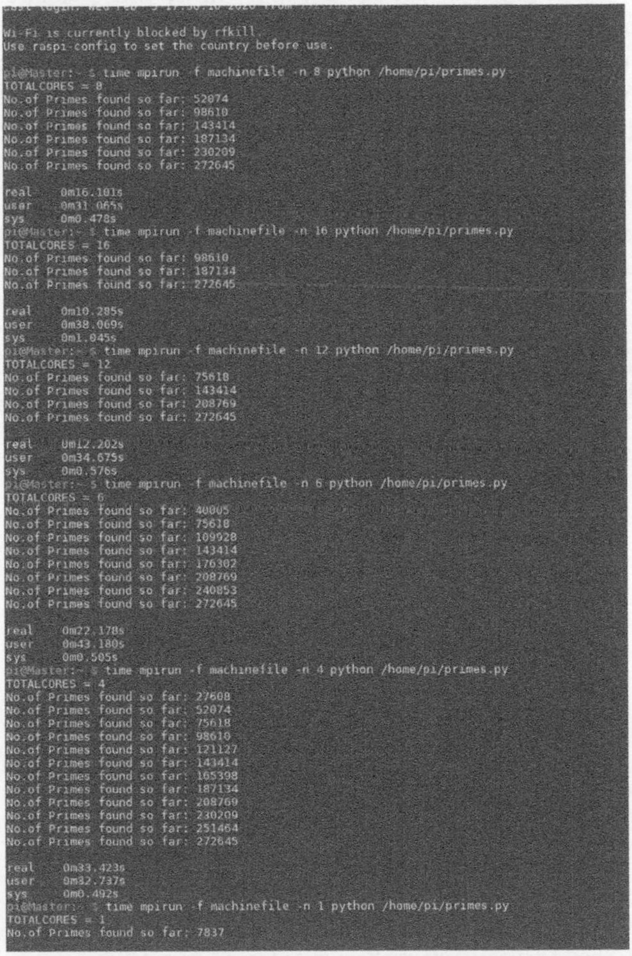

Figure 14.11 Time taken to execute the program on different cores.

14.6   Results and Discussions

1. We have the final output of NextCloud installation on RPi cluster shown as below:
2. Prime number generation to show parallelism on cluster

To explain the parallel computing, we have taken an example of python parallel code which gives output as number of primes found within the given range. Here we can give number of processes in which RPi's execute your computation accordingly. When we execute the code with one process, that means only one core of the processor of master node is utilized. So, the execution time will be more as shown in the below image.

While considering different cores of the processor, i.e. increase in the cores will have less execution time comparatively. Thus, RPi cluster helps in solving large computational problems. Below image shows final execution time.

The execution of code can be done by increasing the given cores in the cluster. Here change of execution time can be seen in the below graph Figure 14.12.

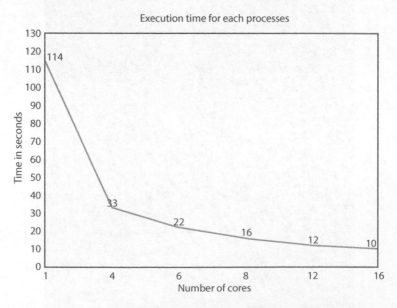

Figure 14.12 Shows the time for execution of code on different cores.

14.7 Conclusion

Design and deployment of super computer cluster with inexpensive hardware like Raspberry Pi, which consume low power which is the major constrain of any cluster has been presented in this work. And also introduced concept of parallel computing and configuration using MPICH and MPI4PY has been presented. This paper also presents an approach to deploy one of the private clouds called as Nextcloud on RPi. A user who is using Nextcloud on his private server has full control on his data. One other approach for performance and workload distribution is that, we can implement RPi Cluster where any number of Rip's can be inter-connected to form a cluster. In order to have more reliability and efficiency we can form a cluster with a greater number of slave nodes like a Raspberry pi cluster with 25 Slave nodes.

References

1. Golden, R., *Raspberry Pi Networking Cookbook*, Packt Publishing, Birmingham - Mumbai, 2013.
2. Govindaraj, V., *Parallel programming in Raspberry Pi cluster, A Design Project Report*, School of Electrical and Computer Engineering, Cornel University, IIT Madras, 2016.
3. Yeo, C.S. *et al.*, Cluster computing: High-performance, high-availability and high-throughput processing on a network of computers, in: *Handbook of Nature—Inspired and Innovative Computing*, A.Y. Zomaya (Ed.), pp. 521–551, Springer, Boston, MA, 2006.
4. Levesque, J. and Wagenbreth, G., *High performance computing: programming and applications*, 1st edition, Chapman and Hall/CRC, California, 2010.
5. Bova, S. *et al.*, Parallel programming with message and directives. *Comput. Sci. Eng.*, 3, 5, 22–37, September/October 2001.
6. Geist, A. *et al.*, *PVM: Parallel virtual machine: A user's guide and tutorial for network parallel computing*, The MIT Press, Cambridge, 1994.
7. Robinson, A. and Cook, M., *Raspberry Pi Projects*, 1st Edition, Wiley, Manchester, UK, 2013.
8. Molloy, D., *Exploring BeagleBone: Tools and techniques for building with embedded Linux*, 1st Edition, Wiley, Ireland, 2014.
9. Kanagachidambaresan, G.R. and Chitra, A., Fail safe fault tolerant mechanism for wireless body sensor network (WBSN). *Wireless Pers. Commun.*, 78, 2, 247–260, 2014.
10. Kanagachidambaresan, G.R. and Chitra, A., TA-FSFT thermal aware fail-safe fault tolerant algorithm for wireless body sensor network. *Wireless Pers. Commun.*, 90, 4, 1935–1950, 2016.

11. Iyer, K., *Learn to build your own supercomputer with Raspberry Pi 3 cluster*, Post on TechWorm, Mumbai, 2018.

12. Dennis, A.K., *Raspberry Pi super cluster*, Packt Publishing, United States, 2013.

13. Saranya, V., Shankar, S., Kanagachidambaresan, G.R., Energy efficient clustering scheme (EECS) for wireless sensor network with mobile sink. *Wireless Pers. Commun.*, 100, 4, 1553–1567, 2018.

14. Morrison, C.R., *Build supercomputers with Raspberry Pi 3*, Packt Publishing— ebooks Account, Mumbai, 2017.

15. https://www.raspberrypi.org/products/raspberry-pi-4-model-b/specifications/

16. Ashari, A. and Riasetiawan, M., High performance computing on cluster and multicore architecture. *TELKOMNIKA (Telecommunication Computing Electronics and Control)*, 13, 4, 1408–1413, 2015.

17. Venkatesh, K., Srinivas, L.N.B., Mukesh Krishnan, M.B., Shanthini, A., QoS Improvisation of Delay Sensitive Communication using SDN based Multipath Routing for Medical Applications, Elsevier. *Future Gener. Comput. Syst.*, 93, 2019, 256–265, 2018.

18. Reddy, V. and Venkatesh, K., Role of Software-Defined Network in Industry 4.0, in: *EAI/Springer Innovations in Communication and Computing- Internet of Things for Industry 4.0 Design, Challenges and Solutions*, pp. 197–218, 2020.

19. Cloutier, M.F., Chad, P., Weaver, V.M., A Raspberry Pi cluster instrumented for fine-grained power measurement. *Electronics*, 5, 4, 61, 2016.

20. Dhulipala, V.R.S. and Kanagachidambaresan, G.R., Cardiac care assistance using self-configured sensor network—A remote patient monitoring system. *J. Inst. Eng. (India): Ser. B*, 95, 2, 101–106, 2014.

21. Esakki, B., Ganesan, S., Mathiyazhagan, S., Kanagachidambaresan, G.R., Design of Amphibious Vehicle for Unmanned Mission in Water Quality Monitoring Using Internet of Things. *Sensors*, 18, 10, 3318, 2018.

22. Grobe, M., An introduction to the Fortran and MPI, University of Kansas, Kansas, November 2013, http://condor.cc.ku.edu/~grobe/docs/intro-MPI.shtml.

23. Drscake, The University of Glasgow's, Raspberry Pi Cloud blog, April 2013. http://raspberrypicloud.wordpress.com/2013/04/25/getting-hadoop-to-run-on-the-raspberry-pi/.

24. Cloutier, M.F., Paradis, C., Weaver, V.M., A Raspberry Pi Cluster Instrumented for Fine-Grained Power Measurement, in: *2014 First International Workshop on Hardware-Software Co-Design for High Performance Computing*, New Orleans, LA, USA, 2014.

25. Padoin, E., de Olivera, D., Velho, P., Navaux, P., Evaluating Performance and Energy on ARM-based Clusters for High Performance Computing, in: *Proceedings of 2012 41st International Conference on Parallel Processing Workshops (ICPPW 2012)*, Pittsburgh, PA, USA, 10–13 September, 2012.

26. Dorr, G. *et al.*, Introduction to parallel processing with eight node Raspberry Pi cluster. *Midwest Instruction and Computing Symposium (MICS)*, 7–8 April, The University of Wisconsin, La Crosse in La Crosse, 2017.

15

Energy Efficient Load Balancing Technique for Distributed Data Transmission Using Edge Computing

Karthikeyan, K.* and Madhavan, P.†

SRMIST, School of Computing, Kattanlathur, Chennai, Tamilnadu, India

Abstract

Nowadays, various IoT devices are connected through the internet to the cloud. With that there is huge amount of data to be transmitted through cloud. Cloud is purely supportable for centralized data processing. In a centralized processing system, handling large amount of data leads to higher latency thereby reducing the efficiency. Load balancing also playing a vital role in the centralized processing. To toggle this problem, edge computing platforms has to be implemented. These kinds of edge computing platforms allow some application to be performed by small edge server positioned between cloud and the user.

The edge computing is a convergence of IT and telecom networking. It is a distributed cloud computing environment which supports offloading of data transmission. The edge computing is not a new concept which is expanded versions of cloud computing, with that all computations are done at the edge of the network. In this, data does not need to be sent to remote cloud or other centralized systems for processing. It removes processing latency as the data need not be sent from the edge of the network to a central processing system. Edge computing is essentially cloud principles applied at network edge close to the user. The usage of distributed algorithm in edge computing platform leverages latency and balances the work load of the request and response.

Keywords: Edge computing, edge server, distributed cloud storage, offloading

Corresponding author: kk9569@srmist.edu.in
†*Corresponding author*: madhavap@srmist.edu.in

G. R. Kanagachidambaresan (ed.) Role of Edge Analytics in Sustainable Smart City Development: Challenges and Solutions (289–302) © 2020 Scrivener Publishing LLC

15.1 Introduction

Nowadays, various IoT devices are connected through the internet to the cloud. With that, there is a huge amount of data to transmitted through cloud. A cloud is purely supportable for centralized data processing. In a centralized processing system, handling a large amount of data has to produce latency request and response timings. Load balancing also plays a vital role in the centralized processing. To toggle this problem, edge computing platform has to be implemented.

These kinds of edge computing platform work by allowing some application processing to be performed by small edge server position between cloud and the user and physically closer to the user. This allows offloading of some of the work from the cloud and low latency response.

The edge computing is a convergence of IT and telecom networking. The edge computing is the distributed cloud computing environment. It also supports for offloading the data transmission. Edge computing is not a new concept and has expanded versions of cloud computing, with all computations are done at the edge of network. In this data does not need to be sent to remote cloud or other centralized system for processing. It removes processing latency as the data need not be sent from the edge of the network to a central processing system. Edge computing is essentially cloud principles applied at network edge close to the user [7].

Edge computing includes compute virtualization, storage virtualization, network virtualization, resources on demand, API Driven Approach, Automated Life Cycle Management, and Uses of Commodity hardware. These principles make edge computing highly principle and programmable.

In this paper, we proposed load balancing energy efficient data transmission and also for offloading data transmission by implementing distributed algorithm consisting of clock frequency, transmission power and offloading strategy selection.

Section 1 discusses about the Energy Efficiency offloading data transmissions, Section 2 discusses about the Energy Harvesting Techniques with Algorithms, Section 3 discusses about the Frameworks and Section 4 about the Communication Techniques, Section 5 discusses about the Networking techniques, and Section 6 discusses about Conclusions.

15.2 Energy Efficiency Offloading Data Transmission

In mobile, edge computing provides offloading capabilities, to potentially avoid the latency, congestion and prolong the life time of mobile devices.

The offloading is proximate physically with Mobile Edge Computing Server and computations are done at mobile devices [1]. For an offloading in edge computing the powerful computational resources, the computation should be compromised due to lack of energy exhausted.to avoid this there is lot of techniques are available [2]. Here we approach green computing with energy efficient data transmission with energy harvesting techniques.

To obtain Energy Efficient Computation Offloading (EECO) we decide which task implementation nodes and allocate radio resources to the offloading devices [1] which are stated as:

Mobile Device Classification: The mobile devices are classified into three types as time, energy cost features and task computing process.

Priority determination: Priorities are determined which are all computations are accessed with offloading concepts with MEC server.

Radio Resource allocation: The Radio resource allocation will allocate the channel allocation of the base stations based on the priorities in the above stages.

15.2.1 Web-Based Offloading

The web-based information gets inputs and processed through the web-based platform which will be performed based on the mobile devices or any other peer devices then the information forwarded to the Edge Server [13]. It will execute before the actual transformation starts so it will required high energy hardware devices to manage this Snap shot web-based offloading techniques.

15.3 Energy Harvesting

Energy Harvesting accomplished with Mobile Edge computing will increase the computation performance and efficient data transmission and offloading performances. To increase the life time of battery power and energy efficient data transmission various offloading framework are accessed. Here we adopt a User Level Online Offloading Framework [ULOOF] [3] with effective data transmissions Mobile Edge Computing Server [MES] with access point mobile devices. The energy harvesting process is shown in the Figure 15.1. For green computing algorithm such as LADCO, Centralized Greedy Algorithm adopted for multi user mobile cloud-edge computing

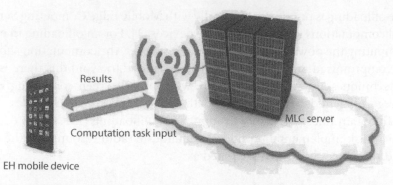

Figure 15.1 Energy harvesting mobile devices with MEC server.

system here we are using LADOO [13], Centralized Greedy Algorithm. The above algorithm will increase the life time of battery, but not focus on CPU Efficiency. The CPU Efficiency is also an important aspect of offloading of which we are using the frequency scaling techniques, which decides offloading policy, task allocation, and Network Interfaces and also for power-delay tradeoff of multi user Mobile Edge Computing Systems [14, 18].

Energy harvesting is mainly use to communication systems for green communication with NON-Casual information, Channel side Information and Energy Side Information [1]. The MEC with Energy harvesting devices are different from communication systems as it mainly focuses on minimizing the energy consumption on the battery power usage and time-related correlation [20–25].

15.3.1 LODCO Algorithm

The Lyapunov optimization-based dynamic computation offloading (LODCO) algorithm is used to solve execution time management problem and also multipurpose mobile edge computing data transmission [5]. The LODCO algorithm has following properties:

- There is no restriction of the system state and feasible action set with low complexity and also no need memory for solving optimal policy.
- There is no need of prior information on channel statistics, energy process and computational task management processes.
- The performance of LODCO algorithm is controlled by two tuples of controlled parameters namely, upper bound parameters and lower bound parameters.

- The LODCO algorithm avoids dropping task by prolonging average completion time in order to achieve a minimal execution cost.
- The LODCO ALGORITHM solves the per-time slots problem by optimal computation offloading solution and Optimal Energy Harvesting.
- The Optimal Energy Harvesting techniques manage that optimal amount of the harvested energy which will incorporate with CPU efficiency. In LADCO Algorithm task being executed locally and CPU cycle should be the same.
- The optimal computation offloading manages the virtual energy efficiency management and also avoids the space limitations and owing correlated with the battery power as space slot.
- The LODCO algorithm produces the asymptotic optimality to manage the efficient data transmissions.

15.4   User-Level Online Offloading Framework (ULOOF)

The User Online Offloading Framework (ULOOF) is equipped with novel algorithms to predict the values of multi-value data transmissions [4]. The main aim of the ULOOF algorithm is to compute the energy consumption values and execution time as well as location-aware capacity estimator. The framework for ULOOF is shown in the Figure 15.2.

Using the ULOOF needs no changes in the operating systems and any other devices which can be adopted to execution in normal way as shown in the figures, without requiring any additional knowledge.

In the mobile devices, the instrument component accesses the candidate method of offloading. Whenever the method starts execution the ULOOF [4] will monitor the execution time and energy consumption. It will estimate both local and remote-based estimations [12]. The decision engine will decide whether the data is to be executed locally and remotely.

The remote execution platform will proceed with remote offloading computations, by means of connector modules. It will be executed and passes the result to the mobile devices by accessing the connector module.

To enable instrumentation orientation process, an offloading application for android has to be prepared. First it will put off loadable methods are marked as annotation, then these methods process with the annotations and the post compiler creates with the offloading logics integrated with virtual machines.

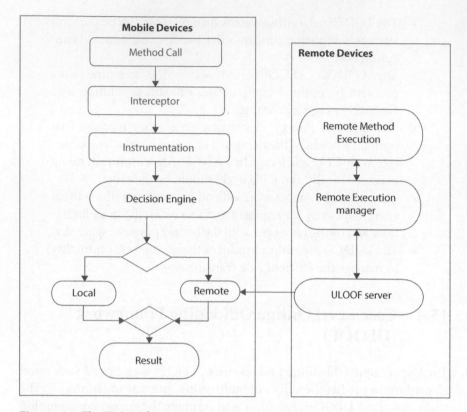

Figure 15.2 The ULOOF framework.

This framework also creates virtual machines which is same as the mobile devices. It will run the android virtual machines with offloading platform and will receive the input from the ULOOF applications.

The MARKOV algorithm is another type of framework algorithm, which will optimal performances of the mobile devise and edge server will joint-optimize the latency and energy in multi-user mobile edge computing systems.

The Markov algorithm performs based on the Markov Chain techniques, to get near optimal solutions. The Markov Algorithm supports both local and remote device processes.

15.5 Frequency Scaling

Frequency scaling is another type of framework technique which will optimize the framework of offloading from a single edge device to multiple

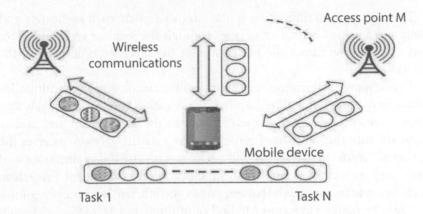

Figure 15.3 Task allocation.

edge devices. This technique can be used to minimize the latency, energy consumption, and task allocation.

The task offloading framework frequency scaling uses the Dynamic Voltage Frequency Scaling (DVFS) [5]. These algorithms will focus on the frequency of the microprocessor and to reduce the mobile device energy consumption. With this, a single mobile will allocate a task to multiple access points and also mainly focus on the CPU Frequency. These can control and monitor the CPU energy consumptions by the CPU Frequency [18], which will be measured with the linear techniques.

Frequency scaling reduces the energy consumption by two ways such as Computational Energy Computations and Wireless transmission energy consumption. Figure 15.3 describes the task allocation for the single devices to multiple access points and also focusing the CPU Frequency to control and monitor the execution latency and energy consumption of the offloading process [18].

15.6 Computation Offloading and Resource Allocation

The Resource Allocation will mainly use to avoid the Big Data problem. To avoid the Big Data issues the capturing of the devices should start with the IoT Edge node. This resource allocation algorithm reduces the fragmentation and also to minimize the throughput problem by effective bandwidth allocation with the joint optimization techniques [6], to focus on the optimization problem to be resolved such as maximize the lifetime of battery, and maximizing the life of the edge nodes.

The computation offloading splits into two aspects such as discrete and continuous values, which can access through the local or remote devices and also consider about the buffer size for the memory utilization of the devices.

The Resource Allocation techniques will focus on the bandwidth allocation to the offloading. The Bandwidth allocation is done at the gateway. Each channel sends the parameter values to the gateway [6] and update remotely once the value has been changed. Once the gateway receives the parameter from the devices it will perform with the linear functions and pairs with each device. For Resource allocation uses Gradient Projection Techniques to maximize the battery power and efficient data transmissions.

The Alternative Direction Method of Multipliers [ADMM] techniques solve the optimization problem which will work based on the spectrum of the system in distributed fashion. To manage the iterative process primal dual interactive process techniques are used for the local data processing. Decentralized resource allocation algorithm is used for the Mobile edge computing offloading process which will start the process at the mobile device itself [9].

The Iterative band with algorithm can be used for minimum bandwidth allocation with that the remaining band width allocation to be monitored and it can be used while partitioning the devices at low power data transmission slots.

At each iteration, the bandwidth finds out the least battery and second least battery life devices, then gateway will allocate more band width to the less battery life devices otherwise it will monitor the power consumptions of the devices [8]. This algorithm deals with fragmentation problem by sharing the bandwidth allocation and also utilizing the remaining the bandwidth by partitioning the devices.

The limited bandwidth in gateway usually shared with multiple Access points which will produce some throughput while using the high range data transmission through the nodes which can be avoided by the novel comparison techniques. It will also lead to more bandwidth allocation problem to avoid these issues partially to allocate with the IoT device itself and remaining will be processed through the gateway.

15.7 Communication Technology

The Communication to edge devices should be optimal to use the Novel algorithm for better communications. Here to apply V2X Algorithm [9], effective communication and rapid development of the technologies should be available. This Algorithm will mainly support for the vehicular Ad-HOC Network and Edge computing devices, communicating with vehicle and mobile edge devices which will collect information to the various sources like vehicle, camera, mobile devices, etc. After getting the input it will forward the data into Edge Devices or edge server after which it will offload the data to the servers by using the VFX Algorithms [9]. This algorithm supports both short range and long-range communications.

A communication-based VFX framework [9], will process real-time data and will process through the edge nodes. Each node will have communicated with the server. Also, it will monitor the CPU-cycle Frequencies and Computation offloading transmission power. The VFX algorithm focus about the:

- Encoding the Offloading Strategies: Which will be encoding the operational-based offloading strategies by using the Genetics Algorithm LODCO Algorithm, to process the data at the hierarchical manner, starts from the mobile devices.
- Fitness Functions and Strategies: The fitness functions and Strategies will monitor and control the offloading process.
- Cross Over Operation: The Cross over operation will monitor the single device and Multiple access point data transmissions.
- Mutual Operation: The mutual operation will monitor the updating process in the mobile devices.

15.8   Ultra-Dense Network

Task offloading in mobile edge computing uses the Ultra Dense Network technique which is wireless networking, addressing the optimization and offloading problem. It includes the Small Base Stations (SBS) and Macro cell Base Stations [9] which will short delay and highly perform with high access capacities. These networks can support both local and remote device processes.

The Ultra Dense Network with edge computing offloading process uses Software Defined Networking [SDN] which achieves the logically centralized controlled on the distributed network. It will provide computation offloading services to the users. The SDN algorithm compares the random and offloading schemes [9].

The SDN are divided into three parts such as User Plane, Data plane and control plane. The user plane will process the information and pass input to the data plane. The data plane will have base stations and sub-stations which will have necessary information and control the devices and the Control plane will manage and control the process. The control plane has an edge computing server.

The SDN Networking needs to maintain the information by the tabular manner so that control management has the information about the table like resource allocation information and offloading information, which also has information about networking devices.

The device table has information about the mobile devices and battery power information and CPU Utilization Information [12]. The base station information table maintains the basic user information to decide which further transmission has to be proceed [12]. The Task Information table maintains the user information and forwards it to the base stations.

The SDN evaluates the decoupling of the information from control plane from the data plane by the virtualization concepts further decides which base station information has to decoupled. The major control functionalities like resource sharing and scheduling are controlled by the SDN Controller.

The SDN Controller [9] maintains the device information and Base Station Information and Task Information Table. The table includes the information as base station information like CPU hopping and the remaining battery power and capacity of the device.

The Task allocation processes the framework of SDN and the mobile device selects nearest sub-stations to forward information to the base stations for task allocations. Then Base Station forwards information to the SDN Controller [9]. The SDN Controller then updates all kinds of the information. It will allocate resources based on the energy consumption and latency of the given task. The SDN Network table is shown in the Figure 15.4.

A Mobile Edge Computing [MEC] server at each base station is able to provide multiple user access at the same time. It will be processed based on the frequency hopping allocation to mobile devices. The server will be

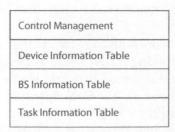

Figure 15.4 SDN network table.

worked based on the spectrum devices which can use the Distributed Best Response Based Multi User Based Algorithm [14].

This Algorithm will be performed based on the distributed linear manner, on the edge server. This Algorithm can allow the user to access the devices to base stations and improve efficient transmissions to the multiple users. It will choose the devices based on the mobile device efficiency.

The remote execution platform will proceed with remote offloading computations, by means of connector modules. It will execute and pass the result to the mobile devices by accessing the connector module [14].

15.9 Conclusion

This paper discussed about the Energy Efficient data transmission with Computation offloading process in edge computing in a distributed manner. Also, comparative study about the Frameworks, Communication protocols, Resource Allocation gateway and Algorithms were used for Offloading data transmission. Energy Efficiency considers both the battery and CPU Utilization for the wired and wireless technologies.

References

1. Mao, Y., Zhang, J., Letaief, K.B., *Dynamic Computation Offloading for Mobile-Edge Computing With Energy Harvesting Devices*, IEEE Xplore, pp. 3590–3605, Dec 2016, https://doi.org/10.1109/JSAC.2016.261196.
2. Xu, J., Chen, L., Ren, S., *Online Learning for Offloading and Autoscaling in Energy Harvesting Mobile Edge Computing*, IEEE Xplore, pp. 361–373, Sep 2017, https://doi.org/10.1109/TCCN.2017.2725277.
3. Neto, J.L.D., Yu, S.-Y., Macedo, D.F., Nogueira, J.M.S., Langar, R., Secci, S., *ULOOF: A User Level Online Offloading Framework for Mobile Edge Computing*, IEEE Xplore, pp. 2660–2674, Nov 2018, https://doi.org/10.1109/TMC.2018.2815015.
4. Zhang, K., Mao, Y., Leng, S., Zhao, Q., Li, L., Peng, X., Pan, L., Maharjan, S., Shang, Y., *Energy-Efficient Offloading for Mobile Edge Computing in 5G Heterogeneous Networks*, IEEE Xplore, pp. 5896–5907, 2016, https://doi.org/10.1109/ACCESS.2016.2597169.
5. Dinh, T.Q., Tang, J., La, Q.D., Quek, T.Q.S., *Offloading in Mobile Edge Computing: Task Allocation and Computational Frequency Scaling*, IEEE Xplore, pp. 3571–3584, Aug 2017, https://doi.org/10.1109/TCOMM.2017.2699660.
6. Samie, F., Tsoutsouras, V., Bauer, L., Xydis, S., Soudris, D., Henkel, J., *Computation Offloading and Resource Allocation for Low-power IoT Edge Devices*, IEEE Xplore, 2016, https://doi.org/10.1109/WF-IoT.2016.7845499.

7. Wang, C., Liang, C., Yu, F.R., Chen, Q., *Computation Offloading and Resource Allocation in Wireless Sensor Networks with Mobile Edge Computing*, IEEE Xplore, pp. 4924–4938, Aug 2017, https://doi.org/10.1109/TWC.2017.2703901.

8. Xu, X., Xue, Y., Li, X., Qi, L., Shaohua, *A Computation Offloading Method for Edge Computing with Vehicle-To-Everything*, IEEE Xplore, Sep 2019, https://doi.org./10.1109/ACCESS.2019.2940295.

9. Chen, M. and Hao, Y., *Task Offloading for Mobile Edge Computing in Software Defined Ultra-Dense Network*, IEEEE Xplore JSAC, pp. 131068–131077, Sep 2019, https://doi.org/10.1109/ACCESS.2019.2940295.

10. Sun, X. and Ansari, N., *Edge IoT: Mobile Edge Computing for the Internet of Things*, IEEEE Communications, pp. 22–29, Dec 2016, https://doi.org/10.1109/MCOM.2016.1600492CM.

11. Wei, F., Chen, S., Zou, W., *A Greedy Algorithm for Task Offloading in Mobile Edge Computing System*, IEEE Xplore, pp. 149–157, Nov 2018, https://doi.org/10.1109/CC.2018.8543056.

12. Sheng, J., Hu, J., Teng, X., Wang, B., Pan, X., *Computation Offloading Strategy in Mobile Edge Computing*, IEEE Xplore, pp. 1–1, Mar 2019, https://doi.org/10.1109/TSUSC.2019.2904680.

13. Jeong, H.-J., *Lightweight Offloading System for Mobile Edge Computing*, IEEE Xplore, Mar 2019, https://doi.org/10.1109/PERCOMW.2019.8730793.

14. Tran, T.X. and Pompilid, D., *Joint Task Offloading and Resource Allocation for Multi-Server Mobile-Edge Computing Networks*, IEEE Xplore, pp. 856–888, Jan 2019, https://doi.org/10.1109/TVT.2018.2881191.

15. Dinh, T.Q., La, Q.D., Quek, T.Q.S., Shin, H., *Learning for Computation Offloading in Mobile Edge Computing*, IEEE Xplore, pp. 6353–6367, Dec 2018, https://doi.org/10.1109/TCOMM.2018.2866572.

16. Li, Y. and Wang, S., *An Energy-Aware Edge Server Placement in Mobile Edge Computing*, IEEE Xplore, July 2018, https://doi.org/10.1109/EDGE.2018.00016.

17. Liu, C.-F., Bennis, M., Poor, H.V., *Latency and Reliability-Aware Task Offloading and Resource Allocation for Mobile Edge Computing*, IEEE Communications, Jan 2018, https://doi.org/10.1109/GLOCOMW.2017.8269175.

18. Mach, P. and Becvar, Z., *Mobile Edge Computing: A Survey on Architecture and Computation Offloading*, IEEE Xplore pp. 1628–1656, Mar 2017, https://doi.org/10.1109/COMST.2017.2682318.

19. Zhou, W., Fang, W., Li, Y., Yuan, B., Li, Y., Wa, T., *Markov Approximation for Task Offloading and Computation Scaling in Mobile Edge Computing*, HINDWAI, 2019, https://doi.org/10.1155/2019/8172698.

20. Feng, W.-J., Yang, C.-H., Zhou, X.-S., *Multi-User and Multi-Task Offloading Decision Algorithms Based on Imbalanced Edge Cloud*, IEEEE Access, pp. 95970–95977, July 2019, https://doi.org/10.1109/ACCESS.2019.2928377.

21. Saranya, V., Shankar, S., Kanagachidambaresan, G.R., Energy efficient clustering scheme (EECS) for wireless sensor network with mobile sink. *Wireless Pers. Commun.*, 100, 4, 1553–1567, 2018.

22. Kanagachidambaresan, G.R. and Chitra, A., Fail safe fault tolerant mechanism for wireless body sensor network (WBSN). *Wireless Pers. Commun.*, 78, 2, 247–260, 2014.
23. Kanagachidambaresan, G.R. and Chitra, A., TA-FSFT thermal aware fail safe fault tolerant algorithm for wireless body sensor network. *Wireless Pers. Commun.*, 90, 4, 1935–1950, 2016.
24. Dhulipala, V.R.S. and Kanagachidambaresan, G.R., Cardiac care assistance using self configured sensor network—A remote patient monitoring system. *J. Inst. Eng. India: Ser. B*, 95, 2, 101–106, 2014.
25. Esakki, B., Ganesan, S., Mathiyazhagan, S., Kanagachidambaresan, G.R., Design of Amphibious Vehicle for Unmanned Mission in Water Quality Monitoring Using Internet of Things. *Sensors*, 18, 10, 3318, 2018.

16

Blockchain-Based SDR Signature Scheme With Time-Stamp

Swathi Singh[1]*, Divya Satish[2] and Sree Rathna Lakshmi[3]

[1]*Anna University, Chennai, India*
[2]*Department of Computer Science and Engineering,*
SKR Engineering College, Chennai, India
[3]*Department of Electronics and Communication Engineering,*
Agni College of Technology, Chennai, India

Abstract

This research chapter presents a new concept using blockchain with time stamp-based support signature schemes. The technique provides enhanced efficiency unlike other hash-based signatures. We propose a forwarded security structural signature scheme as part of industry 4.0, its prerequisites alongside certain approaches for common use in practical and, finally, arrive at a forward-secure approach with few trusted presumptions. We present a detailed design goals and its reasoning for the forwarded security of our proposed scheme. We discuss the detailed survey on hash-based signature schemes with time-stamps and compare the proposed scheme on efficiency parameter with insights on implementation. The ideas of blockchain validation on information structures and its configuration has greater worth and is more valuable for further research.

Keywords: Industry 4.0, blockchain, security system, hash-based signature scheme, cryptography

16.1 Introduction

A unique signature scheme was proposed recently for blockchain [11]. This scheme combined the time stamp strategy based on cryptography with

---

Corresponding author: vk.swathisingh@gmail.com

G. R. Kanagachidambaresan (ed.) Role of Edge Analytics in Sustainable Smart City Development: Challenges and Solutions, (303–320) © 2020 Scrivener Publishing LLC

one-time bound keys. The existing scheme includes the benefits of post quantum security without requiring the dependency on key secrecy. The limitation in this scheme was the pre-generation of keys during every time slot dedicated for signing purposes resulting in less efficient implementation. In real world cases, the keys that are generated on smart cards are not fast. To increase the efficiency, the pre-assignment of keys to the people for respective time-slot can be eliminated and replaced by sequential keys. This signing approach is very efficient during unpredictive slots such as to pay bills where the keys bound by different time lay still. The keys generated sequentially require additional server support. To avoid the reusage of keys it is mandatory to keep track of both server and the signer keys spent during the transactions. The existing procedures would pave way for sequential key management hereby eliminating the need for a trusted server.

The practical approach to combat the limitations of existing signature schemes is mentioned in the proposed Swathi, Divya and Rathna Signature scheme which will be referred as in the forthcoming sections. The scheme can provide non-repudiation with security. Besides, an efficient revocation strategy powered with free cryptographic timestamping, any quantum computer-based known attacks does not occur. The size of the cryptographic keys along with efficient computation will be further compared with the already existing state-of-the-art signature approaches based on various rounds of hash. During the generation of keys, many signatures are created. Similar to the existing hierarchy-less hash approaches, the time of key generation is actually observed when the keys generate 200 or more signatures. A survey of the hash signature schemes with authenticated data structures and server based is depicted in the forthcoming section. Consecutively, the proposed system, the design and its implementation with conclusion is mentioned.

16.2   Literature Study

16.2.1   Signatures With Hashes

The first signature scheme with hashes was given by Diffie & Hellman [15]. This was a one-time based hash approach and the consecutive proposals were made basis this fundamental property [5, 16]. Every signature requires a new pair of keys alongside dispersal of newer public keys. Later, Merkle [21] used the hash tree notion that led to more inputs. These inputs are then connected to one root hash value. Afterwards, the N inputs are connected to $\log_2 N$ based proofs. The successful completion of this process results in the combination of a one-time signature scheme's N instances with N-time scheme. The major limitation of this process is the entire one-time tree build. Merkle [22] also identified a separate method to increase the tree size gradually. The lower or the newer tree nodes can be however authenticated by a chain of single signatures in a non-interactive environment where the public keys are held by the receiver. The same approach has been enhanced in [4, 19]. The stateful limitation of N-time approach where the keys tracked by the signer can only be used once. In such cases, the reuse of keys can lead to major loss of security. A new scheme by Perrig [23] stated a method where only one private key sign many messages and with every addition there is a decrease in the level of security. The optimization scheme with multi-level tree deduced by Bernstein *et al.* [3] is a stateless scheme. This scheme is called SPHINCS where the pseudo-random keys [20] do not track the state.

16.2.2 Signature Scheme With Server Support

In this approach, the signer along with a server creates a unique signature. The major adoptions to use this approach is the high performance and better security. The computations can be performed via a computer with enhanced security to avoid the misuse of keys. A better approach to store the keys is by storing the keys in server or use a separate signature generating process. The best way for this approach is to let the server be operational for every asymmetric key processes' basis signer's request [24]. Here, we use a trusted server. However, it cannot be concluded that the security is enhanced by delegating the key management by the respective end users [12]. Therefore, Asokan *et al.* [2] with additional authors in [17] proposed a method for asymmetric key process. This was server-sided where user tracks the actions of server by signatures. The signature's authenticity can be verified by the user. This approach worked for dispute resolution use cases. This was however not compatible with those applications that required immediate results for instance the authentication in the field of access control. There are various proposed approaches like RSA to overcome the limitation. This leads to an increase in computational power of mobile devices. The private keys were additionally secured [8] during the spilt between devices and servers.

16.2.3 Signatures Scheme Based on Interaction

Anderson *et al.* [1] introduced the interactive protocols between the participating parties or an external time-stamp procedure. This was called

"Guy Fawkes" approach. According to this protocol, the intended message preceded by hash is authenticated. This is done after boot strapping along with a secret hash appended on the previous message. This signature scheme is applicable to a single party only. The property of non-repudiation for sender's origin is an important one to consider. The protocol of Tesla performed authentication of participating parties. The limitation in this approach was inflexibility because it could not extend its support towards verifiers. A new signature scheme based on generic hashes was proposed by Buldas *et al.* [11] that was dependent on the time stamping service. This scheme works on the principle where the signer is associated to a secret key sequence. Every key is allotted a time slot to sign the respective messages which later alters to verifying the key at the time slot completion. To ensure the accurate key usage, time stamping based on cryptography is used [9]. In schemes given in [10], the service provider is trustless and can give time stamping service. In existing schemes [18], the linking of hash and publishing is done. The time stamping of message and keys proves the accurate time of signing process.

16.3 Methodology

16.3.1 Preliminaries

16.3.1.1 Hash Trees

The hash trees were brought into existence by Merkle [21]. This is essentially a data structure that is built by two to one hash denoted as $h:\{0,1\}^{2n} \rightarrow \{0,1\}^n$ shaped like a tree. The tree nodes are denoted by n-bit values. The nodes of the tree are further distinguished into a leaf or an internal node that may or may not have children. The n value is an internal node value denoted as $a \leftarrow h(x_l, x_r)$ where x_l is the left child value and x_r is the right child value. We have a node which is root and will not be a child to any of the tree structure. The hash tree will be denoted as $r_N \leftarrow T^h(a_1, \dots, a_N)$ the leaves are denoted as N comprising of $a_1, \dots, a_N$ values with r_N as root node.

16.3.1.2 Chains of Hashes

The tree-based structure makes it easier to track the sibling nodes of any valid value to prove the participation in r_N root hash. The correctness is determined by tracking the unique path from the respective node to the root. If a_3 is part of the tree depicted in Figure 16.1, the a_4 with $a_{1,2}$ values should be available. This is necessary to compute $a_{3,4} \leftarrow h(a_3, a_4)$,

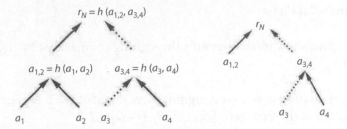

Figure 16.1 The hash tree denoted by $h\,(a_1,...,a_4)$ with its respective chain of hash $a_3 \leadsto r_N$.

$r_N \leftarrow h(a_{1,2}, a_{3,4})$, so that the part of the tree can be re-built. The hash chain h_c links are denoted $a \stackrel{h_c}{\leadsto} r_N$ between a to r_N.

16.3.2 Interactive Hash-Based Signature Scheme

- The device D is secured by the signer to manage the secret keys using trusted functionality.
- The repository R is appended by the server S in static rounds by usage of keys from many signers.
- The signatures are verified by a verifier V using the inputs from repository against the public key p of the signer and round summaries denoted by r^t.

The combination of the signer and repository provides a time-stamping service based on hash and publish scheme. The pre-requisites being the signer, or the verifier does not have to trust the server and only the repository would ensure secure operation for the accuracy as discussed in Figure 16.2.

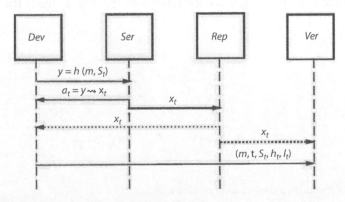

Figure 16.2 Interactive signature scheme and its parties.

Key Generation Phase

The key generation phase prepares the signing of messages by the signer between $1,....\square$,

1. The randomized k-bit signing keys denoted by T is generated as the first step: $(\mathcal{S}_1,....., \mathcal{S}_T) \leftarrow \mathcal{G}(k,T)$.
2. As per the time-slot $a_t \leftarrow h(t,\mathcal{S}_T)$ for $t \in \{1,....,T\}$, each key is bound respectively.
3. The public key p is calculated followed by the aggregation of the bound keys converted into a hash tree: $p \leftarrow \mathcal{T}^h(a_1,.....,a_T)$.

Figure 16.3 depicts the reason as to why the output of the data structure can extract the chain of hashes denoted by h_t. They are linked to the secret key connected to the public key: $h(t, \mathcal{S}_t) \overset{k}{\underset{\sim}{\leftarrow}} p \ t \in \{1,...,T\}$.

Signing Phase

In the signing phase, the message m is signed by the signer at time t:

1. The signer uses the correct key for message authentication: $y \leftarrow h(m,\mathcal{S}_t)$.
2. The authenticators are time-stamped by the signer by giving it to the server to perform aggregation. The hash chain ℓ_t being linked to the authenticator results in: $y \overset{\ell t}{\underset{\sim}{}} x_t$.
3. The signer results in the output tuple: $\sigma \leftarrow (t,\mathcal{S}_t,k_t,\ell_t)$.

Here, post the time-stamping procedure the signature is created and provided to ensure the secure release of the key $\mathcal{S}_t$ from the signer.

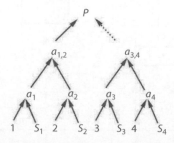

Figure 16.3 Public-key computation specific to N = 4.

The aggregation t comes to an end and further time-stamping of the key S_t cannot be continued anymore.

Verification Phase

During the verification phase, the message m is verified by the verifier x_t using the combination of the signature $\sigma \leftarrow (t, S_t, k_t, \ell_t)$ and public key p.

1. The verifier verifies if the signing key S was committed for the time t: $h(t, S_t) \overset{k_t}{\underset{\sim}{\sim}} p$.
2. The verifier also verifies if the authentication m is completed using the key S at time t: $h(m, S_t) \overset{\ell_t}{\underset{\sim}{\sim}} p$.

16.3.3 Significant Properties of Hash-Based Signature Scheme

The various components of interactive hash-based signature schemes can be used to build several other signature schemes. Few of these properties are depicted below:

i. Proactive Forgery Prevention: During the time of signing, if the keys are expired or revoked they should mandatorily be blocked so that we can proactively prevent the used signature recreation. The status of the keys should be checked right from the detection phase to the time of verification.
ii. Reduced resource requirements of reliable mechanisms: The implementation of various mechanisms requires hardware with strong security and expensive distributed consensus.
iii. Reduction in sharing global data: This approach in distribution with authentication can be expensive.
iv. Strong established security model: These include the security model assumptions, their root of trust etc.
v. Privacy: The entire events of signature should only be viable to the appropriate verifiers.
vi. Efficiency: The efficiency is defined from the use of many signers with fewer servers and one shared trust root.

The additional properties such as revoking keys and proof of signing time also requires the support of server.

16.3.4 Proposed SDR Scheme Structure

16.3.4.1 One-Time Keys

In the hash-based signature scheme, the keys used for signing are bound strictly by time. As a result, due to pre-generation of keys there exists larger overhead. Therefore, the suggested scheme ponders over the sequential use of one-time keys. Initially, for every signature a subsequent time-stamp is associated to prevent forgery. In this approach, the signer can deny any signature making the verification process tedious. When a d document is associated with a z key, there are chances where the signer can sign privately an unauthorized value x and prove that the signature on d document is forged. To avoid such issues, every signer should be associated with respective trusted servers so that the keys can be used for a single transaction only. The need for trusted servers is for non-repudiation. The servers collect the used keys and create additional signatures on the signer's behalf. This can be overcome by accurate auditing and safe logging. The server can only be trusted when it cannot reuse the keys. During verification, this process proves less efficient due to additional data processed. The signer's behavior can also be leaked.

16.3.4.2 Server Behavior Authentication

Every transaction can be presented without trusting the server. The keys are used at the server and by the signer. Hash-trees are created periodically by the server and stores he root hash in a public repository. When the server and a verifier does not contact, the server cannot create valid signatures. However, for the idea to work the signatures are published along with the server gaining access to the used keys. This vulnerability can be removed when the server decreases a used counter (key). The output is signed by z_i which increases the key counter to k. Let us consider that the server and participating signers are not malicious. By neighborhood watch strategy, the signers can notice hash chains, committed root and proof of request legitimate changes from the server. The key counters do not decrease. This method is helpful to detect the malicious activity or forgery but cannot block them. The malicious activity between the server and parties still exist and is not completely eliminated.

The servers are checked by authenticated data structures. If the signatures are equipped with accurate proofs, the signatures can be easily rejected with an invalid proof by the verifiers. This results in larger overhead and the key counters will be continuously validated by the verifiers if the keys are active. The repository, independent auditors and the signers can also validate the signatures. The approach can only detect the presence of a forged signature but not proactively stop them from being created.

16.3.4.3   Pre-Authentication by Repository

The repository can perform server validation. The server must present the updated correctness proof to the repository. The updates can only be accepted by the repository after prior proof validation. The cryptographic methods assist to accept the immutable root hashes and distributes them. The forgery due to decrease in the key counter's usage can be minimized by the signature verification done by repository on the root hashes. The block-chain approach in this scenario is efficient because of linear data growth that is not dependent on the signer's activities. The trusted components are less, input validation is secure, server is not compromised during the time of signing and the continuous tenure of private data log is not required. This approach can act like a byzantine fault tolerance strategy where a single party is not trusted. The scheme is further explained in the below sections.

16.4   SDR Signature Scheme

16.4.1   Pre-Requisites

The proposed scheme depicted in Figure 16.4 comprises of the following:

- **Signer**: A trusted device $\mathcal{D}ev$ is used by the signer for key generation and data signature. Consider the distribution of public keys are authenticated and the $\mathcal{D}ev$, $\mathcal{S}er$ with $\mathcal{D}ev$,

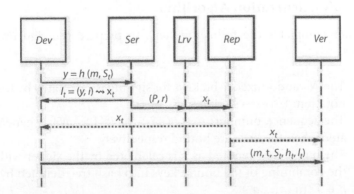

Figure 16.4 Proposed SDR Signature Scheme and its parties.

Rep are linked securely by authenticated channels by the usage of pre-distributed keys in HMAC.

- Server: The signers are assisted by a Server Ser for signature generation. The server holds the counter for the keys that are spent for every participating signer and the results are later shared to the repository.
- Repository: The primary responsibilities of the repository layer L_{rv} are to firstly validate if the Ser operation is accurate before accepting the signature. Secondly, it performs periodic checks for current state summary that can be updated by the public in Rep repository.
- Verifier: The signature verification is done by a separate party called Verifier denoted by Ver.

A hash tree for every party with their respective leaves is maintained by the server. The leaf value is calculated when the (i,y) pair is hashed. Here, the counter of keys spent is denoted by i and the party's last message is denoted by y.

The leaves should be associated with only one public key. This criterion should be met so that signature forging could be avoided. The forging can happen when a server can build many parallel key counters for a party. The counters will increase only for one signature and the remaining ones can easily be forged by using spent keys. The best way to track the path of the tree is when the party shows interest for a service and registers for it. The path is verified while public key distribution. An alternative to this can be the usage of public key bits as a shape. The sparse hash tree is due to the order of bits are not used as the keys.

16.4.2   Key Generation Algorithm

The signer completes the following steps to prepare the sign up to N messages:

1. The N randomized k-bit keys for signing is calculated by the notation: $(S_1,....., S_N) \leftarrow G(k,N)$.
2. The sequence number: $a_t \leftarrow h(t,S_t)$ for $i \in \{1,...,N\}$ is generated when the keys are bound respectively.
3. The public key denoted as p is calculated by the signer with the combining of the bound keys into hash tree denoted by: $p \leftarrow T^h(a_1, ...,a_T)$.
4. The signer also registers itself with the server S.

Here, the public key-based data structure behaves similar to the existing scheme depicted in Figure 16.3. It can extract the chains of hash c_i associated with the bound secret keys for the public key: $h(t, S_t) \overset{k_i}{\sim} p$ for $t \in \{1,.....,N\}$.

16.4.2.1 Server

The server issues a leaf in its tree after the signer provides the registration request. The value is set from i to 0. Here, y is randomly set to a value in the leaf.

16.4.3 Sign Algorithm

16.4.3.1 Signer

The signer signs the message m by following the below steps. The associated signer has the index t of the next key S_t that remains unused in its state.

1. The signer uses the current key for message authentication of: $y \leftarrow h(m, S_t)$
2. The authenticator y is sent to the server by the same signer.
3. The server returns the chain of hash ℓ_t as the signer waits for the step to be completed. The pair (t,y) is then linked to x_t: $h(t, y) \overset{\ell_t}{\sim} x_t$.
4. The signer now verifies if it has received the correct hash chain structure alongside its output matching the value x_t received from the repository.
5. The result is obtained once the validation is correct: (t, i, S_t, k_i, ℓ_t). Here, the index is t, S_t is the i-th key specifically used for signing, c_i is the chaining of hash that is connected to the bound key S_t, the index t is linked to the public key of the signer. The connection between the hash chain ℓ_t and the pair (t,y) with published x_t.
6. The signer then increments the key counter: $t \leftarrow t + 1$.

16.4.3.2 Server

The server performs the following functions after receiving the request y' from the signer.

1. The chain of hash ℓ_t that is associated with the existing client record pair (t,y) with the root r denoted by $h(t, y) \overset{\ell}{\sim} x_t$.

2. The client record pair is converted from (t,y) to $t' \leftarrow t+(1,y')$. The server tree calculates the respective new root hash r'.
3. The server validates and publishes by sending the tuple (t,i,y,ℓ,x,y',r') to the repository.
4. The r_t is published by the server once the repository completes the round.
5. Server considers the r_t of its respective hash tree to receive and broadcast the hash chains ℓ_t of the pending requests. These hash chains connect to (t', y') pair to publish x_t: $h(t', y')\overset{l_t}{\leadsto} x_t$.

16.4.3.3   Repository

The repository in the server tree maintains the current state value in the validation layer $\mathcal{L}_{rv}$ with x^* as root hash value. The server responds with (t,y,i,ℓ,x,y',r') after the validation is completed.

1. The current state of $\mathcal{L}_{rv}$:$x=x^*$ and the to-be state of the signer should be in coordination.
2. The to-be state of the signer requires to comply with the initial state: $h(t, y)\overset{\ell_t}{\leadsto} x$.
3. The counter is incremented $t' \leftarrow t+1$ once the client side is updated.
4. The new state in server tree responds with the alteration in this record: $h(t', y')\overset{\ell_t}{\leadsto} x'$
5. After the above criteria is met, the $\mathcal{L}_{rv}$ can be updated with $x^* \leftarrow x'$.

The functions in rounds. The server updates and validates the state in every round. Once this round is completed, the new state x_t appearing in R additive only public repository.

16.4.4   Verification Algorithm

In the verification phase, the verifier verifies if the message m and the signature $s \leftarrow (t,S_t, k_t, \ell_t)$, matches the public key p by the following steps.

1. The verifier verifies if S is committed as the t-th signing key $h(t, S)\overset{h_t}{\leadsto} p$.
2. It receives the x_t commitment for the subsequent round t from the repository Rep.

3. Finally, the verifier validates the key S that is used to calculate the message authenticator $y \leftarrow h(m,S)$ with the index t: $h(t, S)^{\ell_t}_{\sim} x_t$.

The resulting signature x_t is forwarded after the verification process to the verifier to ensure more security. The key S_t is obtained as part of the signature where the server performs the t counter increment. The consecutive signature is built using $S_t + 1$.

16.5   Supportive Theory

16.5.1   Signing Algorithm Supported by Server

The signatures that are assisted by the server is considered as a high-level one that cannot be compared to the legacy algorithms such as Rivest, Shamir and Adleman algorithm. The highlighted properties are:

- To combat the damages due to key outflow and to manage the forensics it is vital to log all the signing transactions upheld by the server for accurate records.
- A simple key lifecycle control can be obtained by access block done as part of revoking keys ensuring that new signatures are devoid of being created. Here, the server records every key revocation. This is done by imposing sentinel infinite value to the counter belonging to participating clients and providing an update proof post repository commit.
- The use of cryptography for enabling attributes such as time-stamping procedures, policy related IDs, address, etc. can ensure that the server is trusted and cannot be forged.
- The data-dependency based checks can be done by the server, namely the validation of transactions before accepting a signature. The server can only receive the data's hash value where there is no need for the display of the data that has been signed. The server added up with cryptography-based time-stamping procedures can provide non-repudiation.

16.5.2   Repository Deployment

In the proposed approach, the repository is equipped with following properties:

- A valid proof of correctness results in the update acknowledgement.
- Every commitment in the repository is immutable and final.
- The repository-based commitments are public with visibly verifiable immutability.

The blockchain is created to reduce the trust requirements on repository. The pattern to create blockchain can be reused. The approach does not contemplate the proof of work that considered byzantine fault tolerance replication model. The entire transactions are not stored in blockchain. The aggregate hashes of the transactions are only recorded in blockchain. The major advantages of this approach result in the linear growth of blockchain thereby minimizing the dependency on the number of transactions and its size. Also, privacy is achieved by the display and storage of the aggregate hashes. All the transactions within a blockchain is validated prior their execution. For instance, the inhibition of double-spending attacks in various cryptocurrencies with blockchain assistance. The outputs of server are observed and analyzed to validate the correctness of the proofs. The data structures based on authentication are also prone to blockchain validation. There are no trusted components in the repository post blockchain-based byzantine fault tolerance.

16.5.3   SDR Signature Scheme Setup

The real-time deployment of the proposed setup is possible by considering the following scenario. The first layer comprises of distributed cluster of consensus-based blockchain nodes. These nodes function by a permissioned party that are non-dependent. The blockchain is capable of receiving inputs from the servers that perform multiple signing process. They can serve various clients associated with them. The performance is enhanced due to its hierarchical nature. The size and number of blocks are independent of the signatures and participating clients. Every signing server has a certification service with a leaf affixed in the hash tree of the server.

16.5.4   Results and Observation

The proposed scheme depicts an efficient state of the art approach. The client-side management and generation of keys are inherited from the existing approach [11] with the difference of smaller private keys. The signing processes for one day are about 15 requiring 5,475 keys unlike the existing BLT scheme that used about 32 million keys. There is reduction in the overall effort to manage the keys.

The signature size is dependent on two chains of hash. The hash values in the sequences of keys are log_2N which sequentially accounts to about 12 in a year for 5475. Hereby, the hash value of blockchain is about log_2k with K clients for a service. For instance, if about 8 billion individuals perform the signing operation, the hash values reach up to only thirty-three. The hash functions range up to 512 bit and the two chains of hash account to less than 3 Kb totally.

The signature verification requires the recomputation of both chains of hash resulting in about forty-five hash operations. The blockchain query for the committed repository cost is excluded. The approach can be compared to a service equipped with time-stamp alongside an Online Certificate Status Protocol (OCSP) responder for public key infrastructure signature verification.

16.6   Conclusion

The proposed generic hash-based signature approach with blockchain technology is based on cryptographic primitives. The suggested approach for signers and verifiers is highly efficient with smaller public keys and signatures. The server-based scheme integrated with blockchain technology results in immediate revoking of keys and enhanced security without being dependent on the server or the blockchain components. The future enhancements can include the comparison of various blockchain architectures and their use cases in state of the art. The replacement of aggregate hashes with entire transaction record, their associated pre-validation for accurate proofs can also be considered.

References

1. Anderson, R.J., Bergadano, F., Crispo, B., Lee, J.-H., Manifavas, C., Needham, R.M., A new family of authentication protocols. *Oper. Syst. Rev.*, 32, 4, 9–20, 1998.
2. Asokan, G.T. and Waidner, M., Server-supported signatures. *J. Comput. Secur.*, 5, 1, 91–108, 1997.
3. Bernstein, D.J., Hopwood, D., Hulsing, A., Lange, T., Niederhagen, R., Papachristodoulou, L., Schneider, M., Schwabe, P., Wilcox-O'Hearn, Z.,

SPHINCS: Practical stateless hash-based signatures, in: *EUROCRYPT 2015, Proceedings, Part I, volume 9056 of LNCS*, pp. 368–397, Springer, 2015.

4. Buchmann, J.A., Coronado Garcia, L.C., Dahmen, E., Doring, M., Klintsevich, E., CMSS|An improved Merkle signature scheme, in: *INDOCRYPT 2006, Proceedings, volume 4329 of LNCS*, pp. 349–363, Springer, 2006.

5. Buchmann, J.A., Dahmen, E., Ereth, S., Hulsing, A., Ruckert, M., On the security of the Winternitz one-time signature scheme. *IJACT*, 3, 1, 84–96, 2013.

6. Buchmann, J.A., Dahmen, E., Hulsing, A., XMSS|A practical forward secure signature scheme based on minimal security assumptions, in: *PQCrypto 2011, Proceedings, volume 7071 of LNCS*, pp. 117–129, Springer, 2011.

7. Buchmann, J.A., Dahmen, E., Klintsevich, E., Okeya, K., Vuillaume, C., Merkle signatures with virtually unlimited signature capacity, in: *ACNS 2007, Proceedings, volume 4521 of LNCS*, pp. 31–45, Springer, 2007.

8. Buldas, A., Kalu, A., Laud, P., Oruaas, M., Server-supported RSA signatures for mobile devices, in: *ESORICS 2017, Proceedings, Part I, volume 10492 of LNCS*, pp. 315–333, Springer, 2017.

9. Buldas, A., Kroonmaa, A., Laanoja, R., Keyless signatures' infrastructure: How to build global distributed hash-trees, in: *NordSec 2013, Proceedings, volume 8208 of LNCS*, pp. 313–320, Springer, 2013.

10. Buldas, A. and Laanoja, R., Security proofs for hash tree time-stamping using hash functions with small output size, in: *ACISP 2013, Proceedings, volume 7959 of LNCS*, pp. 235–250, Springer, 2013.

11. Buldas, A., Laanoja, R., Truu, A., A server-assisted hash-based signature scheme, in: *NordSec 2017, Proceedings, volume 10674 of LNCS*, pp. 3–17, Springer, 2017.

12. Buldas, A. and Saarepera, M., Electronic signature system with small number of private keys, in: *2nd Annual PKI Research Workshop, Proceedings*, NIST, pp. 96–108, 2003.

13. Coronado Garcia, L.C., *Provably Secure and Practical Signature Schemes*. PhD thesis, Darmstadt University of Technology, Germany, 2005.

14. Dahmen, E., Okeya, K., Takagi, T., Vuillaume, C., Digital signatures out of second-preimage resistant hash functions, in: *PQCrypto 2008, Proceedings, volume 5299 of LNCS*, pp. 109–123, Springer, 2008.

15. Diffie, W. and Hellman, M.E., New directions in cryptography. *IEEE Trans. Inf. Theory*, 22, 6, 644–654, 1976.

16. Dods, C., Smart, N.P., Stam, M., Hash based digital signature schemes, in: *Cryptography and Coding, Proceedings, volume 3796 of LNCS*, pp. 96–115, Springer, 2005.

17. Goyal, V., *More efficient server assisted one time signatures*, Cryptology ePrint Archive, Report 2004/135. 2004, https://eprint.iacr.org/2004/135.

18. Haber, S. and Stornetta, W.S., How to time-stamp a digital document. *J. Cryptol.*, 3, 2, 99–111, 1991.

19. Hulsing, A., Rijneveld, J., Song, F., Mitigating multi-target attacks in hashbased signatures, in: *PKC 2016, Proceedings, Part I, volume 9614 of LNCS*, pp. 387–416, Springer, 2016.
20. Kumar, M.V.R., Bhalaji, N., Singh, S., An augmented approach for pseudo-free groups in smart cyber-physical system. *Clust. Comput.*, 22, 1–20, 2018.
21. Merkle, R.C., *Secrecy, Authentication and Public Key Systems.* PhD thesis, Stanford University, 1979.
22. Merkle, R.C., A digital signature based on a conventional encryption function, in: *CRYPTO'87, Proceedings, volume 293 of LNCS*, pp. 369–378, Springer, 1987.
23. Perrig, A., The BiBa one-time signature and broadcast authentication protocol, in: *ACM CCS 2001, Proceedings*, pp. 28–37, ACM, 2001.
24. Perrin, T., Bruns, L., Moreh, J., Olkin, T., Delegated cryptography, online trusted third parties, and PKI, in: *1st Annual PKI Research Workshop, Proceedings*, NIST, pp. 97–116, 2002.

Index

Accelerometer, 106, 108, 109, 117, 118
Adaptive channel equalizer, 67
Adaptive droop control, 49, 53, 54, 65
Additive white gaussian noise, 67
Adoption technologies, 15
Advanced message queuing protocol (AMQP), 134
Aglet, 31
Amazon EC2 query, 89
Analyzer, 25
Anisotropic magneto resistive, 119
Application programming interface, 226, 236
Arduino mega, 109, 111, 122, 123
ArduPilot, 109, 110, 112, 117, 121
ARMADILLO, 147, 151
Artificial neural network, 68, 69, 72, 75, 78, 82
ATMega 2560, 111
Attribution-based encoding (ABE), 157–161
Auto navigation systems, 119
Autonomous vehicle, 172
Auto-scaling, 94

Back-propagation, 70
Barometer, 108–110
Basic criteria of addiction, 258
Battery, 49, 50, 51, 53, 54, 55, 58, 59, 63, 65, 66
Battery eliminator circuit, 115
Bias, 76

Big data and Hadoop, 88
    see also Hadoop
Bioinspired algorithms, 95
Bit error rate, 69, 72
Blockchain, 303, 311, 316, 317
Bluetooth, 133
Body temperature, 219, 221, 223, 232, 240
Botnets, 248
Bpsk, 77–82
Bridge rectifier, 116
Brushless direct current motor, 105, 106, 111–113

Channel, 67–75, 77, 80–83
Channel model, 72–75, 77, 79, 80–82
Chebyshev neural network, 68
Chebyshev polynomials, 68
Chronic obstructive pulmonary disease, 223
Ciphertext-policy attribute-based encryption (CP-ABE), 158–161
Citrix, 96
Closed loop control, 55, 60
Cloud computing, characteristics, 189
Cloud computing services, 136–137
Cloud interfaces, 89
Cloud load balancing, algorithms, 190–191, 215t
    literature survey, 193–201
    research challenges, 192–193
    strategies, 203t–214t
    survey table, 201–202

CloudAnalyst, 190
Cloud-based servers farms, 192
CloudSim toolkit, 190, 191, 198
CloudStack, 95
Cluster design with Raspberry Pi, 276
    assembling materials to implement cluster, 276–277
    setting up cluster, 278–279
CMOS camera, 113, 114, 125
Color index, 181
Communication system, 67–69, 72, 73, 81–83
Comparator, 25
Competitive layer, 182
Congestive heart failure, 223
Constrained application protocol (CoAP), 134
Convergence, 69, 72, 76, 77–80
Crash override/industry, 250
Crawl manager, 28
Crawler, 25
Cryptography, 303, 306, 315
Cyber attacks,
    bogus information, 152, 163
    GPS spoofing, 164
    impersonation, 163
    replay, 163
    session hijacking, 163, 166
    Sybil, 163, 167

Data analytics, 11, 134–135
Davies–Meyer, 148–149
Decision feedback equalizer, 72, 83
Delay, 72–74, 80
Denial of service, 248
Deployment of private cloud on Raspberry Pi cluster, 281
    about NextCloud software, 281
Depth of discharge (DOD), 53
Desired signal, 68
Differential evolution, 68, 70
Digital motion processor, 118

Dispatcher, 29
Distortion, 67, 68, 71, 72
Distributed denial of service (DDoS), 130, 252
Docker, 89, 94, 95, 98

Eigen value ratio, 71
Eironment perception, 172
Electrically erasable programmable read only memory, 109
Electromagnetic inteference, 111
Electronic speed control, 113, 114
EnergyHarvesting, 297
Equalization, 67–73, 81–83
Equalizers, 67, 69, 72, 77, 79, 80–82
ESP8266, 226–228
Eucalyptus, 96
Evolutionary algorithm, 68, 70
External devices, role in IoT platform, 247–248

Fall detection, 219, 221–222, 225, 230, 236, 238
FCFS, 190
Field oriented control, 55
FIFO scheduling algorithm, 98
Fingerprint, 34
Finite impulse response, 72
Flow control block, 59, 60, 62
Frequency, 49, 50, 54, 55, 60, 66
Frequency scalling, 297
Functional link artificial neural network, 67, 70, 76, 78, 81–83

Gain reduction factor, 75
Global best, 77
Global positioning system, 105, 107, 119, 240
GLUON, 145, 147–148, 151
Gradient descent learning, 71
Gradient model, 196
Greedy algorithms, 297, 301
Gyroscope, 106, 108, 109, 118

Hadoop,
   architecture, 86–89
   performance analysis of, 90–91, 97
Hadoop clusters,
   heterogeneous clusters in cloud
      computing, 96–97
   optimization using cloud platform,
      95–96
Hadoop containers,
   virtualizing, 94–95
Hadoop distributed file system
      (HDFS), 87, 88, 92–93, 96–97,
      99
Hadoop VMs,
   scheduling of, 98–99
Hash-based, 303, 307, 309, 310, 317
HBB-LB, 190, 195
HDFS, 23
HDFS-based distributed cache system
      (HDCache), 96
Healthcare monitoring, 219–242
Heart rate, 219, 221–222, 227–230,
      240
Hidden layer, 71, 75, 76, 80
Hidden neurons, 67
Home healthcare, 11
Honey bee behavior algorithms,
      201–202
HTTP (HyperText Transfer Protocol),
      132
Hypervisors, 89, 95
   cloud computing, 8
   IoT and big data, 5
   RFID, 4
   wearable sensors-head to toe, 7

ICT explosion, 3
IEEE 802.3ad, 95
IIR structure, 71
Implanted sensors, 220
Implementation, 281
   NextCloud on Raspberry Pi cluster,
      281–282

parallel computing on Raspberry Pi
      cluster, 282–286
Indexer, 25
Industry 4.0, 303
Inertial measurement unit, 105,
      109, 118
Influencing factors of addiction
      behavior, 259–262
   environment influence, 260
   family group and society, 262
   media influence, 262
   peers influence, 262
Integral time constant, 52
Integrated circuit, 221, 225–226, 231
Intelligent healthcare, 10
Internal power flow management, 50
Inter-symbol interference, 67, 81
Inverted index, 29
IoT (internet of things), 131–135,
      219–242
   data protocols, 133–135
   key components, 131–133
IoT (internet of things) security
      management,
   significance, 249–250
   tools and legislation, 250–251
IoT architecture, 154
IoT data protocols, 133–135
   advanced message queuing protocol
      (AMQP), 134
   constrained application protocol
      (CoAP), 134
   data analytics, 134–135
   message queue telemetry transport
      (MQTT), 133
IoT systems and devices, protection,
      251–255
IoT-based technology, 129–131
   peer to peer communication
      security, 129–130
   smart city infrastructure, 130–131

Job scheduling, 98–99

Keecak, 146
Klotski, 33
KVM, 89–91, 93–95, 97–98

LBMM scheduling calculation, 199
Lesamanta, 143, 152
Light dependent resistor, 224
Light emitting diode, 224, 229
Lightweight encryption algorithms,
    blowfish, 164
    camellia, 165
    CAST, 165
    proxy-based authentication scheme
        (PBAS), 164–165
Lightweight protocols,
    ARIADNE, 166
    A-SAODV, 166
    authenticated adhoc network
        routing (ARAN), 165
    ECDS, 167
    holistic, 167
    OTC, 166
    RobSAD, 167
    SAODV, 166
    secure and efficient adhoc distance
        (SEAD), 166
Linux, 90–91, 94, 95, 97
Lithium polymer, 112
LM35, 225, 231–232, 234
Load, 49–51, 54, 55, 59, 60, 63–66
LODCO algorithm, 297, 299
LoRaWan (long range wide area
    network), 133
Low cost health monitoring, 219–242
Low pass filter, 54
LXC (linux containers), 90–91, 95

Machine learning-based smart
    decision-making process,
    135–136
Magnetometer, 108, 109, 118, 122
Man-in-the-middle, 130, 248
MapReduce, 90–93, 96, 98

MARKOV chaining techniques, 297,
    298
Masqurader, 129
MATLAB, 50
MCP3208, 234–235
Mean square error, 67, 74
Merkle–Damgard, 145, 148
Mesos, 90–91
Message queue telemetry transport
    (MQTT), 133
Messaging system, 22
Microelectro mechanical systems, 225,
    240
Microcontroller, 219–242
Microgrid, 49, 50, 54, 65, 66
Microsoft hyper-v cloud, 96
Minimal interference maximal
    productivity system (MIMP), 98
Min–Min algorithm, 190–191
Min–Min planning calculation, 199
Mission planner, 110, 116, 117
Mobile agents, 22
Mobility servlet container, 38
Modulation, 68, 72, 73, 77, 79, 80–82
MPPT, 49, 50, 51, 54, 60
MPU6050, 230–232
Multicopter, 106, 109
Multilayer perceptron, 72
Multipath delay spread, 72
Multiple-input–multiple-output
    (MIMO) channel, 68

Navigational LEDs, 116
Near duplicate detector, 28
Neiva, 147, 151
Network gateway, 132
Network packet analyzer tool, 175
Neural network, 67–72, 75–77,
    81–83
Node health degree, 98
Noise, 67, 69, 72, 74, 81
Normal-distributions transform, 181
NOX OpenFlow controller, 197

OGF open cloud computing interface, 89
OLB scheduling calculation, 199
Old database, 25
OpenNebula, 89
OpenVZ, 90, 94, 98
Oscillator, 55
OTR, 156
Output measurement block, 58, 60, 63

Parallel computing and MPI on Raspberry Pi cluster, 279–280
Park's transformation, 57
Particle swarm optimization (PSO), 67–70, 72, 74, 76, 81, 83, 191, 200
Personal best, 77
Personal navigation systems, 119
Phase locked loop, 49, 50, 55, 56, 60
PHOTON, 142–145, 148–149, 168
PI controller, 50, 51, 52, 60
PID controller, 52
Point cloud data, 172
Position vector, 77
Power management, 50, 54, 65
Power transmission line inspection, 105, 107
Pre-learning process, 179
PRESENT, 143–147, 148–149, 152, 155, 169
Priority score, 29
Pulse width modulation, 111
PV/battery hybrid unit, 65

Qam, 68, 77–82
Quadcopter, 105, 106, 124
Quark, 146–147, 150, 169

Radial basis function, 71
Radio controller, 120, 121, 123
Radio resource allocation, 298
Ransomware, 249

Receiver, 67, 72–74
Recurrent neural network, 68, 71, 78, 82, 83
Region of interest, 181
Registration, 181
Remote healthcare, 219–242
Remote recording, 249
Resistive load, 60
RFID, 139, 140, 152–153, 169
Round robin, 190

Scheduler, 29
SDR signature, 316
Self-organized map, 182
Semantic segmentation, 173
   image, 173
   point cloud, 173–174
Sigmoid, 76
Signature, 304–312, 314–317
Smart city-based infrastructure management system, 244–245
Smartphone, 225, 240
Social engineering, 248
Software defined networking, 300
Solar power, 58
Space vector pulse width modulation, 50, 55, 56, 60
Spectrum efficiency, 68
Sponge, 143–144
Spongent, 143, 145–146, 151, 168
Stanford University interim (sui), 74, 75
State of charge (SOC), 50, 51, 53, 54, 55, 63
Support vector machines (SVM), 69

Tapped delay line, 73, 74, 77
Technologies-data cognitive, 13
   deep learning, 14
   image processing, 14
   machine learning, 13
Telemetry radio, 120, 121
TeraSort, 93

Term frequency-inverse document
    frequency, 24
TestDSFIO, 93
ThingSpeak, 236–241
Total harmonic distortion, 56
Traffic analysis, 130
Transfer function, 70, 76
Triton, 250
TWINE, 155–156
Types of addiction and their effects,
    262–269

Uldra dense networking, 300
Universal plug in and play (UPnP),
    255
Unmanned aerial vehicle, 105–109,
    124, 125
Unorganized point, 178
User level online offloading
    framework, 302

V2X algorithm, 303
vCloud, 89

Velocity vector, 77
Virtual hadoop, 89, 95, 97. See also
    hadoop
Virtual machines,
    evaluating map reduce on, 91–93
Virtual technologies, 88–89, 97–98
VMWare, 89, 95
    vCloud, 96
    vSphere, 91, 95, 98
Voltage source control, 50, 54
VPN Filter, 250

Wearable sensors, 219–242
Web-based offloading, 303
Web server database, 24
Weight, 69–71, 74–76, 82, 83
Wind power, 63
Wireless access in vehicle
    environments (WAVE), 161–162
Wireless camera, 120
Wireless communication, 68, 244
Word-of-mouth scouter, 33

ZigBee, 121, 133

Printed and bound by CPI Group (UK) Ltd, Croydon, CR0 4YY